# THE CONTENTIOUS SENATE

## PARTISANSHIP, IDEOLOGY, AND THE MYTH OF COOL JUDGMENT

edited by

## COLTON C. CAMPBELL and NICOL C. RAE

ROWMAN & LITTLEFIELD PUBLISHERS, INC.
*Lanham • Boulder • New York • Oxford*

ROWMAN & LITTLEFIELD PUBLISHERS, INC.

Published in the United States of America
by Rowman & Littlefield Publishers, Inc.
4720 Boston Way, Lanham, Maryland 20706
www.rowmanlittlefield.com

12 Hid's Copse Road, Cumnor Hill, Oxford OX2 9JJ, England

British Library Cataloguing in Publication Information Available

**Library of Congress Cataloging-in-Publication Data**

The contentious Senate : partisanship, ideology, and the myth of cool judgment /
edited by Colton C. Campbell and Nicol C. Rae.
    p. cm.
  Includes bibliographical references and index.
    ISBN 0-7425-0115-9 (alk. paper)—ISBN 0-7425-0116-7 (pbk. : alk. paper)
    1. United States. Congress. Senate. 2. United States. Congress. Senate—Reform. 3.
Political parties—United States. I. Campbell, Colton C., 1965– II. Rae, Nicol C.

JK1161 .C66 2001
328.73'01—dc21                                                    00-059055

Printed in the United States of America

♾™ The paper used in this publication meets the minimum requirements of
American National Standard for Information Sciences—Permanence of Paper for
Printed Library Materials, ANSI/NISO Z39.48-1992.

*For Lily Rae—NCR*

*For C. F. "Budge" Campbell—CCC*

# Contents

*List of Tables and Figures*        *ix*
*Preface*        *xi*

**ONE**    Party Politics and Ideology in the Contemporary Senate    1
*Nicol C. Rae and Colton C. Campbell*

**PART ONE**    DELIBERATION, COMMITTEES, AND PUBLIC POLICY

**TWO**    Senate Floor Deliberation: A Preliminary Inquiry    21
*Roger H. Davidson*

**THREE**    Principle or Party? Foreign and National Security
Policymaking in the Senate    43
*Christopher J. Deering*

**PART TWO**    LEADERSHIP AND MESSAGE POLITICS

**FOUR**    The Senate Leadership Dilemma: Passing Bills and Pursuing
Partisan Advantage in a Nonmajoritarian Chamber    65
*Barbara Sinclair*

**FIVE**    Senate Leaders, Minority Voices: From Dirksen to Daschle    91
*Burdett Loomis*

**SIX**   Message Politics and Senate Procedure    *107*
C. Lawrence Evans and Walter J. Oleszek

**PART THREE**  SENATE REFORM IN HISTORICAL PERSPECTIVE

**SEVEN**  Twentieth-century Senate Reform: The View from
the Inside    *131*
Donald A. Ritchie

**EIGHT**  Twentieth-century Senate Reform: Three Views
from the Outside    *147*
Richard A. Baker

**AFTERWORD**  Reflections on Forty Years of the Senate    *167*
Donald R. Matthews

Bibliography    *171*
Index    *183*
About the Contributors    *195*

# Tables and Figures

**Tables**

**1.1**   Democratic Senate Seats by Region, 1924–1996        *3*

**1.2**   Party Unity and Polarization in Senate Voting,
          1977–1998                                            *6*

**1.3**   Conservative Coalition Votes and Victories in Congress,
          1957–1998                                            *12*

**1.4**   Plan for Democratic Unity                            *15*

**1.5**   Democratic Formula to Succeed in 1999                *16*

**2.1**   Participation in Three Senate Debates                *40*

**2.2**   Party Voting on Three Senate Measures                *42*

**3.1**   Agenda and Party: Senate Key Votes                   *58*

**5.1**   Senate Party Balance, Party Unity, Party Support Scores,
          and the Minority Leader, 1959–1999                   *95*

**5.2**   Divided Government and Filibuster Activity, 1959–2000 *97*

**5.3**   National News Coverage of Minority Leaders, 1959–1999 *100*

**6.1**   Trends in Morning Business: First Five Legislative Days
          in June, 1977–1999                                   *109*

**6.2**    Relevance of Senate Floor Items to Party "Messages,"
           106th Congress, 1st Session                                    *113*

**6.3**    Subject Matter of Rule XIV Measures, 1999                      *117*

**6.4**    Cloture and the Party Message, 1999                           *119*

**6.5**    Filling the Amendment Tree, 1985–1999                         *123*

## Figures

**3.1**    Party and Chamber Ideology                                     *53*

**3.2**    Committee and Chamber Ideology                                 *53*

**3.3**    Foreign Relations Committee Ideology                           *54*

**3.4**    Armed Services Committee Ideology                              *55*

**3.5**    Committee and Chamber Polarization                             *56*

**5.1**    The Constituencies of the Minority Floor Leader                *93*

**6.1**    Rule XIV Measures                                             *116*

# Preface

In a supposed anecdote about the United States Senate, Thomas Jefferson asks George Washington why he consented to the idea of a Senate. "Why did you pour that coffee into your saucer?" asks Washington (quoted in Fenno 1995, 1785). "To cool it," replies Jefferson. "Even so," replies Washington, "we pour legislation into the senatorial saucer to cool it" (quoted in Fenno 1995, 1785). In James Madison's words, that saucer would embody enlightened citizens, whose small number and firmness might fairly interpose against rash councils (Hamilton, Madison, and Jay, *Federalist* No. 62).

The framers of the Constitution were in early agreement that there should be two equal yet distinct and different chambers. As the Senate evolved, their ideas about the Upper Chamber translated into permanent individualistic features, conferring no prerogatives upon a presiding officer, no previous question rule to shut off debate, and no germaneness rule to prevent irrelevant or destructive attachments. By contrast with the impersonal, hierarchical, and disciplined House, the Senate has long tolerated and even promoted individualism, reciprocity, and mutual accommodation. So while the popularly elected House was liable to succumb to partisan public passions, the Senate would always provide a brake, a second look, a longer-run view, and a well-deliberated decision. In short, the myth of "cool" judgment has persisted.

Rising partisanship and ideology in the Senate since the early 1980s, however, indicates a significant reversal of the senatorial tradition toward individualism. Party unity scores and patterns of party voting, for example, culminated in historically high levels during the 104th Congress (1995–1996), and recent developments in both senatorial parties reflect stronger party leadership and an enhanced legislative role for the party caucuses. Many newer senators are from the House, and after having been baptized into relentless and combative partisanship by Newt Gingrich and his Democratic adversaries, they are making the Senate a forum for the party on a national scale. These changes do not dramatically alter the character of the Senate but they do move the Senate closer to the House in terms of the relations between committee leaders, party leaders, and the party groups. Is such an increase in partisanship a temporary or permanent phenomenon? Is a more partisan Senate likely to heighten or overcome the legislative "inertia" that appears to characterize the chamber in recent years? And will this development—contrary to the design of the framers—reduce the effectiveness and legitimacy of the Senate as a governing body? Is the senate becoming more contentious?

These are the issues that this book seeks to address. In their respective chapters, our contributors—all distinguished Senate scholars—address various aspects of increasing partisanship and ideology in the contemporary Senate and their implications for the Senate as an institution. In our introductory chapter, we trace the evolution of partisanship in the Senate in recent decades and discuss several of its ramifications for the functioning of the institution. We conclude that the impact of these developments is largely negative to the body.

The two chapters in part one look more specifically at components fundamental to the legislative process in the Senate. In chapter two, Roger H. Davidson focuses on the rhetoric employed in three recent high-profile Senate floor debates: the Comprehensive Test Ban Treaty Act, the Bipartisan Campaign Finance Reform Act, and the Partial-birth Abortion Ban Act. He concludes that on the evidence of these three cases, the Senate, like the House of Representatives, has become a pervasively partisan institution, casting further doubt on the so-called norm of senatorial courtesy. Chapter three, by Christopher J. Deering, examines the extent to which gridlock, partisanship, and polarization have affected the Senate's unique constitutional role in foreign and national security policy. For Deering, these developments have led to a greater assertion of negative Senate power by the chamber's failure to confirm treaties and presidential appointments to ambassadorships.

The trio of chapters in part two deal with the implications of enhanced partisanship for party leaders in the Senate. All three works also highlight the increasing importance of "message politics" in the day-to-day business of the Senate. In chapter four, Barbara Sinclair examines the dilemma faced by majority party Senate leaders who must fulfill their traditional role in managing the legislative business of the chamber, while simultaneously striving for partisan advantage in a more partisan and polarized Senate. Without the cooperation of the minority leader, high-profile legislation will not pass today's Senate. But while both leaders are under pressure from their party colleagues to pursue partisan advantage, such cooperation has become increasingly difficult to achieve, and as a consequence the Senate often gives the public the impression of being polarized and gridlocked. In chapter five, Burdett Loomis compares the leadership styles of two Senate minority leaders: Republican Everett Dirksen of Illinois in the individualistic era of the 1960s, and Democrat Tom Daschle of South Dakota in the highly partisan 1990s. Both have been seen as particularly effective leaders of the minority, but where Dirksen had to deal with his Democratic opposite numbers to have influence, in a more partisan context, Daschle must heed his primary constituency of Democratic senators as well as pay more attention to delivering a party "message." The advent of "message politics" is also the subject of chapter six, by C. Lawrence Evans and Walter J. Oleszek. Congressional Republicans and Democrats, they suggest, increasingly seek to structure Senate floor action to publicize partisan messages rather to pass legislation. Evans and Oleszek go on to argue that in such a message-driven partisan environment, the traditional Senate practice of unanimous consent—essential to keeping legislative business flowing in a chamber with extremely loose rules for floor debate—has become much harder to achieve.

As the Senate becomes a more partisan body at the beginning of a new century, we felt it appropriate to revisit the issue of whether or not the Senate remains faithful to the vision of the Constitution's framers. To this end, we enlisted Senate Historian Richard A. Baker and Associate Senate Historian Donald A. Ritchie to discuss attitudes toward Senate reform from within and outside the institution during the twentieth century. In chapter seven, Ritchie analyzes oral histories from long-serving Senate staffers to ascertain the effects of various reform efforts on the institution. He concludes that despite these reforms the Senate has remained remarkably unchanged in terms of its powers and procedures during the course of this century, and also reminds us that it is a uniquely powerful upper chamber among national legislatures. Baker, in chapter eight, looks at Senate reform from the perspective of three prominent Senate scholars and political scientists: George H. Haynes, Lindsay Rogers, and George B. Galloway. While these scholars' writings attracted considerable interest in their day, what is more interesting is how little effect these and other various proposals for procedural reform have had on the Senate as an institution. In fact, one common theme emerging from this collection is that Senate change appears to be driven more by changes in the electoral context—the rising influence of national parties, interest groups, and ideological activists on Senate elections—rather than the panaceas put forward by political scientists and reform advocates.

Finally, on the fortieth anniversary of the publication of his seminal work, *U.S. Senators and Their World* (1960), we thought it would be particularly appropriate to ask Donald R. Matthews to contribute some afterthoughts on the evolution of the Senate since his time on Capitol Hill in the late 1950s. Matthews notes that while the resources available to study the Senate have increased tremendously in the intervening forty years, the Senate itself appears to have lost some of its luster in terms of elite and public opinion more generally.

Of course, Matthews also indicates that the decline in popular approval has characterized most American national political institutions not just the Senate. Nevertheless, public disdain for the legislative branch of government appears to be particularly severe. We do not believe that this decline is unrelated to the equally sharp rise in partisanship on Capitol Hill in recent decades, as documented in numerous recent studies of the House of Representatives. This collection makes clear that this holds true for the traditionally less partisan Senate as well. In the current electoral environment, the rise of ideology, partisanship, more partisan leaders, and the predominance of message politics in Senate deliberations appears to make good sense to most senators. Whether this is healthy for the institutional health of the Senate—a chamber, which as Matthews also notes is constitutionally malapportioned and unrepresentative—is another matter. In these circumstances, the Senate's justifying myth of "cool" judgment becomes much harder to perpetuate, and its contentiousness seems certain to increase.

We would like to thank all our contributors for producing such excellent and timely essays as well as for lending their continual wisdom. The Jack D. Gordon Institute for Public Policy and Citizenship Studies gave immeasurable assistance in financing and organizing the project and we are particularly grateful to our strongest supporter, the director of the Gordon Institute, John F. Stack Jr. Special mention should also be given to Elaine Dillashaw for her indefatigable patience and help. We are grateful to Florida International University's provost, Mark Rosenberg, vice president for Sponsored Research, Tom Breslin, the dean of the College of Arts and Sciences, Art Herriott, and the associate dean of the College of Arts and Sciences, Ivelaw Griffith, for their generous financial support.

All of our colleagues in the Department of Political Science were supportive of the project. Particular mention should be given to: Barbara Herrera, Mary Beth Melchior, Keith Dougherty, Sean Foreman, Kevin Hill, and Jenny Chanley. Paul Herrnson of the University of Maryland also contributed valuable comments. Others to whom we owe a special debt of thanks include: Aracelys Montoya, Yolie Saiz, Joyce Peterson, and all the staff at the Roz and Cal Kovens Center.

Jennifer Knerr, Brenda Hadenfeldt, and all the folks at Rowman & Littlefield have been supportive and patient in the production of this book.

Finally, we would like to thank our families and friends for their untiring support of our various academic efforts. Nicol Rae would like to make a particular mention of his mother Lily, and Colton Campbell would like to reiterate his love and respect for his family: parents Budge and Ardis, and sisters Colby and Kenzie.

The help of all the people mentioned here was critical to the production of this book. Hopefully, we have contributed something to the understanding and betterment of an invaluable and uniquely American political institution, the U.S. Senate.

CCC                NCR
*Ukiah, Calif.*        *Miami Beach, Fla.*

# The Contentious Senate

*Source:* National Archive and Records Administration, from the U.S. Senate Collection for Legislative Archives. C. K. Berryman, *Evening Star,* December 10, 1930, cartoon D-90.

## CHAPTER ONE

# Party Politics and Ideology in the Contemporary Senate

## NICOL C. RAE AND COLTON C. CAMPBELL

*With rare exceptions the senators are not beholden to their party leaders; they had little to do with the senators' nomination or election. The tradition of localism and popular reverence for legislative "independence" largely frustrate any efforts by the president, national chairman, or Senate leaders of a party to "purge" unfaithful members. As a result, the political parties in the Senate are, when compared with the parties in most parliamentary democracies and a number of American states, rather disunited organizations. (Matthews 1960, 120–21)*

Since the publication of his classic study of the Senate in 1960, political scientists and other watchers of the U.S. Congress have generally agreed with Donald R. Matthews's conclusions regarding the power of political parties and party leaders in the Senate. By contrast with the impersonal, hierarchical, and disciplined House, the Senate has continued to tolerate and even promote individualism (Ripley 1969 and 1985; Bailey 1988; Sinclair 1989; Smith 1989), reciprocity, and mutual accommodation (Baker 1980). Senators treasure their independence, "which exacerbates the challenges faced by those elected to lead them (Davidson and Oleszek 1998, 166). The chamber's flexible set of forty-two standing rules enhances the power of individual senators by conferring no prerogatives upon the presiding officer, and including neither a previous question rule to shut off debate, nor a germaneness rule to prevent irrelevant or destructive amendments (Fenno 1995; Binder and Smith 1997). Unlike their House counterparts, Senate party leaders have far fewer resources with which to promote party unity. Taken together, these nonmajoritarian features generally ensure individual senators a high degree of independence, dilute partisanship, and limit party government.

1

We join a small but growing set of congressional scholars who focus on the impact of mounting partisanship on party leaders and party caucuses in the Senate (Bullock and Brady 1983; Patterson and Caldeira 1987; Hurley and Wilson 1989; Bader 1998). When partisanship has become most sharply defined in the Senate, it has generally occurred in a specific context (Smith 1993; Loomis 1998). Over the past two decades, both roll call data and personal interviews with senators and their staffs, particularly junior members, suggest an intensifying partisan atmosphere. Party unity scores and patterns of party voting reached historically high levels during the 1990s. Moreover, during the 104th Congress (1995–1996) a number of reforms were passed in the Republican Conference—the crowning achievement of the eleven Republican freshmen senators and their staffs—intended to strengthen the power of the conference as a whole over committee chairmen.

We begin by examining how increasing partisanship has led to more serious efforts to impose party discipline both in the committee rooms and the floor of the chamber, and also how individual senators in both parties have responded to these demands (Mitchell 1997). Additionally, we assess whether the authority of party leaders has been enhanced by comparison with twenty years ago, and examine the effects of increased partisanship on the Senate as an institution. We conclude that party affiliation is indeed playing a wider role in the contemporary Senate (if not nearly to the same extent as it is in the House) and that this is largely attributable to the partisan and ideological cohesion of more recently elected senators. Finally, we see every reason to believe that this growth of partisanship will persist in the Senate, and that absent significant procedural reform, this development is likely to reduce the effectiveness and legitimacy of the Senate as a governing body.

## A MORE IDEOLOGICAL SENATE

From the early 1930s until the mid-1960s, voting cleavages in the Senate were usually based more on region or ideology rather than partisanship. During this period, a conservative majority of Republicans (excluding a handful of northern and western progressives) coalesced with at least one-third of the Senate Democratic Caucus (old guard southern Democrats) in reaction against the New Deal (Manley 1973; Sinclair 1982; Shelley 1983). The security of electoral tenure guaranteed by the southern one-party system effectively made the Senate an institution run by and for southern Democratic senators. Southern Democratic House members were also able to exploit the committee system and the seniority rule to enhance their power, but their influence over the chamber as a whole paled beside that of their Senate counterparts (see table 1.1). When William S. White (1957) and Donald R. Matthews (1960) wrote their contrasting accounts of the workings of the Senate, the one item on which both agreed was the extent to which "southern" mores virtually defined the Senate as an institution. The "folkways" of the chamber—the informal member-to-member understandings about apprenticeship for newcomers, the elaborate courtesies, the institutional pride—all were specifically southern characteristics (Rae 1994). Describing this legislative way of life, former senator Russell B. Long (D-La.) commented:

> In 1948 [when Long first entered the Senate] the South had a lot of influence. There was a gentleman's club, and Dick Russell, Harry Byrd, and Walter George were the key players. They were very talented people and gentlemen in every meaning of the word. In the main they subscribed to a gentleman's code, and they supported it. They would never ask a direct question, but it was implied that there was a condition of reciprocity, that they might have something they had to ask of you. (Quoted in Rae 1994, 98–99)

Leadership in this *communitarian* Senate flowed more from the personal talents and abilities of individual legislators (Fenno 1982; Baker 1988) rather than from the authority of the office they held. A self-selected group of "Senate types" to whom most junior senators deferred, was particularly influential. Richard B. Russell (D-Ga.), for example, who served between 1932 and 1971 was generally regarded as the most respected and powerful figure of the period; "the principal whale" in a Senate that Lyndon B. Johnson divided into "minnows" and "whales." Even Johnson, the most commanding Senate leader of the century who exercised a singular degree of control over the body, held his position largely due to his close relationship with Russell and other members of the "Inner Club" (Fite 1991; Mann 1996).

## TABLE 1.1 DEMOCRATIC SENATE SEATS BY REGION, 1924–1996 (PERCENT)

| Region | 1924 | 1948 | 1960 | 1972 | 1980 | 1988 | 1990 | 1992 | 1994 | 1996 | 1998 |
|---|---|---|---|---|---|---|---|---|---|---|---|
| South | 53.7 | 40.7 | 33.8 | 26.3 | 25.5 | 27.3 | 26.8 | 22.8 | 19.1 | 15.6 | 17.8 |
| Border | 12.2 | 14.8 | 9.2 | 8.8 | 14.9 | 10.6 | 10.7 | 10.5 | 10.6 | 11.1 | 8.9 |
| New England | 2.4 | 5.6 | 7.7 | 12.3 | 12.8 | 12.7 | 12.5 | 12.3 | 12.8 | 13.3 | 13.3 |
| Mid-Atlantic | 7.3 | 5.6 | 3.1 | 3.5 | 8.5 | 7.3 | 7.1 | 8.8 | 8.5 | 8.9 | 11.1 |
| Midwest | 2.4 | 3.7 | 10.8 | 10.5 | 12.8 | 12.7 | 12.5 | 14.0 | 12.8 | 13.3 | 11.1 |
| Plains | 0.0 | 3.7 | 4.6 | 12.3 | 6.4 | 10.9 | 12.5 | 12.3 | 14.9 | 15.6 | 15.6 |
| Mountain | 19.5 | 22.2 | 18.5 | 15.8 | 10.6 | 10.9 | 10.7 | 10.5 | 10.6 | 8.8 | 8.8 |
| Pacific | 2.4 | 3.7 | 12.3 | 10.5 | 8.5 | 7.3 | 7.1 | 8.8 | 10.6 | 13.3 | 13.3 |

*Source:* Adapted from Norman J. Ornstein, Thomas E. Mann, and Michael J. Malbin, *Vital Statistics on Congress, 1999–2000* (Washington, D.C.: American Enterprise Institute Press, 2000).

The Senate has changed a great deal since the time when the Inner Club sup-posedly carried out what White described as the "South's revenge for Gettysburg" (1955, 68). Most notably the grip of the southern Democrats began to erode as the national Democratic party and Democratic presidents embraced the cause of civil rights, southern black voters became enfranchised, and the Republican party became a viable electoral competitor in the South. Large freshman classes of northern Democratic liberal senators elected between 1958 and 1964 moved the chamber in a decidedly more liberal direction in policy terms (Rohde, Ornstein, and Peabody 1985). These new liberal senators also served as the van-guard of a procedural revolution that eroded the old Senate norms of deference to seniority and the committee system. The Senate's new role as the initiator of a national liberal agenda was not immediately accompanied by a rise in the authority of the party leadership, however. Johnson's successor as majority leader, Mike Mansfield of Montana (1961–1977), while sympathetic toward the liber-als saw his role as being more the servant of Democratic senators rather than a leader. He encouraged broad participation, sharing leadership responsibilities, and consulting widely before making assignments or appointments (Davidson 1989). His Republican counterpart for much of this time, Hugh Scott of Pennsylvania, was no more assertive on the minority side.

Thus, rather than centralizing power in the party leadership to advance an ideological agenda, the Senate became more atomized and difficult to manage during the 1960s and 1970s (Baumer 1992). As conservative senators on the Republican side also adjusted to a changing senatorial environment, the increas-ing use of floor amendments and dilatory devices—filibusters, nongermane floor amendments, and holds—and some erosion of the comity traditionally associ-ated with the Senate, frequently combined to bring the chamber to a standstill. Procedural change within the Senate also reflected changes in the wider Washington political community, and in the broader electoral environment of American politics. The rise of the news media and a whole new series of policy-oriented interest groups as a consequence of the further expansion of the federal government during the 1960s interacted with declining party loyalty and the rise of candidate-centered campaigns to create an *individualistic* Senate: a gathering of self-promoting "policy entrepreneurs" in collective disarray (Sinclair 1989). In response to this "new Senate" (Foley 1980; Ornstein, Peabody, and Rohde 1985), party leadership on both sides of the aisle was only intermittently able or willing to assert itself in an "untidy chamber" (Davidson 1985, 225).

Scholarship and commentary on the Senate during the 1980s documented the internal changes in the institution and frequently deplored its unmanage-ability (Peabody 1981; Bullock and Brady 1983; Ripley 1985; Sinclair 1989). In general, it was assumed that Matthews's conclusions regarding the power of party leadership in 1960 were still accurate. Indeed, given the breakdown in internal authority within the Senate, it appeared that party leaders' efforts to lead had become even more fruitless. Several developments within the Senate during the 1980s were not congruent with this analysis, however. For a start, partisan control of the chamber changed hands in 1980 for the first time in over a quarter century. This change not only rallied the new Republican majority behind the program of the newly elected Republican president Ronald Reagan but also initially encouraged more assertive leadership on the part of the new majority leader, Howard Baker of Tennessee. Although Republican cohesion and leadership control eroded dramatically by the end of their six years in control of the chamber, the sharp rise in Senate partisanship evident in the early 1980s persisted throughout the decade and into the 1990s.

## THE CONTEMPORARY SENATE

While the even greater increase in partisan voting in the House has attracted considerable analysis and explanation, the concomitant surge in the contemporary Senate has not attracted the same degree of attention. The rise has been effectively explained in terms of the greater ideological homogeneity of the two parties (Smith 1993; Patterson 1995; Ornstein, Peabody, and Rohde 1997), and indicates the extent to which the number of "centrists" in the chamber have declined (Binder 1996). Since the civil rights revolution in 1964–1965, southern Democrats have become more like national Democrats and conservative southern states and districts now prefer to elect Republicans (Rae 1994). By contrast with the situation during the 1950s, the main line of ideological cleavage in the contemporary Senate now generally parallels the division between the two parties rather than running through the middle of the majority party. The emergence of the budget deficit as the major issue facing the federal government during the 1980s provoked sharp debates between the parties over taxation and reducing the size of government. Moreover, the tendency to address the budget crisis through periodic deficit-reduction packages that have effected major policy change while bypassing the regular federal legislative process also raised the partisan stakes (Sinclair 1997).

During the 1990s, it has become increasingly evident that partisan repositioning has shrunken the ideological center. Sarah A. Binder writes that, "Democrats are perched on the left, Republicans on the right, in both the House and the Senate as ideological centers of the two parties have moved markedly apart" (1996, 36–39). In other words, the two parties are more cohesive internally and farther apart externally than they were in the recent past. Table 1.2 presents party unity scores (with southern Democrats' votes recorded separately) on votes where a majority of voting Democrats oppose a majority of voting Republicans. The overall percentage of these party unity votes expanded under

Presidents Jimmy Carter and Ronald Reagan, reached new highs in 1990 under President George Bush, and soared to 67 and then 69 percent—the highest percentages of any recent president—under President Bill Clinton (Ornstein, Mann, and Malbin 2000).

Ideological shifts and the resulting increase in partisanship depend in part on membership turnover. When the 105th Congress (1997–1998) convened, nearly a majority of senators had been elected in the 1990s. Although the average age and seniority remained fairly steady, respectable turnovers in three successive

## TABLE 1.2 PARTY UNITY AND POLARIZATION IN SENATE VOTING, 1977–1998 (PERCENT)

| Year | All Democrats | Southern Democrats | Republicans |
|---|---|---|---|
| 1977 | 72 | 48 | 75 |
| 1978 | 75 | 54 | 66 |
| 1979 | 76 | 62 | 73 |
| 1980 | 76 | 64 | 74 |
| 1981 | 77 | 64 | 85 |
| 1982 | 76 | 62 | 80 |
| 1983 | 76 | 70 | 79 |
| 1984 | 75 | 61 | 83 |
| 1985 | 79 | 68 | 81 |
| 1986 | 74 | 59 | 80 |
| 1987 | 85 | 80 | 78 |
| 1988 | 85 | 78 | 74 |
| 1989 | 79 | 69 | 79 |
| 1990 | 82 | 75 | 77 |
| 1991 | 83 | 73 | 83 |
| 1992 | 82 | 70 | 83 |
| 1993 | 87 | 78 | 86 |
| 1994 | 86 | 77 | 81 |
| 1995 | 84 | 76 | 91 |
| 1996 | 86 | 75 | 91 |
| 1997 | 86 | 76 | 88 |
| 1998 | 90 | 85 | 88 |

Source: Adapted from Norman J. Ornstein, Thomas E. Mann, and Michael J. Malbin, Vital Statistics on Congress, 1999–2000 (Washington, D.C.: American Enterprise Institute Press, 2000).
Note: Data show percentage of members voting with a majority of their party on party unity votes. Party unity votes are those roll calls on which a majority of a party votes on one side of the issue and a majority of the other party votes on the other side. The percentages are normalized to eliminate the effects of absences, as follows: party unity = unity/(unity + opposition).

elections as well as a high number of retirements in 1996 foretold a changing of the guard not unlike that already witnessed in the House. Less familiar with the institution, the culture, the folkways, or the history of the Senate, these younger members often shun the intraparty or bipartisan comity needed to grease the gears of the senatorial process. When new senators mix ideological intensity with institutional disrespect and a belief that compromise is misguided, the end result is legislative hostility and heightened partisanship (Bader 1998).

Numerous other variables account for recent party voting trends in the Senate. John B. Bader (1998) aptly suggests ideology, presidential politics, party status, and House experience as strong predictors. Patricia A. Hurley and Rick K. Wilson (1989) replicate earlier models developed for the House to describe patterns of party voting, party cohesion, and party strength in the Senate. Accordingly, different forces drive cohesion and strength for the two parties in the Senate. For Democrats, cohesion and strength have been a function of the size of the southern Democratic contingent while for Republicans, cohesion and strength are a product of membership turnover and presidential partisanship.

Absent from these models, however, is the sorting out of the two parties' constituency differences that also help to explain the upsurge in lawmakers' party loyalty. In the South, African Americans are now the Democrats' core electoral constituency, and this has brought southern Democratic senators closer to the national positions of their party. By the same token, the Republican party in the Senate is more uniformly conservative than it used to be (although not to the extent of the Republican party in the House of Representatives). In the South, the most conservative voters now tend to vote for Republicans, not Democrats. In other parts of the nation, such as New England, Democrats have captured Senate seats once represented by Grand Old Party (GOP) liberals.

Although partisan and ideological cleavages in the Senate now largely overlap, this has meant, ironically, that the chamber has become even *harder* to manage, due to the Senate rules that give great power to a determined minority to block legislation on the Senate floor. In addition to making the cooperation between the party leaders essential to the smooth running of the chamber even harder to achieve, "ideologization" of the Senate has moreover entailed that any determined ideological faction can now be extraordinarily effective in derailing legislation. While individualism and obstructionism have always been more characteristic of the Senate by comparison with the House, the decline of the Inner Club and the erosion of the deference and other folkways that at least helped to mitigate these factors have undoubtedly contributed toward the legislative gridlock so characteristic of the contemporary Senate.

To take two examples, filibusters and holds, once regarded as weapons of last resort, have become much more common in the modern Senate, as both individual members and organized factions use the tactic to bring the chamber's business to a halt over relatively minor issues and even for matters of convenience such as scheduling disputes (Sinclair 1989; Binder and Smith 1997; Loomis 1998). Recent congresses have averaged almost thirty filibusters (filibusters are defined as those instances where an attempt to invoke cloture was made). Barbara Sinclair (1999a) observes that in the late 1990s just under 30 percent of major legislation encountered some extended-debate related problem identifiable from the public record.

The distinctly partisan alignment of senators has helped to fuel this "parliamentary arms race" (Binder and Smith 1997, 16). Republicans, for example, defended their use of the filibuster to derail much of President Clinton's congressional agenda in 1993–1994 on the grounds that the Democrats had done the same to Bush and the Republicans in 1991–1992. During the Republican-controlled 104th Congress (1995–1996), the Democratic Senate minority reciprocated by blocking regulatory reform, congressional term limits, and other aspects of the Republican agenda in 1995 and 1996, having learned from the tactics of Republican leader Bob Dole (R-Kans.) in the 103rd Congress (1993–1994) (Binder and Smith 1997).

## A VIEW FROM THE RIGHT

In the perceptions of individual senators, these polarizing changes are becoming readily apparent. During the 1950s when Matthews and White were writing their classic accounts of the "folkways of the Senate," freshman senators were normally quick to adhere to the tradition of the body and its status as the more restrained and deliberative chamber of Congress. In addition to hewing to the legislative ritual and elaborate courtesies of the Senate, it was also generally expected that junior senators should initially maintain a low profile and regard their first term as something of an "apprenticeship." By contrast, many of the members of the Republican Senate freshman class elected in 1994 indicated that they saw their role in far more ideological and partisan terms than most of their more senior Republican colleagues. Many came from the House, after having been baptized by former minority whip Newt Gingrich (R-Ga.) into relentless and combative partisanship. Most of them saw the Senate as another forum to advance the cause of the Republican party and their conservative philosophy on a national scale (Rae 1998, 133). Senator Jon Kyl (R-Ariz.) was typical:

> We're a large group that came together during the early days of the revolution and we have a lot in common. We meet every week, and we work together on special orders on the floor. Most of us are conservatives. In terms of clout we asserted ourselves most clearly on changing the rules of the Senate Republican Conference by sticking together and getting the sophomores to vote with us. (Quoted in Rae 1998, 150)

As Kyl indicated, he and his eleven fellow Republican freshmen worked together as a group to an unprecedented degree, in weekly meetings and on the Senate floor by routinely forming "theme-teams" for morning business debates. Most of the House veterans had engaged in similar partisan activities on the House floor, and sought to bring a similarly combative approach to Senate debate. The so-called freshman "fly-arounds"—where the freshman GOP senators traveled in groups around the country to speak on behalf of Republican Senate candidates for the 1996 elections—was another partisan-driven initiative on the part of the freshmen senators. The brainchild of Michigan senator Spencer Abraham, a public relations expert drawing on his experience at the National Republican Congressional Committee (NRCC), the point of this exercise was to spread the Republican message around the country "unfiltered by the Washington media" and to help elect more conservative Republicans to the Senate (Rae 1998, 153–54).

Troubled by the lack of party discipline and order in the Senate, the Senate freshmen of the 104th Congress made a concerted effort to work together on issues of common interest, particularly issues concerning political reform. Senator Kyl alluded to a direct attempt by his conservative colleagues and one or two similar-minded, more senior members to enforce a new level of party discipline in the Senate by means of rules changes in the Senate Republican Conference. The pretext for these proposals was the critical vote of then Appropriations Committee chair Mark Hatfield (R-Ore.) against the proposed balanced budget amendment to the Constitution in the spring of 1995. Several freshman members felt particularly outraged that a Republican senator in such a pivotal leadership position should vote against an otherwise unified Republican party. They advocated that the conference take disciplinary action against the Oregon senator, including stripping him of his committee chairmanship. According to Senator Kyl, however, some changes along the lines of compelling committee chairs to adhere more closely to the overall party policy agenda were already in the works even before the fracas over Hatfield. "All that was in place before the Hatfield issue came up," he said. "That raised public attention but we were already working on the changes. It wasn't the cause" (Kyl interview, June 14, 1996).

While the effort to sanction Senator Hatfield was eventually beaten back by former Majority Leader Bob Dole, this initiative was important for two reasons. First, the leading proponents of retribution, such as Senators Rick Santorum (R-Pa.) and Connie Mack (R-Fla.), had previously served in the House and felt few qualms about enforcing partisan discipline (Loomis 1998, 102). Second, although Hatfield escaped discipline, Dole was forced to concede the creation of a "task force" headed by Senator Mack to study possible changes in the conference's rules. Mack's task force returned to the conference two months later with eight proposed rules changes designed to substantially reduce the power of the committee chairs, enhance the power of the Republican floor leader, and improve the leverage of rank-and-file members within the party (Dewar 1995; Hosansky 1995).

In July 1995, some of the Mack group's proposals were adopted in modified form by the Senate Republican Conference. Republican committee leaders, like their House counterparts, are now limited to three two-year terms as chair of a full committee. This limitation was also extended to each Republican party leadership position except the floor leader and the largely ceremonial president pro tempore. (This will have only a delayed impact because current committee chairs are able to keep their seats until 2003.) Another noteworthy addition to the Republican Conference rules stated that Republicans who chair a committee cannot simultaneously chair another committee or subcommittee, with the subcommittee chairs of the Appropriations Committee exempted. This opened up about ten subcommittee slots to junior senators, with all eleven Republicans elected in 1994 and five of the eight new senators elected as chairs.

A proposal that would have given the floor leader the power to nominate committee chairs—a process currently managed within committees and strictly according to seniority—was defeated. As a fallback, however, the reformers succeeded in getting the conference to adopt a secret-ballot procedure for the election of committee chairs that would enable the Republican leader to present a nominee in the event that the committee's choice failed to secure a majority from the conference. Republicans also adopted a procedure for establishing a formal GOP "legislative agenda" (requiring the approval of three-quarters of the Republican senators) at the start of each Congress, prior to the election of the committee chairs. Although not binding upon members of the conference, the adoption of the new agenda permits subsequent votes to be taken in the light of members' positions regarding its content. Finally, Republican members of committees may elect the chair by secret ballot followed by another secret ballot "confirmation" by the entire Senate Republican Conference (Evans and Oleszek 1997; Rae 1998).

These new rules did not immediately alter the character of the Senate. But as Christopher J. Deering notes, "they do move the Senate closer to the House in terms of the relations between committee leaders, party leaders, and the party groups" (1999, 97). Secret ballots, for example, enable dissatisfied senators to "send a message" to their colleagues, and term limits force rotation in the system. As Connie Mack, the leader of the task force, put it: "Basically, it's to enhance the leadership's authority and to encourage team play" (quoted in Hosansky 1995, 1382).

Senator Thad Cochran (R-Miss.), chair of Senate Republican Conference from 1990–1996, expressed his concern over the long-term impact of these changes, and certainly believed that the reforms had some impact in his defeat by his fellow Mississippi senator, Trent Lott, in the race to succeed Senator Dole as majority leader in May 1995:

It [reform] has laid the groundwork for an aggressive leadership that has the support of a majority of the caucus and can even pick the senate committee chairmen next time.

In the leadership race, I saw so many chairmen line up to support Senator Lott. All the committee chairmen except two [who did not announce their vote publicly] voted for him over me. Even moderates like John Chafee and Jim Jeffords, who is in-line to be a committee chair. These changes have made the leadership much more powerful by giving them a capacity to insist on party loyalty and discipline. (Rae 1998, 157)

## A VIEW FROM THE LEFT

On the Democratic side, the influence of liberal senators over the party had already become evident during the 1960s and 1970s, when a new generation of Senate liberals were encouraged by Mike Mansfield, the majority leader at that time, to assert themselves against (mainly southern conservative Democratic) committee chairs (Foley 1980; Sinclair 1989). The continuing decline of the party's southern conservative wing and the influence of liberal interest groups in senatorial primaries also operated to move Senate Democrats to the left (Rae 1994). While they held the majority between 1987 and 1994, the leftward movement of Senate Democrats was somewhat disguised by their continuing adherence to Senate individualism and a decentralized leadership structure based around committee chairs and seniority.

Since the election of a Republican Senate in 1994, Senate Democrats under the leadership of Senator Tom Daschle (D-S.Dak.) have become much more cohesive and partisan (see table 1.3). During the 104th and 105th Congresses (1995–1996 and 1997–1998, respectively), for example, the Senate's forty-five Democrats evolved into what some Capitol Hill observers have called "an effective legislative guerrilla force," which has had considerable success in thwarting GOP legislative initiatives (Doherty and Katz 1998, 1822). Minority Leader Daschle has twice been able to mobilize sufficient Democratic votes in the Senate to defeat the balanced budget constitutional amendment (1995 and 1997). In the summer of 1996, Daschle sufficiently held the Democratic minority together behind a series of dilatory floor tactics to stall the Republican legislative agenda, to effectively bring the Senate to a halt, and to force the resignation of Republican presidential candidate Bob Dole as majority leader (Koszczuk 1996, 1205–10). "This is as unified as I've felt the Democrats have been since I've been in the Senate," Daschle himself commented at the time (1205). "If we don't stay unified, we cease to exist" (Doherty and Katz 1998, 1822).

This legislative "guerrilla force" coordinates its activities through regularly scheduled Senate Legislative Directors' (LDs) meetings in the Brumidi Room

## TABLE 1.3 CONSERVATIVE COALITION VOTES AND
## VICTORIES IN CONGRESS, 1957–1998 (PERCENT)

| Year | Votes[a] | Victories[b] | Year | Votes[a] | Victories[b] |
|------|-------|-----------|------|-------|-----------|
| 1957 | 11 | 100 | 1978 | 23 | 46 |
| 1958 | 19 | 86 | 1979 | 18 | 65 |
| 1959 | 19 | 65 | 1980 | 20 | 75 |
| 1960 | 22 | 67 | 1981 | 21 | 95 |
| 1961 | 32 | 48 | 1982 | 20 | 90 |
| 1962 | 15 | 71 | 1983 | 12 | 89 |
| 1963 | 19 | 44 | 1984 | 17 | 94 |
| 1964 | 17 | 47 | 1985 | 16 | 93 |
| 1965 | 24 | 39 | 1986 | 20 | 93 |
| 1966 | 30 | 51 | 1987 | 8 | 100 |
| 1967 | 18 | 54 | 1988 | 10 | 97 |
| 1968 | 25 | 80 | 1989 | 12 | 95 |
| 1969 | 28 | 67 | 1990 | 11 | 95 |
| 1970 | 26 | 64 | 1991 | 14 | 95 |
| 1971 | 28 | 86 | 1992 | 14 | 87 |
| 1972 | 29 | 63 | 1993 | 10 | 90 |
| 1973 | 21 | 54 | 1994 | 10 | 72 |
| 1974 | 30 | 54 | 1995 | 9 | 95 |
| 1975 | 28 | 48 | 1996 | 12 | 97 |
| 1976 | 26 | 58 | 1997 | 8 | 92 |
| 1977 | 29 | 74 | 1998 | 3 | 100 |

Source: Adapted from Norman J. Ornstein, Thomas E. Mann, and Michael J. Malbin, Vital Statistics on Congress, 1999–2000 (Washington, D.C.: American Enterprise Institute Press, 2000).
[a]The percentage of all roll call votes on which a majority of southern Democrats and a majority of Republicans opposed a majority of northern Democrats.
[b]The percentage of conservative coalition votes won by the coalition.

located immediately off the Senate floor. The office once occupied by Lyndon Johnson is used each Friday during the legislative session to discuss matters of party policy, to organize, identify, and guide legislative priorities, and to formulate strategies and tactics against Republican measures. Tightly guarded, Democratic LDs discuss ways to dramatize the Democratic party's difference from the Republicans on upcoming floor activities. During one such briefing, Daschle's aides noted that over one hundred proposals had been brought to the caucus by members, but that leadership would only choose measures that would "help us [Democrats] on effectiveness for forwarding our agenda, on credibility, on the ability to hold unity, and the ability to contrast us with the Republican agenda" (authors' personal observation during a meeting for Senate Democratic Legislative Directors, January 15, 1999, U.S. Senate).

A final indicator of the degree of Democratic unity in the Senate was the unanimous Democratic vote against both counts of impeachment at the conclusion of President Clinton's 1999 Senate impeachment trial. Democratic solidarity ensured that the Republican House managers never had a serious opportunity to get the constitutionally required two-thirds vote for the conviction and removal from office of the Democratic president. "If the Republicans really want witnesses," noted one leadership aide during a Senate Democratic LDs meeting, "our strategy is to let them produce the votes to depose witnesses and drag this [impeachment] out" (authors' personal observation during a meeting for Senate Democratic Legislative Directors, January 15, 1999, U.S. Senate).

## PARTY LEADERS AND PARTY CONFERENCES

Personal inclinations and institutional context broadly shape the styles of party leaders (Oleszek 1995). Factors such as leaders' view of their roles, their colleagues' expectations, and the size of their party's majority in the Senate define leadership opportunities and constraints. Senate Republicans share a full enough sense of partisan identity to encourage or support a leader who is more aggressively partisan. Elected the new majority leader in June 1996, Trent Lott is younger and considered more ideologically conservative and energetic than his predecessor, Bob Dole. "He does a better job at cajoling, intimidating, and influencing committee chairs," commented one longtime Senate aide (West interview, June 10, 1998). "Dole was an institutionalist who put the institution [Senate] before the party. He was a 'Lone Ranger' with no consultative system" (1998). As majority leader, Lott has instituted a form of leadership similar to his days as Senate Republican whip: congressional party leadership as a team enterprise (Sinclair 1999a). He relies more on sharing duties with other elected leaders, attempting to provide more structure but also more openness to leadership endeavors, and striving to include senators in possible party-based activities (Davidson and Campbell 2000). This approach promotes party loyalty, noted Senator Mack, who observed that relying on the "Conference becomes a means to an end" (quoted in Cohen 1996, 2733).

The Republican Policy Committee (RPC), which is composed of the GOP Senate leaders, the chairs of the Senate's standing committees, and such other senators appointed by the Majority and Policy Committee chair, is an apparatus that Lott has used to achieve policy integration as well as to promote party unity. Loosely constructed, yet consistently chaired by a conservative Republican, the RPC is, in the words of its staff director, the "analytical arm of the GOP leadership" (West interview, June 10, 1998). In existence since 1946, it provides summaries of GOP positions on specific issues; researches procedural and substantive issues; and drafts policy alternatives. Its more informal style of operation has long reflected the party's minority status in all but one Congress during the 1950s and 1960s. As the RPC's functions have evolved, its emphasis has changed depending on whether the GOP held the majority in the Senate. Under the helm of Senator Don Nickles of Oklahoma (1991–1996), the RPC became more ingrained in the party's leadership operations (Ritchie 1997). When Republicans returned to the majority in the Senate in 1995, the RPC saw strategic adjustments and prominent use of new technology to advance the party's message and agenda (1997). The in-house television station (RPC–TV), for example, broadcasts scheduling information and other party messages from the leadership whenever the Senate is in session.

In addition to serving as a communications network, the RPC is an important educational forum in the Senate. It participates in the orientation programs for new senators by coordinating the leadership orientation programs for the new Republican freshman class. The committee also sponsors a series of orientations for staff. Weekly luncheon meetings are held every Tuesday that the Senate is in session where Republican senators gather in the Russell Senate Office Building to review the Senate's schedule, to discuss policy options, and to survey partisan strategies. Majority Leader Lott and RPC Chairman Larry Craig of Idaho created policy task forces, which are composed of senators and select staffs and are assisted by RPC policy analysts who address specific issues and recommend unified Republican approaches to them.

On the Democratic side, there has generally been a tradition of more centralized leadership, with the Democratic leader also serving as conference chair and policy committee chair as opposed to be the more dispersed Republican leadership structure where these offices are elected separately by the conference. In 1960, Matthews drew a distinction between the Senate parties' attitude toward leadership: Democrats were "personalized, informal, and centralized," whereas the Republicans were "formalized, institutionalized, and decentralized" (1960, 123–24). These distinctions are no longer so clear in the 1990s. Recent changes in the Senate GOP rules appear to indicate a more centralized approach, while since the election of George Mitchell (D-Maine) in 1988, the Democratic leader has ceded the chairmanship of the Democrats' Steering Committee (which makes committee assignments) and only "cochairs" the Democratic Policy Committee with another Democratic senator. Nevertheless, the Senate Democrats still showed signs of a more partisan approach when Senator Charles S. Robb (D-Va.) was dropped from the Senate Budget Committee as a consequence of his support for fiscal conservatism and the Persian Gulf War.

Dashcle has been a very effective minority leader through deft use of Senate rules and maintaining an extraordinary degree of partisan cohesion on crucial votes (Ornstein, Peabody, and Rohde 1997, 19). In building party unity, Daschle has employed a "carrots to sticks" approach—"I want to induce unity rather than force it," he has said (quoted in Doherty and Katz 1998, 1822)—but he does not hide his displeasure with senators who obstruct the party's agenda. "He doesn't make it painless . . . he has a high capacity to induce guilt," noted Senator Joseph I. Lieberman of Connecticut after he and fellow Democrats John B. Breaux of Louisiana and Robert G. Torricelli of New Jersey defied the party by voting to shut off debate on a GOP-backed education bill (quoted in Doherty and Katz 1998, 1822).

Certainly every indication during the 1990s has been that the Senate Democrats exhibited as much party cohesion and obstructive capacity as their Republican counterparts. Tables 1.4 and 1.5 present marching orders issued by Minority Leader Daschle to all Senate Democrats early in the 106th Congress (1999–2000). As with the Republicans, the number of "centrist" Democrats elected to the Senate has been diminishing and the policy positions of the predominant liberal wing are largely

### TABLE 1.4 PLAN FOR DEMOCRATIC UNITY

*Agenda*
Pursue unfinished business (HMOs, CFR, Public Schools, etc.).
Develop new initiatives.
Prepare legislative strategy.

*Unity*
Protect each other's rights—Stand together on ALL procedural votes.
Stay in sync with House Democrats and White House.
Expand Caucus participation and continue inclusion.

*Message*
Promote our positive ideas.
Anticipate GOP attacks.
Stay focused—Maintain discipline.

*Commitment*
Early, aggressive recruitment of candidates (Task Force).
Substantial financial support for challengers and Class of 2000.
Increase participation and appearances at events.

*The Criteria*
Credibility of proposal to meet concerns.
Unity among Democrats.
Importance of the issue to voters.
Contrast with Republicans.

## Table 1.5 Democratic Formula to Succeed in 1999

Define the *Message* early—Prepare to shape the debate.

Drive our *Agenda*—Demonstrate contrast and force the Republicans to respond to us.

Message and agenda cannot succeed without *Unity*.

Majority within reach with total *Commitment* to Class of 2000.

reflected by a party leadership that has been as active and effective as that on the Republican side of the aisle. Whether greater ideological homogeneity and enhanced party discipline serves the interests of the Senate as an institution is, of course, another issue.

## Conclusion

On the House side, it is generally agreed that the greater levels of partisanship enhance the power of the party leadership (Kiewiet and McCubbins 1991; Cox and McCubbins 1993; Sinclair 1995; Binder 1996). In 1994, the new Republican majority in the House quickly devised procedural reforms that counterbalanced, and in some cases contradicted, the earlier norm of deference to committees that was encouraged by weak party cohesion. By giving priority to the party's agenda, under the new Republican House regime, committees work to enhance the reputation of their party and to achieve their party's policy goals (Kiewiet and McCubbins 1991; Cox and McCubbins 1993; Sinclair 1995; Binder 1996). On the Senate side, however, the indubitable rise in partisan unity and its effect on Senate party leadership has not been as thoroughly examined. Perhaps this dearth of attention is attributable to the Senate's small size and its tradition of viewing members as "ambassadors" from sovereign states. Most Senate observers still share the view of former Senate Republican leader Everett Dirksen (1959–1969) who once stated, "There are one hundred diverse personalities in the U.S. Senate. O Great God, what an amazing and dissonant one hundred personalities they are! What an amazing thing it is to harmonize them. What a job it is" (quoted in Oleszek 1995, 1269). The media's focus on practices that characterize the power of individual senators, such as holds and the powers asserted by committee chairs like Senator Jesse Helms of North Carolina on the Foreign Relations Committee, also tends to mask the underlying trend towards greater ideological cohesion and stronger party leadership.

During the 1980s and the early 1990s, however, it became clear that the Senate became a more partisan body in every sense of the term, even if this trend was disguised by the Senate norms of courtesy in debate and civility between senators by comparison with the more rambunctious and combative tone of the House over the past decade. At the level of both voting data and the individual perceptions of members, the advent of greater partisanship in the Senate since 1980 is marked. The driving force behind the current political transformation in the Senate is the changing face of its membership. Senators known for compromise, moderation, and institutional loyalty have been replaced with more ideological and partisan members who see the Senate as a place to enhance their party fortunes. As a consequence, life on Capitol Hill has become commonly acrimonious (Uslaner 1993). The notion of Senate leadership has long been a contradiction in terms within an institution that serves its individual members. Leadership in the contemporary Senate, however, is slowly reversing this assumption. "Today's Senate is a reflection of its leaders," observed a longtime Senate parliamentarian (Dove interview, June 25, 1998).

For many members and observers of the Senate, this may appear to be a positive development. Adherents of the "responsible party government" school of American government have asserted that more ideologically coherent and programmatic parties with the ability of implementing a program of policy measures through party discipline are to be commended (Burns 1963). If this means that the most individualistic, slow-moving, exasperating, and obstructive element of the legislative process—the U.S. Senate—has become a more shrill and partisan chamber then, according to this school, this should be a welcome step for the American political system as a whole.

In fact, given the powers provided to the minority and the Senate's freewheeling tradition of floor debate, any rise in partisanship in the Senate is likely to have the reverse effect by enhancing the prospects of obstruction and legislative gridlock, as evidenced by the fate of the Republicans' Contract with America on the Senate floor during the 104th Congress. Of course, rules changes that eliminate some of the obstructive practices—primarily the filibuster—would enhance the effectiveness of a partisan approach, but given that such changes require a two-thirds majority under Senate rules, this appears unlikely to happen anytime soon. Thus, perversely, more partisanship in the Senate is likely to lead to more gridlock and frustration inside the chamber, among the wider public in Washington, and beyond.

The framers of the Constitution had certain ideas about the Senate. The House would succumb to transient public passions, but "the use of the Senate," said Madison in his *Notes on Debates in the Federal Convention of 1787*, "is to consist in its proceeding with more coolness, with more system and with more wisdom, than the popular branch" (Madison 1999). In short, the framers had planned for the Senate to check certain unhealthy developments in the lower ranks of society, to take a politically reactive posture to the popular passions in the House, and to provide an opportunity for greater deliberation and reconsideration of legislative proposals (Swift 1996).

Given the increasingly large role played by ideological activists and affiliated single-issue groups in the senatorial nominating politics of both parties, there is little prospect that this trend toward more ideologically committed and partisan freshman classes in the Senate is likely to be reversed. The imperatives of political action committee–fund-raising and conciliating party activists in low-turnout primary elections in contemporary congressional elections pulls senators toward more partisan positions and enhances the influence of party leaders and party conferences in the Senate. Thus, unless there is a sea change in the universe of American electoral politics, the partisan trend in the Senate will likely be maintained over the next decade.

The danger of a more partisan and ideological Senate, however, is that the authority of the chamber will be undermined as its rhetoric becomes more partisan. Failing the extraordinary situation of a Senate majority in excess of the sixty votes needed to impose cloture, the outcome of such partisan debate is likely to be endemic legislative gridlock because of the nature of Senate rules. Eventually, this is bound to have an adverse impact with the public as a whole. Indeed, there is some evidence that this has already occurred (Hibbing and Theiss-Morse, 1995). If a more partisan Senate is perceived to be less effective under the current Senate rules, then there may be pressure from the media and other shapers of American public opinion, such as parties and interest groups, to make major changes in Senate rules so as to make the Senate a majoritarian chamber on similar lines to the House of Representatives. As scholars concerned about the necessity for greater deliberation in American government, as opposed to the shrill partisanship, scandal-mongering, and ideological posturing so prevalent in recent times, we do not view a more partisan, and therefore less effective Senate, as a welcome development.

## NOTE

In addition to the references cited, this chapter is based on interviews and observations conducted by the authors.

# PART ONE

## Deliberation, Committees, and Public Policy

## CHAPTER TWO

# Senate Floor Deliberation:
# A Preliminary Inquiry

## ROGER H. DAVIDSON

To obtain a current snapshot of the state of floor proceedings in what is styled "the world's greatest deliberative body," I have elected to examine a sequence of three high-profile debates that occurred in October 1999. These debates were among the most important held in the chamber during the 106th Congress (1999–2000): the Comprehensive Test Ban Treaty Act, the Bipartisan Campaign Finance Reform Act, and the Partial-birth Abortion Ban Act.

Rather than relying upon the extensive media coverage, I have chosen to carefully examine the text of the debates themselves. Although much is known about the Senate, and there has been a resurgence of interest in the chamber over the last few years, it seemed to me that few if any specialists have taken the time to carefully read what is said, or prepared, in connection with floor deliberations. Such a direct, even naïve, approach would be a way of reacquainting ourselves with the chamber and its members, and might even yield insights about the social dynamics and the state of deliberation within the body. Certainly, textual analyses by such distinguished colleagues as Ralph K. Huitt (1954), Richard F. Fenno Jr. (1976), and Charles O. Jones (1994, chapter 7) have yielded important insights. Replicating such an approach ought to yield similar insights of current relevance, even at this advanced stage of our scholarly research on Congress.

All three of these debates concerned highly visible and contentious subjects. All received extensive media coverage. All invited participation by a large number of senators eager to place their views on record. They occurred late in the session, when the leadership was struggling not only to dispose of these matters but also to gain closure on the "must-pass" appropriations bills for fiscal year 2000.

No claim is made that these three debates are typical of the contemporary Senate, or even of the 106th Congress. However, as I will demonstrate, these debates offer instructive insights concerning the character and texture of contemporary Senate deliberations. They suggest, moreover, some of the prevalent patterns of interpersonal relations and certainly of partisanship. They may also offer insights about the relationship between elements of the deliberative process—especially problem solving, persuasion, and bargaining.

## COMPREHENSIVE TEST BAN TREATY

The Senate's rejection of the Comprehensive Test Ban Treaty (CTBT) on October 13, 1999, was the result of a misadventure on all sides that ended in a major train wreck. From the moment that President Clinton had forwarded it to the Senate two years earlier, the treaty had encountered surprisingly widespread and intense resistance. Senate conservatives suspected that the pact jeopardized the nation's nuclear superiority and would weaken our deterrence against would-be nuclear powers. Initially, Foreign Relations Chair Jesse Helms (R-N.C.) refused to schedule any hearings, under the pretext that two other treaties—the Antiballistic Missile Treaty and a global warming agreement—ought to have been submitted first.

President Clinton publicly urged the Senate to take up the treaty, as did prominent Democratic senators. Seeking to embarrass their Republican colleagues, Democrats threatened to keep harping on the matter, even to the point of bringing floor business to a halt until CTBT ratification was placed on the agenda. After withstanding such taunts, Majority Leader Trent Lott (R-Miss.) and his allies, including Helms, suddenly reversed course at the end of September 1999 and quickly arranged for brief hearings on the treaty—three days in the Armed Services Committee and only one day in the Foreign Relations Committee—and then an equally speedy floor vote.

Treaty supporters realized, albeit too late, that they had fallen headlong into a trap of their own making. As Lott explained it: "for two years there has been this agitation to get this treaty up and have a vote on it. So finally they got what they said they wanted, and then they didn't want what they said they wanted. Then they said: Wait a minute, wait a minute, no, we didn't mean 'now.' Like this thing was just sprung on us" (*Congressional Record* 1999, S12285).

Lott scornfully described the plight of the treaty's advocates: "What they found, when they actually got what they said they wanted—that is, the treaty was going to come up—[was] that the treaty is flawed and it is going to be defeated." Unbeknownst to CTBT's supporters, their adversaries had been quietly mobilizing behind the scenes over a period of some months—gathering factual information, refining their arguments, collecting expert opinion, and then meeting face-to-face with colleagues to share their information and sow doubts about the pact. Among the key persuaders were John Kyl (R-Ariz.) and James M. Inhofe (R-Okla.).

## The Floor Debate

The debate itself was a surprisingly tidy affair: "nasty, brutish, and short," as one commentator put it (Silverberg 1999, 16). It proceeded under a unanimous consent agreement (UCA) propounded by Majority Leader Lott and was provided with fourteen hours of debate, equally divided between proponents and opponents, with four additional hours, if needed, to debate up to two amendments—one allowed for each side. Later—when it became obvious that the treaty was doomed—no less than sixty-two senators went on record as wanting to postpone the debate, at least until the 107th Congress (2001–2002). For a time, Lott gave the impression he might consider a postponement. But mutual distrust precluded a good-faith agreement: President Clinton would not promise unequivocally not to raise the subject in the 2000 election year, something the opponents feared. Moreover, CTBT's hard-core opponents, eager to sink the treaty once and for all, had no reason to let the protreaty forces off the hook. As Inhofe observed:

> This was done by unanimous consent . . . That is the way the Senate is run . . . So anyone could have stopped it. And they did not do it. But they could have. It takes unanimous consent to vitiate that unanimous consent agreement . . . in the event someone asks for a unanimous-consent agreement to delay this vote, I will object. I want everybody to know right now. I will object to that. (*Congressional Record* 1999, S12271)

Why did the treaty's supporters acquiesce to the UCA in the first place? Several considerations no doubt contributed to the fiasco. For one thing, treaty advocates simply misread the number and intensity of the opposition, and were apparently wholly unaware of the quiet but effective consolidation of sentiment that had taken place within the Republican ranks. For another, supporters could perhaps have believed that a dramatic, media-covered public debate, coupled with a full-court press from the Clinton administration, would turn the tide in favor of the treaty. Throughout the Cold War era, after all, the causes of arms control and nuclear nonproliferation had enjoyed widespread support among the public and the policy elites. "If we had had a normal process," President Clinton remarked following the defeat, "you would have seen a much more extensive public campaign. There was simply no time to put it together" (quoted in Silverberg 1999). The administration's efforts, such as they were, proved to be too little too late. The treaty did not seem to have been treated as a White House priority until the last moment; even then, the usual public relations effort—

including creation of task forces and enlistment of expert support—was not mounted. Finally, protreaty strategists reasoned that if they lost their nerve at this juncture, the hard-core opponents—Lott, Helms, and their allies—would certainly not give the treaty another chance.

## Making the Case for the Treaty

The case for the treaty was managed on the floor by Senator Joseph R. Biden Jr. (D-Del.), ranking minority member of Foreign Relations. A scrappy and resourceful debater, Biden engaged a number of the treaty opponents in colloquies, answering their points in a colorful if somewhat disjointed style.

Facing certain defeat, CTBT advocates deplored the limited time for floor debate and pleaded that the vote be postponed. "Unfortunately, we embark on this debate effectively shackled, gagged, and to a considerable extent, blindfolded," complained Robert C. Byrd (D-W.Va.) (*Congressional Record* 1999, S12301). "Are we seriously going to cede, without a murmur, our duty to advise and consent to the ratification of treaties?" (S12302) Byrd then proceeded to lecture his colleagues—at some length and with eloquence not often heard in today's chamber—on the subject of the Senate's fallen estate:

> I have spent 41 years of my 82 years right here in this Senate, and I have respected its rulings, its precedents, its rules, its history, and its customs. And I have to say to senators that I often bow my head in sorrow at the way this Senate has changed since I came here.
>
> I cannot imagine that Senator Russell, Senator Dirksen, Senator Fulbright, Senator McClellan—I cannot imagine that those senators would have been . . . satisfied. They would have been restless. They would have been very uncomfortable with saying that we have to go through with this unanimous consent request which was sent around on the telephone to all senators' offices on a Friday—I believe it was Friday. . . .
>
> Mr. President, I come not to bury Caesar nor do I come here to call Lazarus from the tomb. I do not come here today to make a case for or against the treaty. I am here only to plead that we have more time so we can study it and be better prepared to render a proper and right judgment. (S12302–3)

When the final vote was taken on ratification, Byrd answered "present"—for the first time in his Senate career, so he said.

Treaty proponents had their own substantive arguments to put forth. Many speakers cited officials and experts who favored the treaty—including not only Clinton administration appointees but also national security officials (five former chairmen of the Joint Chiefs of Staff, directors of national weapons laboratories), Nobel laureates, and a large number of scientific, international affairs, religious, and public interest groups. In an extraordinary op-ed article that appeared in the *New York Times* as the floor debate began, three heads of government—Prime Minister Tony Blair of Britain, President Jacques Chirac of France, and Chancellor Gerhard Schroeder of Germany—urged the Senate to ratify the treaty (Chirac, Blair, and Schroeder 1999). Senators noted that the Clinton administration had spearheaded the treaty and urged other nations to sign it, following a bipartisan record of presidential leadership stretching back to the Eisenhower administration. "[T]his treaty is symbolic," declared Chuck Hagel (R-Nebr.), who voted against CTBT but argued for postponing the vote. "It represents 50 years of America's leadership throughout the world in dealing with our allies and, yes, our adversaries, in trying to curb nuclear proliferation" (*Congressional Record* 1999, S12269).

Advocates recited the continuing U.S. efforts to limit the development, testing, and use of nuclear weapons, cooperation between the two major nuclear powers (the United States and Russia), and efforts to thwart would-be nuclear powers such as India, Pakistan, China, or Libya. As Daniel Patrick Moynihan (D-N.Y.), a former ambassador to India, expressed it: "[S]hould we turn this treaty down, the forces in New Delhi and Islamabad will say: 'You see, there are the western imperialists demanding their own liberties to do anything they wish—tests, they have already the 1,030 tests—and they want now to deny them to us? No, that day is over' " (*Congressional Record* 1999, S12269). Closing the debate, Biden returned to this theme:

> We cannot tell what the precise consequences of our actions are going to be this time, but the world will surely watch and wonder if we once again abdicate America's responsibility of world leadership, if we once again allow the world to drift rudderless into the stormy seas of nuclear proliferation. . . .
>
> I end by suggesting to all that the chance being taken by those who are worried about our ability to verify compliance and our ability to verify the stockpile is far outweighed by the chance we take in rejecting this treaty and saying to the entire world: We are going to do testing and we do not believe that you can maintain your interests without testing, so have at it.
>
> We should all consider that this may be a major turning point in world affairs. If we should reject this treaty, we may later find that "the road not taken," in Robert Frost's famous phrase, was, in fact, the last road back from the nuclear brink. (S12543)

### Begging to Differ

The manager for the CTBT opponents was John W. Warner (R-Va.), chair of the Armed Services Committee, although Foreign Relations Chair Helms was in evidence later and closed the debate. Kyl and Inhofe were frequent contributors, and Kay Bailey Hutchison (R-Tex.) delivered a couple of speeches.

The opponents' statements were tightly constructed and clearly researched briefs supporting the proposition that, as Helms put it, "This is a dangerous treaty, contrary to the national security interests of the American people" (*Congressional Record* 1999, S12311). The CTBT's foes argued, first, that the treaty's laudable goals would not halt nuclear proliferation; aspiring countries such as India, Pakistan, Libya, or North Korea would have no interest in curbing their nuclear development programs and would probably ignore the treaty, even if they could be persuaded to sign it. Second, the United States therefore needs to maintain credible nuclear superiority in order to deter nations that might harbor aggressive goals. Third, only by testing—or at least retaining the option of testing—could this nuclear deterrence be maintained in the future. Finally, alternatives to testing, especially the government's "Stockpile Stewardship Program," have been underfunded and by no means operational, much less reliable.

Nearly all of the treaty's foes cited their own lengthy lists of national security officials in agreement with their position—including six former secretaries of defense, four former National Security advisors (including Henry Kissinger), four former directors of Central Intelligence, and two retired chairmen of the Joint Chiefs of Staff. Most of these figures, to be sure, had served in Republican administrations; but the list also included James Schlesinger, who held national security posts under Jimmy Carter.

Many speakers took pains to defend and describe the Senate hearings convened prior to the debate—however hastily arranged and perfunctory (four days total). Majority Leader Lott insisted that the time allocated for floor debate was not out of line with similar ratification debates. A recurring theme voiced by treaty opponents was that senators had indeed studied the matter and made their decisions, and that prolonged floor debate was unlikely to alter. In minimizing the importance of floor deliberation, Paul Coverdell (R-Ga.) argued in the following way:

> In the modern Senate, in my judgment, individual senators come to decisions on monumental issues, such as this treaty, far more from their personal and internal counsel than they do whether or not there have been a series of hearings. Not very many senators are able to attend those hearings, but they are gathering the information unto themselves, and they have been weighing the facts about this treaty for a long, long time. That is where the personal decision is likely to be made. (*Congressional Record* 1999, S12295)

## Bargaining

No substantive bargaining was in evidence during floor deliberations on the treaty. Sending the treaty to the Senate in August 1995, President Clinton had added a series of six conditions, or safeguards, designed to make the agreement more palatable to those who were concerned about protecting the nation's nuclear deterrence. The most important of these provisions was that the president, consulting with the Senate, would withdraw from the treaty if he found that "nuclear testing is necessary to assure . . . the safety and reliability of the U.S. nuclear weapons stockpile" (*Congressional Record* 1999, S12361). Apparently for tactical reasons, GOP leaders failed to attach these conditions when the treaty was sent to the floor. Acting for Minority Leader Tom Daschle (D-S.Dak.), Biden proposed an amendment adding the safeguards to the document to be acted upon. Biden's amendment was accepted without objection, the request being made by Jesse Helms, of all people. But the treaty's foes were quick to observe that the amendment was meaningless. "We accepted [the amendment] because it is what is being done anyway," Kyl explained. "It would have added to the treaty. The president theoretically is pursuing these things. He should pursue them. But they [the six conditions] are not going to make the treaty any better or worse" (S12368).

No one stepped forward to suggest serious modifications in the language of the treaty—a failure no doubt shared jointly by the Clinton administration, Senate Democrats, and even those Republican senators who could normally be expected to play a constructive role. To avoid the kind of humiliation suffered by Woodrow Wilson when the Senate rejected the Versailles Treaty, modern presidents have usually informed the Senate during the process of negotiating a major treaty, often appointing key senators as "observers" to monitor the process. This process has been especially advisable in the case of arms-reduction agreements, which raise sensitive questions concerning the sufficiency of national defense. Typical was the Senate's 1988 consideration of the Intermediate Nuclear Force (INF) Treaty signed the previous winter by President Ronald Reagan and Premier Mikhail Gorbachev of the Soviet Union. Select senators formally served as observers during the negotiations; certain senators' questions about procedures were sent to U.S. and Soviet officials to make the bargaining table work out the details. After four months of deliberation and two weeks of floor debate, the treaty was ratified, ninety-three to five.

Once treaties have been signed, the Senate has shown no timidity in demanding that certain conditions be met. (Even in the case of the Versailles Treaty, opposition senators proposed a series of reservations—which Wilson turned aside.) During debate over the controversial Panama Canal Treaty in the 1970s, fully half of the members of the Senate traveled to Panama to meet with the country's president, and a freshman senator proposed a change that forced the president to initiate further negotiations with the Panamanians.

The CTBT was accorded no such careful treatment. For whatever reason— perhaps because this was a multilateral agreement—the administration failed to cooperate closely with senators during the negotiations. And once the treaty was in the Senate's hands, the chamber's leaders were not inclined to make any attempts to perfect the document. The residue of distrust from the Clinton impeachment debate earlier in the year no doubt poisoned the atmosphere of White House–Senate relations. Indeed, the price of Clinton's Senate acquittal in February may have been defeat of his treaty in October.

## Personalities

Before debate resumed on the third and final day, Majority Leader Lott made a tactical misstep when he allowed unrelated legislative business to intervene. A required motion to return to the executive calendar—that is, the treaty debate—was adopted by a straight party line vote, fifty-five to forty-five. However, just before the vote on this motion, Senator Byrd asked unanimous consent to speak for fifteen minutes—presumably for yet another appeal to postpone the final consideration of the treaty. Lott objected in order to hasten the proceedings, and so after the vote Byrd took the floor to upbraid the majority leader. "I think it comes with poor grace," Byrd complained, "to object when a senior member of the Senate who wishes to speak before a critical vote" (*Congressional Record* 1999, S12505).

> Mr. President, what is the majority leader afraid of? Is he afraid to hear an expression of opinion that may differ from his? As majority leader, I never did that. When I was majority leader, I sought to protect the rights of the minority. That is one of the great functions of this Senate, one of its reasons for being. I would defend to the death the right of any senator in this body to speak. Fifteen minutes? Consider the time we have spent. We haven't spent a great deal of time on this treaty.

After some time, Byrd yielded to Lott, who launched into a lengthy defense of his action while seeking to placate his irate colleague. He noted that at least three hours remained to debate the treaty.

> Majority leaders have to balance time schedules and view of senators and different bills, appropriations bills, the desire to get to campaign finance reform. I gave my word to more than one senator that we would begin today on campaign finance reform. I am still determined to keep that commitment. But if it is 8 or 9, they will say: Well, you didn't keep your word. It is too late. All of that comes into play. (S12506)

Byrd was not mollified by this explanation. For some minutes he continued his lecture on free speech and Senate traditions. Reminding Lott that the Senate operates by courtesy, he warned that "there will come a day when he will need the help of the minority" (*Congressional Record* 1999, S12507). "I think I have said enough," Lott replied when Byrd finally yielded to him. "I appreciate the fact that he has said his piece and we will move on about our business" (S12507). By the time the two senators finished and shook hands, the exchange had consumed far more time than the fifteen minutes Byrd had requested. And the time was charged against the treaty proponents: when Biden asked unanimous consent that the colloquy not be charged to either side, Inhofe objected. "I thank my friend," Biden retorted sarcastically. "I thank him for the courtesy" (S12507).

### The Outcome

As for the Senate's public debate on the nuclear proliferation treaty, Coverdell was surely correct: senators had obviously reached their decisions, for or against the treaty, long before the floor debate. Still, nearly two-thirds of the senators, sixty-one in fact, came to the floor to speak on the matter. Among the Senate's acknowledged foreign policy specialists, the most conspicuous no-show during the floor debate was Richard G. Lugar (R-Ind.)—who nonetheless voted against the treaty and issued a press statement explaining his reasons. In the final vote, the treaty failed, forty-eight to fifty-one—short of a majority, much less the required two-thirds. It was mainly a party line affair: all Democrats supported the treaty, except for Byrd, who voted "present." Four Republicans left their party to vote for the treaty: John H. Chafee (R.I.), James M. Jeffords (Vt.), Gordon H. Smith (Ore.), and Arlen Specter (Pa.).

### Partisanship

The debate, not to mention the vote, betrayed the distrust Republicans harbored toward President Clinton—who had escaped removal from office in the Senate just seven months earlier. "There is a certain lack of trust between Capitol Hill and the White House," Specter observed, "and that is a fact we have to take into account in our calculations" (*Congressional Record* 1999, S12266). Foreign Relations Chair Helms could not curb his animosity toward Clinton, referring to the president repeatedly in contemptuous and sarcastic terms. It was Helms who had dismissed British Prime Minister Tony Blair's message on the treaty with the added comment, "Monica sends her regards." It was as much a measure of Helms's character as of President Clinton's.

The Republican leadership's decision to attack an important global treaty won them a short-term victory. What remains unclear is the potential fallout from the domestic and international arms-control community. In the view of at least one commentator, the summary partisan dismissal of the treaty was at odds with Senate norms. "While there was nothing improper or illegal in their parliamentary tactics, it was nonetheless a nasty and contemptuous way of doing business quite out of character with the stately, sometimes ponderous way of doing business" (Silverberg 1999, 16). However, as the other cases discussed here indicate, stateliness or even ponderousness are far from being the norm in contemporary Senate floor deliberations.

## CAMPAIGN FINANCE REFORM

The McCain-Feingold Bipartisan Campaign Reform Act of 1999 came to the Senate floor on the heels of the nuclear testing treaty. When the measure came up late in the evening, coauthor Senator John McCain (R-Ariz.) complained that he had been promised five days of debate. "Even the staff is gone. Most of the members have gone," McCain noted. "The Senate majority leader knows that" (*Congressional Record* 1999, S12550). Majority Leader Lott conceded that "starting at 7:30 at night is not, obviously a day of debate and discussion." Explaining that the treaty had taken longer than expected, however, he detailed the pressures he experienced. "We are getting down to the end of the session," he said, "and I have a lot of people pulling on me to do [various pending legislative proposals]" (S12550).

### Campaign Reform Advocates

Serious debate began the next morning when Senator McCain explained the purposes of his bill: to ban soft-money contributions to political parties and to codify federal court holdings that guarantee union members the right to withhold that portion of their required dues that is used for political purposes. The first element was opposed by most Republicans: although the party has traditionally led its rivals in contributions, GOP leaders have opposed what they term "unilateral disarmament." Thus the second, antiunion provision was aimed at mollifying Republicans, although it could presumably apply to organizations other than unions. The bill's coauthor, Russell Feingold (D-Wis.), conceded that their bill was narrower than previous versions: "It is clear that this Senate . . . will not pass a comprehensive bill to deal with all or even most of the problems with the current system. We have known this for some time. In fact, the bill we considered in the last Congress was even significantly narrower than the comprehensive bill Senator McCain and I first introduced in 1995" (*Congressional Record* 1999, S12578).

The sponsors presented charts showing the growth of soft-money contributions and the overall growth of campaign spending, and cited the statements of bipartisan sources—including former senators Walter Mondale and Nancy Kassebaum Baker—about the need for campaign finance reform (CFR).

Advocates of CFR, following the example of McCain and Feingold, drew upon their own experience to detail the endless search for campaign money and its results. Richard Durbin (D-Ill.) recounted that, running in 1996 for the Senate while a House member, he would take off during the day, drive a block away to a small cubicle he had rented, and make fund-raising phone calls. "When I received my beeper notification, I would race back to the floor of the

House . . . to cast a vote and then back to make more phone calls and raise more money" (*Congressional Record* 1999, S12597). Incumbent officeholders should favor reform because: "[W]hen we are up and it is our cycle, we can't do a good job of representing people because every day we have to spend two and three hours on the phone. We miss debate that we should be involved in; we miss committee work we should be involved in; we miss a lot of work that we should be doing, representing the people of our states" (S12606).

Barbara Boxer (D-Calif.), another CFR supporter, made the opposite argument: that incumbents are loathe to change a system they had learned to use so successfully. "Why am I standing here?" she asked. Her answer: "I know how to work the system. I have been at it a long time. It is in my benefit to keep it the way it is . . . But the system is broken, and we have to clean up our act" (*Congressional Record* 1999, S12608).

The scope and bias of money-fueled lobbying on Capitol Hill was delineated by Paul Wellstone (D-Minn.), the former Carlton College political scientist turned liberal lawmaker:

> When we debated the telecommunications bill, the anteroom outside the chamber was packed with people. I could not find truth, beauty, and justice anywhere. Everybody was representing billions of dollars there. And when we had a debate about the welfare bill—whatever you think about the welfare bill—where were the poor mothers and children? Where was their powerful lobby? They were nowhere to be found. (*Congressional Record* 1999, S12603)

### Defensive Strategies and Tactics

Mitch McConnell (R-Ky.), the Republican point man against CFRs, opened the opposition to McCain-Feingold by observing sarcastically that the bill had been drastically cut back over the two years it had been considered. "If it were whittled down any further, only the effective date would remain. As it is, McCain-Feingold now amounts to an effective date on an ineffectual provision" (*Congressional Record* 1999, S12852). But his major assault on the proposal was that it targeted free speech. "Soft money, issue advocacy, express advocacy, PACs, and all the rest are nothing more than euphemisms for first-amendment-protected political speech and association means of amplifying one's voice in this vast nation of 270 million people." When Fred Thompson (R-Tenn.), a reform supporter whose hearings had detailed campaign irregularities in the 1996 presidential contest, wondered why thirty-seven companies had given $50,000 or more to both parties in the first six months of 1999, McConnell replied: "I am grateful they did because it gave us an opportunity to compete with the newspapers and the special interest groups that have a constitutional right to participate in the political process. . . . And anybody who wants to make an issue out of it, it is fully disclosed, which is why my friend from Tennessee has the list" (S12601).

McConnell and his allies quickly shifted their attack to McCain's long-term assault on pork-barrel legislation, described as a byproduct of financial corruption of the policymaking process. McCain's website (under headings like "It's *Your* Country" and "Daily Outrage") had cited numerous examples of spending that was alleged to result from special-interest pressures. "We are all corrupted" by this system, McCain had declared. Now McConnell wanted to know: "Who is corrupt?" (*Congressional Record* 1999, S12586) And specific targets of McCain's criticisms came to the floor to defend their records. Robert Bennett (R-Utah) claimed to be the target of a McCain barb regarding an unauthorized federal appropriation for sewer upgrading in preparation for the 2000 Winter Olympics in Salt Lake City. "Who paid me to lobby for [this]?" Bennett wanted to know. "I think the charge that I am corrupt should be withdrawn . . . I want an apology." "The senator is incorrect," McCain retorted. "I did not accuse him of being corrupt. No apology or withdrawal is warranted." Bennett was unappeased, remaining on the floor for some time to defend his honor. Meanwhile, Slade Gorton (R-Wash.) challenged McCain's criticism of a federal grant to help defray Seattle's cost for the 1999 World Trade Organization meeting. McConnell took exception to McCain's criticism of tobacco subsidies. "These are hard-working farmers engaged in producing a legal crop that representatives of Kentucky, regardless of party, seek to defend," he declared (S12589). None of McCain's detractors were in any hurry to conclude their attacks. Goading McConnell to explain how corruption could exist without individual senators being corrupt, McCain complained that "either the senator from Kentucky did not listen to what I said, or doesn't care about what I said" (S12601). (McCain subsequently removed the offending references from his website.)

These objections no doubt reflected personal animus toward McCain by way of his critique of pork-barrel measures; but they also were a deliberate diversion from the issue at hand. "I ask my colleague from Kentucky," Wellstone challenged, "for those of us who want to debate this larger question, how long will you continue with this attack of Senator McCain on the floor? How much longer is that going to happen?" (*Congressional Record* 1999, S12590) Later, Wellstone praised McCain for pointing out that "we have a systemic corruption that is, unfortunately, far more serious than the wrongdoing of individual office holders" (S12605). The only concrete result of McConnell's line of attack was an amendment he offered (which was later accepted without a record vote) "requiring senators to report credible information of corruption."

## Parliamentary Posturing

The second full day of debate opened with parliamentary maneuvers aimed at setting up votes to clarify party positions. First, Minority Leader Tom Daschle (D-S.Dak.) introduced a substitute consisting of the campaign reform bill passed by the House earlier in the year, a bipartisan measure cosponsored by Christopher Shays (R-Conn.) and Martin T. Meehan (D-Mass.). Broader than McCain-Feingold, it not only banned unregulated "soft money," but closed a legal loophole on "issue ads" provided for expanded, speedier disclosure of contributions and expenditures, and forbid both direct and indirect foreign contributions. Then Minority Whip Harry Reid (D-Nev.) put forward a perfecting amendment to the Daschle substitute dealing with "soft-money" contributions to parties, increased contribution limits to parties, codification of a court decision concerning union members' withholding of contributions to their unions' political activities, and expedited reporting and publicity for contributions and expenditures. Then the two filed cloture petitions on their measures to ensure at least symbolic votes on broader CFR. McConnell and his allies subsequently charged that the Democratic leaders had "filled up the amendment tree" in order to polarize the debate and especially to prevent consideration of other amendments. Whatever the Democrats' strategy, a single substitute and an amendment to that substitute do not in fact exhaust the number of amendments that would be in order procedurally. "It was chosen [by CFR opponents] as a matter of tactics not to offer amendments and then talk about the fact that they were not able to offer amendments," Reid explained. "In fact, the majority could have offered all the amendments they wanted" (*Congressional Record* 1999, S12807).

The third full day of debate was essentially a period of marking time before the cloture votes could be called up. Some seventeen senators delivered speeches for and against the various pending measures. Several senators presented their own amendments that, however, were not voted upon. One was an amendment on Internet free speech sponsored by Bennett and Conrad Burns (R-Mont.). Another, from Wellstone, was aimed at encouraging voluntary state public financing of campaigns. Still another, from a group of GOP senators, would prohibit out-of-state contributions to congressional campaigns.

## The Result

The fourth and final day of debate ended the Senate's consideration of CFR for 1999—the third such debate in as many years. In two rapid cloture votes, the Senate refused to end debate on the Daschle substitute (Shays-Meehan) and the Reid amendment. The votes on the substitute and the amendment were fifty-two to forty-eight and fifty-three to forty-seven, respectively—bare majorities that fell short of the sixty votes required to invoke cloture. Partisanship, especially on the Democratic side, marked both votes. All forty-five Democrats supported cloture; on the Republican side, McCain and Thompson voted for cloture in both instances, along with a group of moderates (John Chafee, R.I.; Susan Collins, Maine; James M. Jeffords, Vt.; Olympia Snowe, Maine; and Arlen Specter, Pa.). Sam Brownback (R-Kans.) supported cloture on the Reid amendment.

Opposing forces immediately sought to put a positive spin on the results of the two votes. Noting that the final vote was the twentieth failed cloture attempt on the subject since 1987, McConnell saw "no momentum whatsoever for this kind of measure which seeks to put the government in charge of what people may say, when they may say it, and attempts to take the two great American political parties out of the process" (*Congressional Record* 1999, S12806). Reid countered: "[My friend from Kentucky] can spin it however he sees proper, but the numbers don't lie. We are picking up Republican senators every time we have a vote on this issue. We have eight now. That is a victory for campaign finance reform" (S12807).

Majority Leader Lott immediately steered the Senate toward the next items of business: a continuing appropriations bill (adopted without objection) and the so-called partial-birth abortion bill. When CFR supporters objected to Lott's unanimous consent request, he introduced a motion to proceed to consider S.1692, the abortion bill.

Debating Lott's motion, McCain-Feingold supporters especially voiced their anger at abandoning the subject of campaign finance. No less than fourteen senators, all but four favoring campaign reform, addressed the chamber before the debate ended. "Do we have a good debate or not?" Daschle asked. "The majority leader said no" (*Congressional Record* 1999, S12804). Agreeing that an abortion debate would take place, Feingold protested that the vote to proceed "is about whether we will keep working on the campaign finance bill after a short hiatus to do other business" (S12862).

The author of the late-term abortion bill, Rick Santorum (R-Pa.), had not spoken on the two previous measures. Now he sought to persuade senators that it was time to move on. "I am hopeful we can recognize that we had a good debate on campaign finance reform . . . and it is time to move on to other business . . . I hope we can have some sort of comity here that would allow the business to continue" (*Congressional Record* 1999, S12861).

McCain complained that "we have not been treated fairly in this process by either side" (*Congressional Record* 1999, S12805). He and Feingold had pared down their bill in the hopes of achieving close to the sixty votes they needed to close debate. The result had flung them in the middle of a fierce partisan struggle for leverage on the issue. Hard-core opponents of changing campaign laws could be expected to vote against their bill. Advocates of reform supported their bill but preferred to vote on more comprehensive alternatives. Both sides belittled their pared-down measure, called "McCain-Feingold Lite."

## "Partial-birth Abortion" Ban

Like campaign finance, the so-called "partial-birth abortion" debate was a repeat of earlier Senate battles. Santorum's bills had been passed twice before (in 1995 and 1997), only to be vetoed by President Clinton. Two override attempts had failed, although in 1998 the supporters were only three votes short.

The two measures were alike in other ways as well. Both the McCain-Feingold and the Santorum bills had been pared down in scope and refined in language to attract as many votes as possible. In his opening remarks, Santorum described his bill as "a straightforward piece of legislation that deals with a specific procedure," and not part of a grand strategy to chip away at abortion rights or overturn Supreme Court rulings. In fact, the current version of the bill, Santorum explained, had been specifically designed to conform with *Roe v. Wade*—because the procedure involves babies that are "outside the mother," that is, no longer in the womb. There were exceptions, moreover, when the life or health of the mother was jeopardized by the pregnancy.

Yet, like the McCain-Feingold bill, this circumscribed proposal had become, and would remain, a symbol in the wider debate over abortion rights, a cause that produced heated rhetoric inside and outside the chamber, and fueled fund-raising efforts on the part of interest groups on both sides of the issue. Santorum's colorful language (he spoke contemptuously of abortionists, calling them "executioners") reflected not only his personal passion but a cultural agenda that went beyond the specific language of his bill:

> The agenda [of our side] is very simple. At a time when we are faced with sense-less, irrational violence, with a culture that is insensitive to life and promotes death through our music, through videos, just a little beacon of hope, a little grain of sand of affirmation that life is, in fact, something to be cherished, not to be brutalized; that there are lines in our society that we can't blur, that we should-n't cross, because when we do that, we throw in doubt . . . the issue of, well, maybe this isn't so wrong. We cloud the issue . . . of life for children that are three inches away from constitutional protection. Don't you think that is a good place to draw the line? Don't you think that is a reasonable place to say, OK, enough is enough? . . . I tuck five little ones in bed every night. I wonder . . . what is in store for them, if we continue as the Senate, the greatest deliberative body in the world, to allow this wanton destruction of the most vulnerable in our society. Where are we headed? (*Congressional Record* 1999, S12866)

Santorum's detractors derided the measure as "a political exercise," in Richard Durbin's (D-Ill.) words. "It is not an attempt to pass a bill which will become a law. . . . This is all about raising this issue for public consciousness and a record vote. . . . Some people want a scorecard" (S12871).

Abortion rights supporters, for their own part, clothed their cause in broad language. At one level, they described their concern for, as Barbara Mikulski (D-Md.) put it, "the right of women facing the most tragic and rare set of compli-cations affecting her pregnancy to make medically appropriate or necessary choices" (*Congressional Record* 1999, S12885). These senators at the same time regarded Santorum's bill as the camel's nose under the tent, threatening a woman's right to choose. Tom Harkin (D-Iowa) declared that "we do need to send a strong message that the freedom to choose is no more negotiable than the freedom to speak or the freedom to worship" (S12887).

The ostensible target of the Santorum bill was a specific abortion procedure, called intact dilation and extraction (D&E, or D&X)—that is controversial and gruesome, but apparently infrequently employed. Nearly everything about the procedure is disputed. Many medical experts claim the procedure is never the only alternative in an abortion; others claim it is the easiest and safest procedure in certain cases. Pro-choice experts had long claimed that the procedure was used in very few cases, but prior debates had revealed that the numbers had been minimized. As before, the Senate debate featured charts produced by speakers from both sides—including grotesque photos and diagrams of the abortion procedure (including what one detractor called "cartoons of a woman's body"), photos of women whose difficult pregnancies had made them grateful for the availability of the procedure, and charts portraying the estimated numbers of such abortions. Pro-choice groups had summoned some of these families to Capitol Hill to meet senators and tell their stories. One speaker, Robert C. Smith (R-N.H.), defended his use of scissors and what he called a "medical doll" in describing the grim abortion procedure.

The rhetoric on both sides of the question frequently employed two devices: the use of *anecdotes*, or individual stories, and the abundance of *personal references*—to experiences of family, of children, grandchildren, and other relatives or loved ones. This set the abortion discussions apart from the other two debates, although we did note that a number of political experiences were aired in speeches concerning the McCain-Feingold bill.

As she opened debate for the bill's opponents, floor manager Barbara Boxer (D-Calif.) introduced individual cases of women who had sought late-term abortions to end troubled pregnancies. "I want you to meet a real person," Boxer said. "I want to picture a real face—not a cartoon, but a real face—on the floor of this Senate" (*Congressional Record* 1999, S12869). This was the first in a parade of such cases—complete with large photos of the women and their families. (President Clinton had cited similar cases in defending his first veto of the late-term abortion measure.) Santorum and his supporters, such as Mike DeWine (R-Ohio), had their own anecdotes to share: tragic stories of babies born following a D&E procedure, many of whom died and some of whom miraculously survived. Both sides not only employed anecdotes; each accused the other of arguing by anecdote. At one point Boxer challenged Santorum on this matter. "I say . . . with no hate in my heart whatsoever, you call these stories anecdotes. I say these stories are these families' lives" (S12950). Santorum responded by explaining the dictionary definition of the term.

Personal and family stories abounded in the debate. During a particularly tangled colloquy, concerning exactly when a baby is "born," Santorum and Boxer had a testy exchange:

| | |
|---|---|
| *Boxer:* | I had two babies, and within seconds of them being born— |
| *Santorum:* | We had six. |
| *Boxer:* | You didn't have any. |
| *Santorum:* | My wife and I did. We do things together in my family. |
| *Boxer:* | Your wife gave birth. I gave birth. I can tell you, I know when the baby was born. (*Congressional Record* 1999, S12879) |

Other family stories were poignant. Frank Lautenberg (D-N.J.) related that one of his daughters had a fetus that died in her womb (*Congressional Record* 1999, S12983). "She called me and said: Daddy, I've got bad news. . . . Nothing hurt me more. Nothing hurt her more." He drew a pro-choice lesson: "We are not the kind of family that casually looks at abortion and says everybody ought to have one. This is the right of privacy, is it not?"

## Bargaining and Amendments

As in the campaign finance debate, certain senators on both sides of the divide tried to steer an independent course and present alternatives that would attract their colleagues' votes. In a couple of cases their efforts were successful. One effort at staking out a somewhat different position was a substitute, submitted by Richard J. Durbin (D-Ill.), that would have forbid doctors from aborting viable fetuses unless the physician certified that the act was necessary to save the mother's life or prevent injury to her health. Santorum's motion to table this alternative was adopted by a sixty-one to thirty-eight vote; all but three Republicans supported the motion, and all but ten Democrats opposed it. On the other side of the issue, Smith of New Hampshire proposed an amendment that would have established strict reporting requirements for fetal tissue obtained from abortions. The amendment was rejected by a forty-six to fifty-one vote; seven moderate Republicans opposed the amendment, while one southern Democrat supported it.

Another tactic was advanced by Mary Landrieu (D-La.), the object of opposing pressures from women's organizations and her Catholic background and constituents. Landrieu's amendment would have expressed the sense of Congress that the federal government should fully cover educational, medical, and respite care expenses of families with special-needs children—the reasoning being that parents should not hesitate to bear such children because of financial worries. Her amendment was rejected by a vote of forty-six to fifty-one. Landrieu supported other Democratic initiatives, such as language expressing support for *Roe v. Wade*, but her vote in favor of the Santorum bill itself led EMILY'S List, a pro-choice Democratic women's organization, to withdraw their support (Malcolm 1999). (Blanche Lincoln [D-Ark.], also fell from the group's good graces. Landrieu's colleague, John Breaux [D-La.], voted consistently for the partial-birth abortion ban.)

The most successful effort to counter the thrust of the Santorum bill was a joint effort by Boxer and Harkin to, as Harkin put it, "see if there was support in the Congress for *Roe v. Wade*." Boxer's amendment expressed the sense of Congress that "consistent with the rulings of the Supreme Court, a woman's life and health must always be protected in any reproductive health legislation passed by Congress" (*Congressional Record* 1999, S12886). To this affirmation, Harkin proposed to add a sense-of-Congress resolution that the Supreme Court's 1973 *Roe v. Wade* decision was "an appropriate decision and secures an important constitutional right." Santorum complained that Harkin's amendment "has nothing to do with the bill that is before us" (S12890). But the amendments were accepted by fifty-one to forty-seven, after Santorum's motion to table was turned down, forty-eight to fifty-one. On the vote on Harkin, forty-three Democrats (all but Breaux and Reid) were joined by six Republicans (Chafee, Collins, Jeffords, Snowe, Specter, and Ted Stevens of Alaska). The liberals' success turned out to be the biggest story of the entire debate, and it gave pro-choice forces tangible grounds to boast that the political layout of the long-standing debate over abortion had shifted significantly.

### The Outcome

Inasmuch as the Senate had twice before gone on record as opposing the partial-birth procedure, the final vote on S.1692 was no surprise. The Santorum measure was adopted by a vote of sixty-three to thirty-four—still four votes shy of a veto-proof margin. Forty-nine Republicans were joined by no less than fourteen Democrats (Evan Bayh of Indiana, Biden, Breaux, Byrd, Kent Conrad of N.Dak., Daschle, Byron Dorgan of North Dakota, Ernest F. Hollings of South Carolina, Timothy P. Johnson of South Dakota, Landrieu, Patrick Leahy of Vermont, Lincoln, Moynihan, and Reid). In opposition were thirty-one Democrats and three Republicans—Collins, Jeffords, and Snowe (Chafee was absent).

### FINDINGS GLEANED FROM THE THREE DEBATES

The three recent cases of deliberations investigated here—the CTBT, CFR, and partial-birth abortion—by no means exhaust the subject. They may or may not accurately represent of the Senate's floor business. Nonetheless, they suggest several generalizations about the state of floor debate in the contemporary Senate.

Several of these observations serve to confirm the knowledge, or at least the impressions, that close students of the institution undoubtedly agree upon. In other respects, however, the findings are counterintuitive, even surprising.

## Scheduling

In none of these debates did the Senate behave as the stately, leisurely body it is normally thought to be. Formal or de facto time limits restricted deliberations in all three cases. In the late weeks of a congressional session, the Senate, like the House, is under stringent time pressures—exacerbated in this case by the lingering budget negotiations between the White House and congressional leaders.

Scheduling was largely the domain of the Republican leadership, although outside pressures dictated the majority's tactics. Majority Leader Lott was subject to importuning from all sides to schedule these contentious issues, and at the same time to move with dispatch to other issues. The Republican leadership's decision to execute a quick about-face and schedule the CTBT was, of course, a strategic move to catch the treaty's advocates off guard and to scuttle the treaty. The partial-birth abortion ban gave conservatives yet another opportunity to satisfy an important segment of their core constituency and to sharpen their record of disagreement with the president. Although CFR was an issue the GOP leadership would have preferred to avoid, the bipartisan support attracted by the issue, not to mention public and media interest, suggested that a strictly limited period of debate, culminating in failed cloture votes, would serve to marginalize the issue well before the 2000 election year.

## Debate and Persuasion

Despite the fact that all three issues were highly visible and politically potent, not all senators were heard during the floor debates. The CTBT attracted the most attention, as sixty senators delivered speeches or inserted statements for the record (see table 2.1). Forty-three senators participated in the CFR debate, whereas only thirty-four were led to speak on partial-birth abortion. Participation was virtually evenly matched between the parties in all three cases.

In all three debates, a small number of senators seemed fully engaged in the matter at hand. The treaty debate was managed by Democrat Biden (in favor) and by Republicans Warner and Helms (opposition). McCain and Feingold obviously managed debate on their campaign finance bill; McConnell was its chief opponent. On partial-birth abortion, Santorum argued for his bill, while Boxer seemed to act as point person for the opposition. Party leaders were very much in evidence in all three debates, engaging in procedural maneuvers as well as a measure of substantive debate. Most senators spoke on at least one of the

40 ROGER H. DAVIDSON

## TABLE 2.1 PARTICIPATION IN THREE SENATE DEBATES (OCTOBER 1999)

| Number of Participating Senators | |
|---|---|
| Comprehensive Test Ban Treaty (Oct. 8, 12, 13) | 60 |
| Campaign Finance Reform (Oct. 13, 14, 15, 18, 19) | 43 |
| Partial-Birth Abortion Ban (Oct. 19, 20, 21) | 34 |
| | |
| *Senators' Rates of Participation* | |
| All three debates | 20 |
| Two debates | 27 |
| One debate | 31 |
| None | 22 |

Source: *Congressional Record* (106th Cong., 1st sess., vol. 145, nos. 136–144, 1999) (daily edition), Oct. 8–21. Numbers include speeches and statements delivered or submitted during or after the periods of debate.

issues; twenty senators participated in one way or another on all three debates. However, twenty-two senators were silent on all three issues.

These figures reflect significant variations in senators' participation in floor deliberations. Several factors seem to be in play here. First, the eventual outcome in all three cases was generally known, even though the precise votes (on final passage or cloture) were of considerable interest. Second, and relatedly, two of the issues—CFR and partial-birth abortion—had been debated on the Senate floor on two previous occasions; only the CTBT was an issue not previously debated in the chamber. Thus, both sides tended to treat the debates as symbolic engagements designed to appeal mainly to specific outside constituencies. Finally, the time constraints bore down on the senators, especially on the Republican side. Lott and his lieutenants were committed to strict limits on the time devoted to all three issues, and were able to convey their tactics to GOP senators (most of whom were on the majority side of the controversies).

Senators' speeches and statements on these issues were well rehearsed and extensively documented—perhaps no surprise in the case of the two issues that were up for repeat performances. Eloquence was in short supply, but competent discussions of legislative histories, court cases, and expert opinions were found throughout the debates. Occasional bursts of personal passion, if not eloquence, were seen. Charts, photographs, and even display objects appeared on the Senate floor in all three cases. Two frequent argumentative techniques were anecdotal cases and personal and family recollections.

All three debates were highly rehearsed set pieces, in which the two opposing sides (mostly following partisan lines) spoke their lines and appealed to their respective constituencies. To the extent that the speeches embodied persuasive efforts, they were directed toward outside clienteles—interested groups, core constituencies, and the media. Within the chamber, the debates were less occasions for persuasion than for argumentation: stating and restating long-held and well-publicized positions.

## Partisanship

No observer of the contemporary Congress can be unaware of its intense partisanship (Binder 1996). The House of Representatives is often cited for its partisanship, and of course for the close balance between the two parties in the 106th Congress. Some people are tempted to believe that the Senate's famous norm of courtesy—not to mention its different conditions of coalition building —means that it is a calmer, less partisan body than the House. During the impeachment battle if 1998–1999, the contrast between the two chambers was repeatedly drawn by media commentators.

The three controversies studied in this chapter dispel this impression of muted partisanship. In all three cases, party leaders planned and orchestrated the proceedings, and party lines remained relatively firm in voting. Of the 1,321 votes cast by individual senators in the fourteen record votes during the course of the three debates, nearly nine out of ten (87.6 percent) followed the normal party positions on the issues (see table 2.2). The figure for Democrats was 90.4 percent, for Republicans 85.2 percent. The disparity was the result of GOP defections on campaign finance and several of the ancillary votes concerning late-term abortions. Party line voting was especially marked in the vote on the CTBT—which, given the GOP edge, denied the treaty a majority vote, much less the required two-thirds. Two key amendments to the CFR bill actually garnered bare majorities, but in both cases the issue was cloture and a supermajority would have been required. Senator Santorum's partial-birth abortion bill attracted an impressive (though not veto-proof) majority because of the defection of a number of Democrats, but votes on most (though not all) of the amendments went more closely along party lines.

These debates, admittedly on high-profile and partisan issues, seem to indicate that the concept of "senatorial courtesy" may have become an oxymoron. Personal animosities were so evident that the norm of courtesy hardly concealed them. The hardly concealed animosity displayed by many Republican colleagues toward John McCain had both substantive and personal roots: not only was he threatening the GOP's superiority at campaign fund-raising, but he seemed to have accused his fellow senators of "corruption" for supporting pet constituency projects. Santorum's single-minded passion on the abortion issue seemed to make a number of his colleagues uneasy; although his measure prevailed, he was virtually alone in guiding its course on the floor. Inhofe's hardball tactics—insisting that the CTBT debate go forward—were quite proper procedurally but aroused bitterness on the other side of the aisle.

## TABLE 2.2 PARTY VOTING ON THREE SENATE MEASURES (OCTOBER 1999)

| Issue | Matter Voted On | Result | Party Votes[a] | Nonparty Votes | | |
|---|---|---|---|---|---|---|
| | | | | R | D | Total |
| Treaty | Motion to proceed | 55–45 | 100 | 0 | 0 | 0 |
| | Adoption | 48–51–1 | 95 | 4 | 0 | 4 |
| Campaign Finance | Contribution disclosure (McCain amendment) | 77–20 | 63 | 34 | 0 | 34 |
| | Cloture: Shays-Meehan bill (Daschle substitute) | 52–48 | 93 | 7 | 0 | 7 |
| | Cloture: soft money, union dues (Reid amendment) | 53–47 | 92 | 8 | 0 | 0 |
| Abortion | Motion to proceed | 52–48 | 89 | 7 | 4 | 11 |
| | Table: reconsider above vote | 53–47 | 90 | 6 | 4 | 10 |
| | Table: sense of Congress (Santorum amendment) | 36–63 | 82 | 4 | 13 | 17 |
| | Table: postviability abortions (Durbin substitute) | 61–38 | 86 | 3 | 10 | 13 |
| | Table: Roe v. Wade (Harkin amendment) | 48–51 | 89 | 8 | 2 | 10 |
| | Adoption: Harkin amendment | 51–47 | 88 | 8 | 2 | 10 |
| | Fetal tissue disclosure (Smith, NH, amendment) | 46–51 | 89 | 7 | 1 | 8 |
| | Special needs children (Landrieu amendment) | 46–51 | 74 | 12 | 11 | 23 |
| | Passage of bill | 63–34 | 80 | 3 | 14 | 17 |
| Total | Roll-call votes (n = 14) | | 1210 | 111 | 61 | 172 |
| Party-line Votes | 87.6% | | | | | |
| Republicans | 85.2% | | | | | |
| Democrats | 90.4% | | | | | |

Source: Congressional Record (106th Cong., 1st sess., vol. 145, nos. 136–144, 1999) (daily edition), Oct. 8–21.
[a]Party votes are those cast in accord with the majority of the senator's political party.

On the evidence of these three cases, at least, one must say that the Senate, like the House of Representatives, has become a pervasively partisan institution. Moreover, the partisanship has cast further doubt on the so-called norm of senatorial courtesy—on historical grounds, a questionable principle at best.

# CHAPTER THREE

# Principle or Party? Foreign and National Security Policymaking in the Senate

## CHRISTOPHER J. DEERING

In the spring of 1997, President Bill Clinton settled upon Republican William Weld, governor of Massachusetts, as his nominee to be the next U.S. ambassador to Mexico. In June, Jesse Helms (R-N.C.), the chairman of the Senate Foreign Relations Committee, decided it was a bad idea. "I don't think that he is ambassador quality and neither do a great many of the conservatives and Republicans in the State of Massachusetts" (Doherty 1997). Helms subsequently refused to hold hearings or to allow a vote on the Weld nomination and, despite pressure from within his own party and by fellow committee members, none ever occurred. By September, Weld, who had resigned from the office of governor to fight for his confirmation, asked that his nomination be withdrawn.

Is this just another example of "Senator No," as Helms is frequently referred to, gumming up the works of foreign policymaking? Maybe. But in 1997, the Senate Foreign Relations Committee also gave its advise and consent to 119 other nominees, approved 1004 promotions in the foreign service, passed 37 bills, and approved 15 treaties—including a chemical weapons treaty that Helms stoutly opposed (Cassata 1997a, 296). The effort was concerted. And it was aimed at overcoming both Helms's reputation as a roadblock and the committee's growing reputation for irrelevance.

Ideology, partisanship, interinstitutional competition, and parochialism long have colored the making of U.S. foreign and national security policy. Episodically, fits of cooperation and bipartisanship emerge, or, foreign and national security simply fade from the national agenda. But the notion that "politics stops at the waters' edge" is more a political ploy than an empirical verity. Indeed, the Pacificus-Helvidius debate between Alexander Hamilton and James Madison, an

43

extension of their disagreements regarding constitutional design, was simply the first such high-profile dustup about the relative power of political institutions and ideas in making foreign and security policy. The War of 1812, the imperialist expansion of the late nineteenth century, and a variety of wars and policy matters throughout the twentieth century have done nothing to change that. In the midst of all this, of course, is that exceptional institution, the U.S. Senate.

The Senate's changing role in foreign and national security policy is a function of institutional change, agenda change, and membership change. The principal institutional change during the postwar era has been a shift from the traditional, committee-dominated chamber of the 1950s and 1960s to the more individualist institution of the 1980s and 1990s (Sinclair 1989). The principal agenda change that has impacted these committees is first the rise and then the demise of the Cold War confrontation between the Eastern and Western blocs. And, finally, the primary change in Senate membership was a gradual shift toward northern liberal Democratic domination of the party and the institution and then a sea change to Republican, conservative domination. As will be demonstrated in this chapter, partisanship in the Senate generally declined from the 1950s through the end of the 1970s. But that decline halted and reversed in the early 1980s, first with the Republican takeover in the Senate, and then with Republican control of both chambers in 1995. Because the party polarization is evident in so much of what Congress does these days, it is tempting to assume that polarization has infected foreign and security policy as well.[1]

This chapter examines the extent to which gridlock, partisanship, and/or polarization represent a fair characterization of these policy areas. It proceeds first by examining the constitutional principles that create the foundation for the Senate's role in foreign and security policy. It then turns to a more detailed treatment of the institutional, agenda, and membership changes that have already been noted.

## THE SENATE AND NEGATIVE POWER

In September 1997, President Clinton submitted the Comprehensive Test Ban Treaty to the Senate. Support for the treaty was lukewarm at best and it faced outright opposition among conservative Republicans. For two years the treaty simply sat on the Senate's executive calendar. Then, in the early fall of 1999, the Clinton administration sought a vote on the treaty. The president's Democratic colleagues in the Senate voted unanimously to ratify the document but only four Republicans did likewise leaving the administration far short of the two-thirds vote needed for ratification. On March 6, 2000, Representative Ron Paul (R-Tex.) introduced a resolution calling for U.S. withdrawal from the World Trade

Organization. If both chambers passed the resolution, it would have had embarrassing consequences for U.S. trade policy. House leaders gave the resolution some chance of passage inasmuch as it united conservative Republicans and liberal Democrats in rare common cause. They consoled themselves, however, that a successful House vote would only prove to be symbolic since no one believed it could pass the Senate. Ultimately, House defeat of the measure rendered Senate action moot. But the anticipated role of the Senate, negative in both cases, had very different implications for U.S. foreign policy.

By design, there is little positive power in American legislative institutions—that is, the power to define, advance, and pass legislation opposed by others. There is, however, considerable negative power—the ability to defend the status quo against proponents of change (Deering and Smith 1997; Smith 1989). Neither chamber can act without the concurrence of the other. And, of course, only by marshaling a supermajority can the two chambers overcome the determined opposition of the chief executive. If, as Thomas Jefferson is alleged to have said, the Senate was to be the saucer in which House-passed legislation would cool, its role would be primarily negative. Before proceeding, it will be useful to briefly examine several key institutional features that bear on the Senate's role in foreign and security policy. These are rules, electoral mechanisms, and peculiar constitutional responsibilities (which are discussed in the following section).

Sarah A. Binder and Steven S. Smith (1997) have distinguished between the "original" Senate of the founders of the Constitution and the "traditional" Senate that emerged during the nineteenth century. The original Senate, they argue, was designed to be more mature, stable, temperate, and protective of state interests. In practice, the original Senate met behind closed doors, acted upon previous House decisions, and protected the status quo. While structure defined the original Senate, the traditional Senate had procedure at its core—in particular the absence of a previous question rule and, ultimately, adoption of the supermajority institution of cloture (1997).

Because only a third of the Senate's seats is contested at each national election and because most senators, like their House counterparts, have safe seats, turnover rarely exceeds very modest levels. By design, the Senate was to be the more stable of the two legislative chambers. By design, the Senate was to check the vulnerability of a House "sufficiently numerous to feel all the passions which actuate a multitude" (Hamilton, Madison, and Jay 1961, 309). And by design, the Senate was to operate in a fashion that would protect state interests. In concert, the electoral structure of the Senate was intended to shape the preferences of the members who would populate the institution. And although turnover was much greater than expected during the Senate's first century, it remains the primary mechanism for altering that balance of preferences (Brady and Volden 1998; Krehbiel 1998).

## DIPLOMACY AND DEFENSE IN THE CONSTITUTION

The post–Cold War era makes sharp distinctions between foreign and military policy (diplomacy and defense) difficult to enunciate clearly. Although arguments that favor an energetic and independent executive role where security policy is concerned frequently lump these two separate points together, the founders almost certainly distinguished between diplomacy and defense in the Constitution. The new Constitution needed to be drafted carefully to provide for a true national government that would overcome the weaknesses recognized in the Articles of Confederation. But it had to be limited enough to satisfy those who harbored fears about centralized power. It also needed to stand a chance of actual ratification.

The founders adopted a *consolidated deterrence* approach to foreign and defense policy. Consolidated deterrence meant combining several national strengths in order to deter foreign aggression and diminish national weaknesses. In *Federalist* No. 4, John Jay gives an apt characterization of this notion:

> If [foreign nations] see that our national government is efficient and well administered, our trade prudently regulated, our militia properly organized and disciplined, our resources and finances discreetly managed, our credit re-established, our people free, contented, and united, they will be much more disposed to cultivate our friendship than provoke our resentment. (Hamilton, Madison, and Jay 1961, 49)

For Jay, national security was best achieved through a common commercial policy, stable governing institutions, and "discreetly" managed finances. A strong, unified, national government and an attendant strength in commerce were the two most important requirements for safety from British, French, and Spanish rivals. A well-organized militia and a competent navy were simply added measures of security.

The founders also enumerated for Congress, in Article I of the Constitution, an explicit set of foreign and national security responsibilities including the obvious—declaring war, establishing an army and a navy, controlling immigration, and regulating foreign commerce—and the not so obvious—granting letters of marque and reprisal.[2] The Constitution contains a single explicit limitation on Congress's power in this area: "no appropriation of money to [raise and support armies] shall be for a longer term than two years." In total, the Constitution offers a wide-ranging, clear-cut, and explicit grant of legislative policymaking authority to Congress where national security is concerned.

By contrast, the founders provided a brief grant of authority to the president where foreign and national security policy was concerned. The president's powers are stated in Article II, Section 2; his duties and responsibilities in Section 3. The president's only explicit national security power consists of the following:

"The President shall be Commander and Chief of the Army and Navy of the United States, and of the Militia of the several States, when called into the actual Service of the United States." The president is also granted two diplomatic powers: the power to make treaties and the power to appoint ambassadors (each with the advice and consent of the Senate) in addition to the general grant of "executive power." Section 3 adds the diplomatic responsibility of "receiving ambassadors and other public ministers"[3] and, of course, the responsibility to "take care that the laws be faithfully executed."

In sum, Congress is given the bulk of powers that are necessary for assembling this early strategic triad of consolidated deterrence: defense, foreign commerce, and economic policy. By contrast, the president is asked to execute these laws, command the military if and when called into the actual service of the United States, and perhaps to take the lead in national diplomacy. This division makes logical and historical sense. The profound distrust of monarchical power, especially when conjoined to military power, led them to circumscribe that combination. The diplomatic environment, on the other hand, was more difficult to hand to the "popular branch." Hence, the practical concession to secrecy, dispatch, energy, and efficiency where diplomacy was concerned.

This rough division between diplomacy and defense is generally overlooked today. The *Federalist Papers* scarcely mention the president's role as commander in chief.[4] But both Hamilton and Jay discuss the president's peculiar advantages where diplomacy is concerned. In fact, it is frequently (perhaps conveniently) forgotten that Jay's reference to secrecy and dispatch is a reference to the diplomatic requisites of treaty making and touches not at all upon war making (No. 64). Hamilton extols those same virtues (No. 70) but without mention of either diplomacy or defense: "Decision, activity, secrecy, and dispatch will generally characterize the proceedings of one man in a much greater more eminent degree than the proceedings of any greater number" (Hamilton, Madison, and Jay 1961, 424). Nonetheless, modern commentators have adopted Jay's language and applied it in a much broader fashion to describe the presidency's supposed advantages in diplomacy and in defense.[5]

## INSTITUTIONAL CHANGE

Institutions can take the form of either structures (e.g., committees and parties) or procedures (e.g., appointment processes and rules for bill consideration). Institutions may also be formal or informal. Informal norms of behavior, such as apprenticeship or restraint, are every bit as important as Senate Rule XXII, which governs the cloture procedure used to limit floor debate. Once adopted, rules constrain or condition the behavior of the institution's members and the rules themselves are likely to be resistant to change. If, however, there is substantial turnover in membership or some other exogenous shock occurs (e.g., a war or depression) then the balance of preferences within the institution may change sufficiently to permit alterations in structure or procedure. As we will see in the next section, the level of polarization, the ideological character of the two parties, and the balance of preferences within and across the committees changed in significant ways during the second half of the twentieth century. These changes, in turn, affected the character of a variety of Senate institutions. In this section, two significant changes are addressed: the shifting pattern of statutory authorizations for activities in foreign and defense policy and the alteration of norms governing member participation in policymaking.

### The Ebb and Flow of Authorizations

As with most committees, the institutional role (and import) of the Foreign Relations and Armed Services Committees is closely tied to money. During the Seventy-third Congress (1933–1935), the Foreign Relations Committee—and its House counterpart—passed legislation authorizing the expenditure of $103,000. In the decade immediately following World War II, these same two committees constructed and passed annual foreign aid bills that authorized the expenditure of more than $50 billion. In one congress alone, the Eighty-third (1943–1945), the committees authorized $8 billion (Carroll 1966, 20). The dramatic shift in the amount of money authorized by Foreign Relations was, of course, more than matched by Armed Services for defense. And for both Foreign Relations and Armed Services, these authorizing activities were critical elements of their institutional power. That said, the trends for the two panels would run in opposite directions.

Throughout most of the nineteenth and the first half of the twentieth century, defense legislation provided liberal grants of authority to the military departments to provide for the national defense. And, in the immediate post–World War II era, little had changed. For example, before 1962 the committees authorized the military services an aggregate active duty personnel ceiling of five million even though actual peacetime, active duty personnel levels rarely reached half these authorized levels (Blechman 1990, 29–30).

The practical impact of open-ended grants of authority, and the presence of a large standing army, was to eliminate the Armed Services Committee from any serious role in national security policymaking. By contrast, Foreign Relations' annual foreign aid authorization bill gave that panel a consistent opportunity to influence policy. Only in military construction, 100 percent of which was authorized annually, did Armed Services have a comparable role (Blechman 1990, 30–31).[6] By the early 1960s, therefore, the committees faced a dual threat to their power. The Pentagon was authorized to operate within very permissive programmatic authority, a circumstance that reduced Armed Services to the status of defense cheerleader. Meanwhile, the Appropriations subcommittees undermined the authority of Armed Services by establishing a pattern of *annual* appropriations—a process that frequently also included programmatic guidance.

Thus, the committee seized upon the procedural device of annual authorization of appropriations to ensure its capacity to effectively participate in defense policymaking. The trend toward annual reauthorization began in 1959 with the so-called Russell Amendment—named after the venerable chair of the Senate Armed Services Committee, Richard Russell of Georgia. The Russell Amendment required the annual authorization of appropriations for the procurement of aircraft, missiles, and naval vessels. From 1962 through 1982, the annual authorization requirement was expanded eleven more times. By one estimate, only 2 percent of defense appropriations required annual authorization in 1961—virtually all accounted for by military construction while today the figure stands at nearly 100 percent (Blechman 1990, 30). As a result, the Armed Services Committee produces, each year, what most observers regard as a "must" piece of legislation, the annual defense authorization bill. This bill authorizes the appropriation of roughly 15 percent of the annual federal budget—$289 billion in fiscal year 2000. Unlike the foreign aid bill, this bill has been passed successfully in all but one year for the past three decades or more. Indeed, existing law virtually requires passage.

As Armed Services' role expanded through the late 1960s and into the 1970s, Foreign Relations suffered a comparable decline. Ideological and partisan differences regarding foreign aid ultimately ended in stalemate as the committee was unable to report a foreign aid bill that could garner majority support in the chamber. Foreign aid programs did not disappear, but Foreign Relations' influence was ceded to the Foreign Operations subcommittee of the Appropriations Committee. Weakly led and without an annual authorization bill, Foreign Relations had become a shadow of its former self. As Senator Christopher J. Dodd (D-Conn.) put it: "By frittering away its authorizing function, the Foreign Relations Committee became a largely irrelevant debating society" (Goshko 1985, A12). To arrest this decline, Foreign Relations simply emulated Armed Services by expanding its use of the State Department authorization bill.

### The DeConcini Syndrome

Barbara Sinclair (1999d) has persuasively argued that increases in staff, rules changes, expansion of the interest group community, and the intrusion of mass media combined with membership change alter the traditional Senate in fundamental ways. Rather than the clubby, apprenticeship-driven, institution dominated by committees, the Senate of the 1960s and 1970s was much more individualistic. As Senate norms, which previously proscribed broad, dilatory participation in opposition to committee products, gave way to an expectation of aggressive individualism, legislating in the Senate focused increasingly on the floor (Matthews 1960). Steven S. Smith (1989, 179) documents this move toward floor activity as a sea change in amendments by committee and non-committee members targeted bills on the Senate floor. And, although, Foreign Relations' legislation was a target throughout the postwar era, Armed Services steadily rose as a target for floor amendments to its bills.

Although many recent examples could be marshaled in support of this trend, not least Jesse Helms's scuttling of the Weld nomination, an earlier incident will serve to anchor this trend more nearly at its beginnings. In 1977, the Carter administration submitted to the Senate a treaty that would relinquish control of the Panama Canal to the Panamanians. The canal is, of course, primarily a commercial enterprise, but U.S. warships also use the canal for rapid transit between the Atlantic and Pacific Oceans. The treaty itself was not a Carter administration initiative. Rather, it had been negotiated over a long period of time by both Republican and Democratic administrations. Upon submission, the treaty became controversial in several respects but one senator in particular, the newly elected Dennis DeConcini (D-Ariz.) determined that he would not vote for the treaty unless it was amended. Knowing the vote was close, the Carter administration was forced to take DeConcini's objections seriously. But an amendment would require Panamanian approval, through a plebiscite, and thus threatened to scuttle a treaty that had been constructed over a thirteen-year period. After some hard bargaining, DeConcini agreed to back off the amendment in favor of a "reservation" that would not require further action. DeConcini's reservation was not an isolated attempt, but it was perhaps the most widely publicized.[7] The treaty ultimately passed.

Senate individualism also emerges in the context of expanded use of the filibuster. And, although legislation on foreign policy and particularly on defense policy is generally viewed as must pass by senators, it then becomes a convenient target for amending activity and peculiarly liable to filibuster threats. Thus, Binder and Smith found that only a single piece of legislation on foreign and defense policy has actually been killed by a filibuster since the cloture rule was adopted in 1917. But of the thirty-four Senate actions that were influenced by filibusters from 1985 to 1995, nearly a third involved legislation on foreign and security policy (Binder and Smith 1997, 135, 144).

## MEMBERSHIP CHANGE

Because senators' preferences matter and because most evidence suggests that senators' preferences are relatively stable, membership change is a key element to understanding policy change in general and foreign and security policy change in particular. By wide agreement, institutional and policy shifts of the late 1960s and 1970s were not merely a function of changing public opinion or simple replacement of senators and representatives. Newly elected legislators differed from their predecessors with respect to their attitudes about institutions *and* with respect to their policy preferences. In this regard, we are interested in the overall balance of preferences within the Senate, the balance of preferences within the two key committees, and the relative differences between the parties and party contingents. Moreover, due to the deference accorded to committee leaders—again, particularly the deference to negative power—separate consideration of those individuals is necessary in what follows.

### Committee Leaders and Leadership Change

The Foreign Relations and Armed Services Committees were created in 1816 along with other stalwarts of the Senate committee system—Judiciary, Finance, Appropriations, and so forth. Thus, they have played an important institutional role for the better part of two hundred years. During the immediate postwar period, Foreign Relations Committee chair and ranking minority member Arthur G. Vandenberg (R-Mich.) was an invigorating force for bipartisanship and interbranch cooperation. Later, Senator J. William Fulbright (D-Ark.) similarly marshaled the committee to play an important role in debates about U.S. policy in Southeast Asia—though arguably he paid the ultimate political price in his failure to be renominated in 1974. Likewise, the Armed Services Committee has long been led—indeed more consistently so—by a string of Senate luminaries: Senators Richard B. Russell (D-Ga.), Leverett Saltonstall (R-Mass.), John C. Stennis (D-Miss.), John G. Tower (R-Tex.), Barry G. Goldwater (R-Ariz.), Sam A. Nunn (D-Ga.), and J. Strom Thurmond (R-S.C.).

Does personality and ability matter? It certainly seems to. Throughout the postwar era, the tide of fortunes of Foreign Relations appear to be a function of leadership: ebbing during the recent stewardship of Senators Jesse A. Helms (R-N.C.) and Claiborne D. Pell (D-R.I.) and flowing under Senators Thomas T. Connelly (D-Tex.), Vandenberg, and Fulbright.[8] By most accounts, Helms saw the committee as a brake on policy change. Thus, under his stewardship the committee had been much more likely to utilize its negative power—failing to act on certain nominations or to fund U.S. dues to the United Nations—than its positive power. For Pell, deference to Helms's senatorial prerogatives and the lack of a compelling agenda permitted the committee to drift.

By contrast, Armed Services' role in annual authorizations helped to carve out a more stable institutional role, one less dependent on personality, aided by a Cold War consensus on defense issues, and buttressed by a uniformly conservative membership. As a result, even the least distinguished of its chairs maintained an air of authority within the chamber. Only age, it would seem, can seriously threaten the institutionalized position of the committee's chair—as it did with Stennis, Goldwater, and Thurmond.

## Membership Evolution and Change

From the Eightieth to the Eighty-fifth Congresses (1947–1959), only two Democratic members—Lester C. Hunt (Wyo.) and Henry M. Jackson (Wash.)—were not from the South or states bordering the South. By contrast, half or less than half of the Democrats on Foreign Relations were from the South. Republican contingents on Armed Services had a decidedly northeastern cast, while those on Foreign Relations were dominated by the upper Midwest and the Northeast. By the middle 1970s, six of the ten Democrats on Armed Services were nonsoutherners while Foreign Relations included liberal Democrats such as Edmund Muskie (Maine), George McGovern (S.Dak.), and Hubert Humphrey (Minn.). In and of themselves, the names evidence the sort of changes experienced by the chamber and by the committees.

But, partisan and ideological changes in the chamber and in the committees can be examined more systematically through the use of Keith T. Poole and Howard Rosenthal's (1997) comprehensive analysis of congressional voting. They use a sophisticated statistical technique to array members of each Congress along significant voting dimensions. The liberal-conservative dimension is by far the most consistent and encompassing of those they document. In general, the Poole and Rosenthal scores range from –1, the most liberal members, to +1, the most conservative members.[9] In addition, they are able to generate a presidential score based upon the announced position of the president on various matters pending before Congress. For present purposes, the Senate scores have been combined with information about senators' committee assignments and party affiliations during the post–World War II era.[10]

As noted earlier, and documented in figure 3.1, the Senate gradually became more liberal from the Eightieth (1947–1949) to the Ninety-second Congress (1971–1973). Although both parties contributed to this trend, the data clearly indicate that moderation in the Republican party accounts for the bulk of the change—a shift from .47 to .07 for Republicans compared to a more modest shift of –.20 to –.32 for Democrats. As a result, the ideological difference between the two parties was at its narrowest during the Ninety-second Congress having fallen from .67 in the Eightieth Congress to only .39. Beginning with the Ninety-third Congress, that gap steadily increased again until the 105th Congress (1997–1999) when it reached .73. Clearly, the congresses of the early 1970s marked the nadir of institutional partisanship in both the House and Senate. What of the two committees?

The Foreign Relations and Armed Services Committees share a common trait in that they are consistently among the most ideologically extreme committees of the Senate. But they are distinctly different in that Foreign Relations consistently ranks among the most liberal and Armed Services among the most conservative committees in the Senate (Deering and Smith 1997, 110, 112).

**FIGURE 3.1   Party and Chamber Ideology**

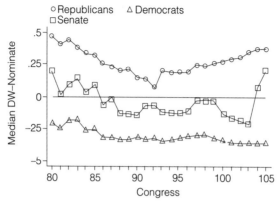

Source: See note 10.

Although the committees did not differ substantially from one another during the immediate postwar period (the Eightieth to the Eighty-third Congresses), they diverged sharply in the Eighty-fourth Congress as each moved to opposite poles in the Senate (see fig. 3.2). Of course, it was the Eighty-fourth Congress in which the Democrats regained control of the chamber, control they would not relinquish until 1981. From the Eighty-fourth (1955–1957) to the Ninety-fifth Congress (1977–1979), the membership of Foreign Relations became steadily more liberal as demonstrated in figure 3.3. This trend is generally reflective of the overall chamber shift in a liberal direction during that time period.

**FIGURE 3.2   Committee and Chamber Ideology**

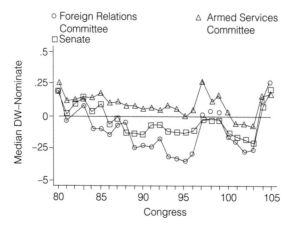

Source: See note 10.

**FIGURE 3.3    Foreign Relations Committee (FRC) Ideology**

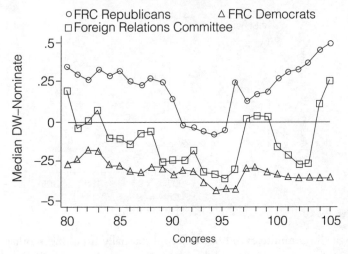

*Source:* See note 10.

As the median liberalism-conservatism scores tracked in figure 3.3 demonstrate, the reverse for Foreign Relations was dramatic and it was one-sided. At the conclusion of the Ninety-fifth Congress, Republican Senators Clifford Case (N.J.), James B. Pearson (Kans.), Robert P. Griffin (Mich.), and John C. Danforth (Mo.) left the committee and were replaced by Howard H. Baker Jr. (Tenn.), Jesse Helms (N.C.), S. I. Hayakawa (Calif.), and Richard G. Lugar (Ind.). Thus, while the ideological shift among Democrats on the committee was slight and in the liberal direction (from a median of –.42 to –.43), committee Republicans shifted sharply to the right (from –.05 to .25) and the ideological difference between the two party contingents diverged dramatically (from .37 to .68).[11] For Republicans, the replacement members not only meant a shift in the conservative direction, one that has continued unabated to the present day, it also meant a change in the internal dynamics of the committee. Senior Republicans on the committee had been inclined to cooperate with their Democratic colleagues—to the point that they did not even press hard for their share of increased staffing resources that were made available by committee reforms adopted in 1976. But together, Helms, Hayakawa, and Lugar pushed their senior colleagues to demand the staff and, over time, to stake out positions in opposition to committee Democrats.[12]

Armed Services also floated in a generally more liberal direction during the early postwar era but the trend halted and reversed in the Ninetieth Congress (1967–1969) (see fig. 3.4). The Armed Services' median ideological position bottomed at .12 in the Eighty-eighth Congress and then rose steadily through the Ninety-fifth Congress when it reached .46. The membership of the com-

**FIGURE 3.4   Armed Services Committee (ASC) Ideology**

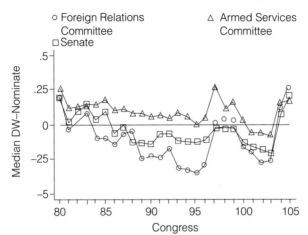

*Source:* See note 10.

mittee also became polarized more sharply—with differences between the party medians jumping from .25 to .61 between the Eighty-eighth and the Ninety-first Congresses—though it closed a bit subsequently as Democratic views moderated. And although debates about certain defense issues—not least, the military policy in Southeast Asia—remained heated, the two party groups generally worked together to produce each year's defense authorization bill. Unlike Foreign Relations and most other Senate committees in the aftermath of the Stevenson Committee reforms, Armed Services retained a combined, bipartisan committee staff. Foreign Relations' minority staff gave into demands from the newly added conservatives on the panel. Senators Jacob K. Javits (R-N.Y.) and Charles H. Percy (R-Ill.) were inclined to stick with the bipartisan approach and, hence, with the unified staff. Separate minority staff are first identified, in the *Congressional Staff Directory,* in 1979. Even so, it was not until 1983 that a separate minority staff is identified for Armed Services (Brownson and Brownson 1979 and 1983).

In sum, polarization (measured by the difference between the median Democratic and Republican ideological scores and tracked in fig. 3.5) in the Armed Services Committee remained lower than that for either chamber or the Foreign Relations Committee until the Ninetieth Congress (1967–1969). Polarization in Foreign Relations, by contrast, tracked along with chamber polarization during that same period before diminishing to distinctly lower levels. As noted earlier, the addition of three conservative senators in the Ninety-sixth Congress reversed that trend. And since then, the ideological distance between the two parties has steadily increased in the chamber and on the two committees.

**FIGURE 3.5**    **Committee and Chamber Polarization**

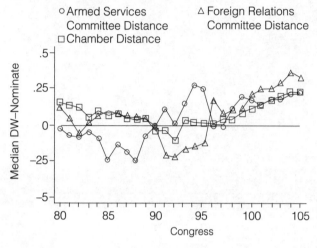

*Source:* See note 10.

## Agenda Change, Gridlock, and Divided Government

As we have seen, membership change and institutional change are important and interrelated components where policy change is concerned. But a third component, the policy agenda, also requires attention. Agenda change can affect policy change in two ways. First, the distribution of Senate preferences on the active agenda may differ from the distribution of preferences on the inactive agenda. Should new issues emerge or existing but inactive issues become active, policy change may result (Brady and Volden 1998, 24–29).[13] Second, to the extent that changing agendas affect electoral outcomes, they may also shape the distribution of preferences within the institution. The latter sort of shift has been addressed, what of agenda change?

While agendas appear to be at the heart of virtually all models of policy-making, they are, at best, imprecisely and differentially defined. In her recent work on gridlock, Binder recognizes this difficulty and has adopted a characterization of the agenda as the list of "potential enactments" that are before Congress at any given time (Binder 1999a, 520). She operationalizes the systemic agenda by using daily, unsigned editorials in the *New York Times* that addressed legislative issues. With the rough parameters of the agenda set, she is then able to determine Congress's level of success and failure at addressing agenda items. That effort is useful in the present context in two ways. First, by breaking down the systemic agenda into foreign and domestic issues we are afforded some measure of the changing size of the foreign policy agenda over time. Second, by examining the level of success and failure we can see whether the membership and institutional changes noted earlier are related to Senate policymaking activity.[14]

As we might expect, the proportion of the entire agenda comprised by foreign and security issues dropped after the Truman administration—from 34 percent to about 15 percent—and remained low until slight up ticks occurred during the Bush and Clinton presidencies. And there is little difference if we constrict our view to the most salient items on that agenda. The minor exceptions being slightly elevated proportions during the Nixon-Ford years.[15] Consistent with common images of postwar trends, the level of foreign policy failure (excepting the Eighty-seventh Congress) rose from the Truman through the Nixon administration.

The rising salience of the war in Southeast Asia and opposition to it had the affect of bringing larger numbers of war opponents into the Senate in the late 1960s and the early 1970s. Likewise, concerns about abuses of power in the Nixon administration diminished the interparty conflict and the ideological distance. By most estimates, the agenda also moved away from traditional arenas of Republican-Democrat conflict—most obviously on the environment. Do trends in membership change relate to agenda change? At best only weakly as the correlation between domestic failure and Senate interparty nominate distance is virtually zero. On foreign policy, however, the correlation between foreign policy failure and nominate distance is negative. That is, as the distance between the two parties declined, foreign policy failure increased.[16] As noted earlier, the relationship can be attributed to larger numbers of antiwar members being elected to both parties. Thus, while the distance between the two parties declined, opposition to Johnson and then Nixon simultaneously increased.

Senate key votes, produced by the *Congressional Quarterly Weekly*, offer an alternative means of measuring the size and content of the foreign policy agenda. Table 3.1 presents a summary of these votes for the last three administrations. Consistent with Binder's findings about the foreign policy agenda, key votes make up a modest proportion of the salient agenda. Data available here do not reflect gridlock in the same way as Binder's but the level of party votes (a majority of Republicans voting against a majority of Democrats) on foreign and security policy issues is quite high across the three administrations and there is no substantial distance, given the relatively small number of votes on which it is based, between partisanship generally and partisanship on the foreign policy agenda.

As for substance, the key votes identified by the *Congressional Quarterly Weekly* are heavily weighted toward Cold War defense issues—the MX missile, B-1 bomber, and the Strategic Defense Initiative—and disagreements in foreign policy that split Republicans and Democrats—aid to the Nicaraguan contras, for example. During the Clinton administration, the salient agenda was characterized by incidence of

**TABLE 3.1 AGENDA AND PARTY: SENATE KEY VOTES**

| President (years) | Key Votes | Foreign/Defense Key Votes (%) | Party-based Key Votes (%) | Foreign/Defense Key Votes (%) |
|---|---|---|---|---|
| Ronald Reagan (1981–1989) | 117 | 34 (.29) | 89 (.76) | 28 (.82) |
| George Bush (1989–1993) | 63 | 21 (.33) | 42 (.67) | 14 (.67) |
| Bill Clinton (1993–1999) | 99 | 22 (.22) | 75 (.76) | 13 (.59) |

Source: Congressional Quarterly Weekly Report and CQ Weekly.

U.S. troop use overseas—Haiti, Ethiopia, and Bosnia—and trade issues such as the North Atlantic Free Trade Agreement and fast-track authority.

## WHITHER THE COMMITTEES: PARTISANSHIP AND INDIVIDUALISM

Changing agendas and shifts in personnel appear to have ushered in a new era for both the Foreign Relations and Armed Services Committees. The two panels have been led for most of the last decade by aging senior senators—and ironically, since the Republican takeover of the Senate in 1995, by conservative southern Republicans. But ninety-five-year-old J. Strom Thurmond relinquished his post in 1999 to be succeeded by John W. Warner (R-Va.) and Jesse Helms devolved power within Foreign Relations to a vigorous set of Republican conservatives (Towell 1998; Pomper 1998).

Thurmond's replacement by Warner is consistent with postwar trends in that the chair is a sympathetic defender and promoter of the military's interests. Warner has ample experience with security issues after having served in the military during World War II and as secretary of the navy. Nonetheless, he came to the position under a bit of cloud having alienating some conservatives because of his lukewarm support for former senator John Tower (R-Texas) when he was nominated to be secretary of defense and failing to back Oliver North's candidacy for the Senate from his home state of Virginia. But Thurmond was under pressure and faced the prospect of a revolt by his own colleagues in 1995. Initially, he relinquished some of the power available to the chair in allowing the subcommittee chairs to establish their own agendas and organize their own hearings. This decentralized approach was a sharp break with the committee's long tradition of centralized operations (Hook and Cassata 1995, 466).

In the fall of 1998, Thurmond announced that he would relinquish his position entirely at the outset of the 106th Congress (1999–2000) and despite occasional rumblings about opposition within the Republican ranks Warner acceded to the post. Warner recognized that his leadership would be challenged by inter-party disagreement and by the reduced salience of defense issues. Speaking before a group of defense experts, Warner said, "We start from a base [among members] that is rapidly dwindling in terms of interest and in terms of background association with military and security affairs" (quoted in Towell 1998, 3183). Put differently, Warner recognized that the agenda had changed and that it would be a continuing challenge for the new panel chair.

The pattern on Foreign Relations was very much the same although it started a bit earlier. "Foreign Relations has been kind of a wasteland. It is not a particularly strong committee to fund-raise from," says Chuck Hagel (R-Neb.), chair of the Subcommittee on Economic Policy. "You can't deal with foreign policy like you dealt with it 20 years ago. Everything is foreign policy now" (quoted in Pomper 1998, 3208). Helms's loosened reins allows the several subcommittee chairs to trumpet their positions on policy issues even if Helms continues to utilize his negative power to block initiatives he opposes. And ranking minority member Joseph Biden (D-Del.) sees a Republican advantage in this. "These guys find themselves in very fortunate circumstances. They find themselves in critical positions at a time when their party is making up its mind on foreign policy. The Republican Party finds itself at a foreign policy crossroads similar to the domestic policy crossroads Democrats found themselves in during the '80s and early '90s" (quoted in Pomper 1998, 3208).

Thus, agendas, members, and institutions will continue to matter. So long as the Senate's new norms of tolerance for the dispositions, even eccentricities, of its membership are maintained, negative power will remain ascendant. Likewise, polarization within the chamber makes it likely that gridlock on status quo policies is likely to continue—again making positive actions difficult. This means that action on fast-track negotiating authority may well be dead for the foreseeable future, that agreements such as the Comprehensive Test Ban Treaty will face tough sledding, and that willful members will continue to make life difficult for appointees with differing points of view. But the Senate will also dampen the *majoritarian* instincts of the House—on continued U.S. membership in World Trade Organization, for example. Most importantly, simple partisan control will not be the key to policy change. Rather, the character of membership change and the status of issues on the national agenda will remain important variables in the role of the Senate.

## NOTES

The author wishes to thank Sarah A. Binder, Colton Campbell, Kevin Hill, Keith T. Poole, Nicol C. Rae, Priscilla Regan, Charles Stewart III, and Paul Wahlbeck for generous assistance in the preparation of this chapter.

1. James M. Lindsay, for one, suggests that it would be a hasty assumption (1999, 173–83).

2. Letters of marque and reprisal are now obsolete. In 1856, the European powers agreed to end privateering. And, as a general practice, nations no longer authorize private third parties to "exact justice." See Louis Henkin's *Foreign Affairs and the Constitution* (1972, 68).

3. Hamilton describes this duty as "more a matter of dignity than of authority. It is a circumstance which will be without consequence in the administration of the government; and it is far more convenient that it should be arranged in this manner" (Hamilton, Madison, and Jay 1961, 420).

4. Hamilton does have a brief discussion in No. 69 in which he characterizes the role as a limited one and compares it to similar grants of authority in existence at the time of the convention (Hamilton, Madison, and Jay 1961, 417–18). Hamilton may also have remained silent on the issue for fear of raising a contemporary red herring. Either that or he experienced a sudden shift of opinion in writing as "Pacificus."

5. For example, in a broad discussion of the War Powers Act before the Senate Foreign Relations Committee's Special Subcommittee on War Powers (100th Congress), Robert F. Hunter adds a section on "The Need for Secrecy." The discussion that follows focuses primarily on foreign affairs and then quotes at length from Jay's discussion of treaty making. At this point, Hunter is making a case for a tradition of congressional "deference to the President in *foreign affairs*" (emphasis mine). It is not at all clear that that same deference was present where defense policy was concerned by either the Congress or the courts (Turner 1989, 832–41).

Another example, but with a more pro-Congress bent, is Nicholas deB. Katzenbach's "The Constitution and Foreign Policy" (1987, 59–75).

6. The construction portion of the defense budget was only a very small percentage of total annual appropriations.

7. California's junior senator, S. I. Hayakawa, a seventy-year-old freshman, semanticist, and former college president, announced his opposition to negotiating with Panama about the canal by opining that "we stole it fair and square" (quoted in Cannon 1977, A1). Details on the treaty ratification process can be found in Thomas M. Franck and Edward Weisband's *Foreign Policy by Congress* (1979, 275–88).

8. On the impact of Pell's stewardship see, Helen Dewar's "Senate Foreign Relations Panel Founders" (1989, A1). On Helms and the brief tenure of Senator Richard G. Lugar as chair, see Pamela Fessler's "Helms Sweeps Through Panel, Fires Nine GOP Staff Aides" (1992), and John M. Goshko's "Virtuoso Performance Surprises Hill" (1985, A12).

9. It is important to note that the scores reported here are for all votes that comport to the liberal-conservative dimension. They are not restricted to foreign or to defense issues. Rather they are broader indicators of members' liberalism and conservatism.

10. Committee assignment data used in this chapter are combined from the following sources: Garrison Nelson's *Committees in the U.S. Congress, 1947–1992* (1993), and Charles Stewart III and Jonathan Woon's *Congressional Committee Assignments, 103rd to 105th Congresses, 1993–1998* (1998). These data are combined from a membership file and an assignment file that can be downloaded from: <ftp://cabernet.mit.edu/sm10501.txt> and <ftp://cabernet.mit.edu/sa10501.txt>. Ideological scores were obtained from Keith T. Poole and Howard Rosenthal, *DW-NOMINATE Scores 80th–105th Congresses*. The data file used here is SL01105B.DAT and was downloaded from: <http://voteview.gsia.cmu.edu/dwnomin.htm>. Poole has since removed that file. It is replaced by SL01105C.DAT, which includes DW-NOMINATE scores for the First through 105th Congresses.

11. The mean ideological score for the group of departing members in the Ninety-fifth Congress was –.1 while the mean score for the incoming group in the Ninety-sixth Congress was .37. Of the exiting group only Griffin, with a DW-NOMINATE score of .26, could be considered a conservative. Of the four new Republicans, only Baker's score of .2 was more "liberal" than Griffin's.

12. Helms, Hayakawa, and Lugar are listed here in order of their committee seniority. Although they joined the committee on the same day, Helms had come to the Senate four years earlier than his colleagues. Hayakawa's higher status was, presumably, simply a function of alphabetization since he and Lugar were elected at the same time. Though Hayakawa would soon leave the Senate, the close seniority status of Helms and Lugar (duplicated in the Agriculture Committee) has proven to be an irritant ever since because of Lugar's desire to chair the Foreign Relations Committee and Helms's refusal, save for one Congress, to relinquish the chair. Friction between the two has been nearly constant throughout their careers.

13. Brady and Volden call this "the shifting of policy realizations over time." That is, status quo policies may no longer work or they may become outdated as exogenous changes occur in the political system. They use the minimum wage as an example of a policy that can become outdated with changes in the macroeconomy. In this context, a U.S. policy of containment or deterrence may succumb to changes in the international system caused by the end of the Cold War.

14. See Binder (1999b) for details on the construction of the agenda and gridlock measures. The breakdowns for foreign and domestic policy were generously provided by Binder (1999b, chapter 3).

15. Binder uses the number of editorials written about each issue as an indicator of salience (1999b, appendix B).

16. The coefficient is –.34 but the relationship is not quite significant at conventional levels.

# PART TWO

## Leadership and Message Politics

## CHAPTER FOUR

# The Senate Leadership Dilemma: Passing Bills and Pursuing Partisan Advantage in a Nonmajoritarian Chamber

## Barbara Sinclair

As legislative leaders are elected by their members, they need to satisfy their members' expectations. For the Senate's central leaders that means keeping the Senate functioning legislatively and, because they are chosen by their party colleagues and not by the Senate as a whole, pursuing partisan objectives. In the contemporary Senate, characterized as it is by individualism and high partisanship, those imperatives often conflict and thus create a dilemma for the leaders, especially for the majority leader. In this chapter, I examine the origins and contours of that dilemma as well as analyze how leaders attempt to cope with the difficult tasks set before them and explore its impact on the legislative process in the Senate.

## THE CONTEXT OF SENATE LEADERSHIP

The Senate operates under the most permissive floor rules of any legislature in the world. Senators can offer as many amendments as they like to any bill and, in most cases, the amendments need not even be germane. A senator can hold the floor as long as she wants and a supermajority—now sixty votes—is required to shut off debate.

The extent to which senators exploit the rules has varied over time (Oppenheimer 1985; Binder 1997; Binder and Smith 1997). The classical literature on the Senate of the 1950s depicts a clubby, inward-looking body in which members were restrained in how they used the great prerogatives Senate rules gave them (Matthews 1960; White 1957; Huitt 1965). The serious legislative work was done in fairly autonomous committees led by quite powerful committee chairs; most senators offered few amendments on the floor, in a narrow range of areas, and seldom to bills from committees on which they did not serve. Junior senators were especially restrained (Sinclair 1989). Senators seldom exploited their right of extended debate for strategic reasons, to try to kill legislation, for example; filibusters were infrequent and reserved for the serious issue of civil rights.

Membership change and a transformation in the broader political environment changed the Senate (Sinclair 1989; see also Foley 1980; Rohde, Ornstein, and Peabody 1985; Loomis 1988). The liberal Democrats elected in large numbers in highly competitive races between 1958 and 1964 found a Senate that did not serve either their policy or reelection needs. The explosion of issues and of interest groups in the 1960s fundamentally altered the political environment and that new environment gave most senators incentives to change their behavior and the Senate. The myriad of interest groups needed champions, spokespeople, and the media, which had become increasingly important, and they needed credible sources to represent issue positions and for commentary. Because of the small size and prestige of the Senate, senators fit the bill. However, to take on those roles and become significant players on the broader stage, senators would have to change their behavior and their institution.

From the mid-1960s through the mid-1970s, senators did just that. The number of positions on good committees and the number of subcommittee leadership positions were expanded and distributed much more broadly. Staff too was greatly expanded and made available to junior as well as senior senators. Senators were able to involve themselves in a much broader range of issues and they did so. Senators also became much more active on the Senate floor, offering more amendments to a wider range of bills. Senators exploited extended debate to a much greater extent and the frequency of filibusters shot up (Sinclair 1989 and 1997; Beth 1995). The media became an increasingly important arena for participation and a significant resource for senators in the pursuit of their policy, power, and reelection goals.

A *Washington Post* story from 1987 illustrates the character of the individualist Senate and the challenges it presented to leaders charged with keeping the Senate as a legislature functioning. "Colleagues Tell of Chiles' 'Martyrdom' on Bill," the *Post* headline read (Auerbach 1987). The story recounted events surrounding the Senate leadership's attempt to work out an agreement to schedule final action on a trade bill, one of the Democratic congressional leadership's legislative priorities. Senator Lawton Chiles (D-Fla.) intended to offer an amendment that would have banned ships from U.S. ports for six months after visiting Cuba, a proposal attractive to the large anti-Castro Cuban population in Florida, where he faced reelection in less than two years. However, Lowell Weicker (R-

Conn.) threatened to filibuster the bill if the amendment was offered. After much "anguish" and a promise from the Democratic and Republican leaderships to bring up his proposal as a free-standing resolution as soon as possible, Chiles agreed to withdraw his amendment and let the trade bill proceed. "This action on the part of Mr. Chiles is a demonstration of reasonableness that we too often fail to see here," said Majority Leader Robert C. Byrd. "Without it, this trade bill would be around here a long, long time," he added. "It was not entirely fair" to ask him to give up his amendment, Republican leader Robert Dole conceded. No other senator had been asked to do likewise. "It is one of those unfortunate circumstances where—if you are reasonable and want to see the Senate do its work—then you are at a disadvantage," Dole continued.

A body in which individual senators are willing and able to disrupt the legislative schedule of the joint leadership and possibly block enactment of high-priority legislation, one in which a senator's act of self-restraint is labeled a "martyrdom" by his peers and considered worthy of news coverage is a very different institution from the clubby, restrained Senate of the 1950s. The individualist Senate was a body whose members had different expectations and so presented its leaders with quite different problems. Every senator regardless of seniority considered himself entitled to participate on any issue that interested him for either constituency or policy reasons. Senators took for granted that they—and their colleagues—would regularly exploit the powers Senate rules gave them. Senators became increasingly outward-directed, focusing on their links with interest groups, policy communities, and the media more then their ties to one another. Senators came to expect that their leaders would fully accommodate if not facilitate their individualist strategies and yet still keep the Senate functioning.

With increasing partisanship in the Senate in the late 1980s and 1990s, senators' expectations of their leaders became even more complex. Party realignment in the South and the growing conservatism of Republican party activists and, to some extent, Republican voters had by the late 1980s begun to change significantly the character of the political parties in the Senate. Few conservative southern Democrats remained; over time, most were replaced by even more conservative—and more unabashedly ideological—southern Republicans. In the rest of the country, as a result of the changing character of the Republican party, moderate Republicans were gradually replaced by Democrats or conservative Republicans. In the 1990s, a number of veterans of Newt Gingrich's (R-Ga.) House Republican party were elected to the Senate.

The growing partisanship manifested itself in voting in committee and on the floor. In the late 1960s and early 1970s, Senate committees seldom split along party lines (only 4 percent on major legislation in the Ninety-first Congress); in the Republican congresses of the 1990s, partisan committee splits were common; they occurred on 34 percent of major measures in the 104th

(1995–1996) and on 25 percent in the 105th (1997–1998) (Sinclair 1999c). In the late 1960s and early 1970s, only about a third of Senate roll call votes pitted a majority of Democrats against a majority of Republicans. By the 1990s, from half to two-thirds of roll calls were such party votes. The frequency with which senators voted with their partisan colleagues on party votes increased significantly as well. By the 1990s, a typical party vote saw well over 80 percent of the Democrats voting together on one side and well over 80 percent of the Republicans on the other (*Congressional Quarterly Weekly Report,* various dates).

Senators, unlike members of the House of Representatives, gave their party leaders no significant new powers as the parties became more ideologically homogeneous internally and moved further apart. Yet senators' expectations of their leaders were affected. As party leaders, the majority leader and the minority leader, the Senate's only central leaders, have since the inception of these positions been expected to further their party colleagues' collective partisan interests (Gamm and Smith 1999). Still, as partisan divisions and partisan rivalries became sharper, these expectations also intensified and fulfilling these expectations conflicted more frequently with the imperative that leaders keep the Senate functioning.

## KEEPING THE SENATE FUNCTIONING

Whether a senator seeks reelection, policy, or power or all three, for the senator to attain her goals, the Senate must be capable of legislating. Even the senator who pursues his goals primarily through a strategy of blocking requires that the Senate be capable of passing bills in order to gain advantage from using his prerogatives to prevent specific legislative actions.

For the Senate to legislate, a number of coordination tasks must be performed and, as in the House, the central leadership is charged with carrying those out. The majority leader, although not an officer of his chamber as the Speaker of the House is, is as close as the Senate comes to having a central leader. He, however, lacks the powers that can derive from being presiding officer and must contend with a membership that commands enormous individual prerogatives. The triumph of individualism in the Senate dictates a highly accommodating leadership style in a chamber already so inclined.

The core of the majority leader's coordination tasks is the scheduling of legislation for floor consideration. To bring legislation to the floor, the majority leader uses his right of first recognition, a prerogative he has had under Senate precedents since the 1930s. He can move that a bill be taken off the calendar and considered, but the motion to proceed is a debatable, and thus filibusterable motion. Since the 1950s, the Senate has usually operated by unanimous consent (Evans and Oleszek 1999; Oleszek 1996). Obtaining recognition before any other senator seeking it, as is his right, the majority leader asks unanimous consent that a bill be taken off the calendar and considered.

Ensuring that unanimous consent will be forthcoming requires an elaborate consultation process, one that has become more elaborate and more difficult with the development of the individualist Senate. The majority leader must, of course, consult with the chairs of the relevant committees and subcommittees; other senators known to be especially active on the issue will also be consulted. With the increase in senators' expectations of participation, a good deal of the consultation process has become semi-institutionalized. The party secretaries, employees of the Senate political parties and their leaderships, are charged with keeping lists of those senators who have requested to be consulted before a given bill or nomination is brought to the floor. When the majority leader has cleared his plans with all the relevant actors on his side of the aisle, he consults with the minority leader, who must then consult with the relevant actors among his members. If a complex unanimous consent agreement (UCA) is at issue, the majority may convey an offer in writing to which the minority may then respond with a counteroffer. When the majority and minority leaders have a tentative agreement, they put it on the "hot line," a direct phone line to the offices of all senators. A recorded message specifies the terms of the UCA and asks any senator who has objections to contact his leader within a given period of time.

Such broad consultation is a necessity in the contemporary Senate. Any one senator can destroy the floor schedule by objecting to unanimous consent requests and senators are much more willing to do so than they were in the Senate of the 1950s. The threat to object to a unanimous consent request on a specific matter has become semi-institutionalized in the practice of "holds." Senators inform their leader directly or through the party secretary, who keeps the list of "holds." In order to obtain a unanimous consent request, the leaders must satisfy all interested senators sufficiently to keep them from objecting. From the leaders' perspective, the "hold" system at least provides information on who has a problem that needs to be addressed.

Keeping the Senate functioning as a legislature requires broad accommodation; it dictates satisfying every senator to some extent. To be sure, there are "holds" a majority leader cannot honor and threats to filibuster he cannot give in to. "Must-pass" legislation such as appropriations bills literally must pass even if that requires suffering and breaking a filibuster. But, as a senior staffer explained, "If there are going to be cloture votes and the like, it can take days to ram something through this place. You can't do it on every bill. You can only do it on a selected few bills."

Leaders can and do use "threats" to persuade senators to limit their individualism: "we'll be here till Christmas" is a frequent leadership refrain. A few recalcitrants will be subjected to considerable peer pressure when time is short.

Leaders themselves, however, are under pressure from senators to limit the inconvenience to which they are subject. The dominant strategy for leaders tends to be one of accommodation.

The passage of the legislation incorporating the appropriations deal between Congress and President Bill Clinton in 1999 illustrates the problems facing contemporary Senate leaders and their strategies for coping with them. Administration negotiators and congressional Republicans reached a deal on the five unfinished appropriations bills on Wednesday night, November 17. This was weeks after the October 1 beginning of the fiscal year and many days after the leaderships' target for adjournment of the first session of the 106th Congress (1999–2000) so everyone was eager to finish and go home. The deal was wrapped into the conference report on the District of Columbia appropriations bill, the House leadership scheduled a quick vote, and the House approved it the following day.

In the Senate, in contrast, the individual senators who had problems with aspects of the deal could and did delay action. Senator Max Baucus (D-Mont.) objected to the dropping of a $1.25 billion loan guarantee provision designed to help satellite companies expand local programming into rural areas. Baucus threatened to filibuster the appropriations package but relented after being assured by Majority Leader Trent Lott (R-Miss.) that the Senate would vote on this provision as a stand-alone bill by April 1. Senator Robert C. Byrd (D-W.Va.), outraged at the exclusion of a provision overturning a court case adverse to his state's coal mining industry, a provision that the Clinton administration strongly opposed, was mollified by an immediate vote on his legislation as a free-standing measure. Similarly, North Carolina Senators Jesse Helms (R) and John Edwards (D) got a vote on additional disaster aid to their state.

By Friday, only the senators from Wisconsin and Minnesota were still objecting to a vote on the appropriations package. They vehemently objected to the inclusion of the Northeast Dairy Compact, which, they believed, put their dairy farmers at a disadvantage. Led by the usually mild-mannered Herb Kohl (D-Wis.), these senators were prepared to sink the entire agreement. The party leaders worked together to find a solution. Minority Leader Tom Daschle (D-S.Dak.) talked to Kohl, urging him to end the filibuster so as not to derail the agreement on spending. "Obviously they had leverage," said Daschle, when asked about his conversation with Kohl. "It was a question of how to appropriately use that leverage" (quoted in Preston 1999 and Bresnahan 1999a, 1, 15). Lott filed a cloture petition and set the vote for 1:01 A.M. on Saturday. Meanwhile, he and Daschle continued to talk to the four senators about what could be done. The four could hardly be unaware that their ninety-six colleagues were eager to get home and would become increasingly annoyed as the impasse stretched on. As Lott said, "A lot of Senators have commitments and they [were] very disturbed that we couldn't find a way to complete this without being here until 2 or 3 o'clock in the morning. Senator Kohl, I believe, realizes he can get commitments now and can affect the debate next year that he might not be able to get at 1 [A.M.] or 2 [A.M.]" (quoted in Preston and Bresnahan 1999, 1, 15).

Kohl and his colleagues relented and allowed a vote on passage of the spending bill on Friday afternoon. In return, they received a promise of hearings and legislation in the second session from Agriculture Committee Chairman Richard Lugar (R-Ind.), public statements by both Daschle and Lott that they opposed the current way of setting milk prices embodied in the compact, and a commitment to make developing a different system a high priority for the second session.

The close working relationship between the majority leader and the minority leader, the use of both procedural and peer pressure to encourage the recalcitrant to deal, and the accommodation to some extent of all senators with problems all characterize the leadership enterprise in the contemporary Senate. They are necessary to keeping the Senate functioning. After the Senate finally adjourned, Majority Leader Trent Lott said of the body, "If there is any place in the world that is like good wine, I guess it is the Senate. It just takes time, and in due time you will get a result. But until the Senate is ready and Senators are ready, you can't make it happen" (quoted in Preston and Bresnahan 1999, 1, 15). Less mellow, Sheila Burke, for many years Senate majority and minority leader Bob Dole's top staffer, contends, "The Senate is frighteningly hard to manage" (Dole Institute Conference, July 16, 1999).

## PURSUING PARTISAN OBJECTIVES

Asked to describe the job of the majority leader, a senior Lott aide replied, "It consists of, well, one is traffic cop. The majority leader is the gatekeeper. No major legislation gets considered on the floor without the majority leader's okay. He's the voice of 54 other members, and this is a more political role. He's a sounding board. Ideas filter up to him, and he pretty much decides what the party position on the floor will be."

A high-ranking aide to Minority Leader Tom Daschle responded to a similar question by saying, "To try to protect the rights of our caucus on issues of concern to them. Second, to make sure that Democrats' priorities are considered by the Senate. And the third task is spokesperson for the president, especially where we think that his perspective is not getting a fair shake up here; [when] it's not getting represented."

Not surprisingly, given that they are elected by their party colleagues, pursuing partisan objectives is seen as a major part of the two leaders' jobs. With the increase in partisan polarization, the narrow margins, and the shifts in partisan control of the chamber, senators' expectations that their leader promote their collective partisan interests have intensified. Yet senators also expect their leaders to impose few constraints on their individualist goals—advancing strategies despite the potential that such individualist strategies may conflict with party promoting efforts and with simply keeping the Senate functioning as well. "It's a tough role," a Lott aide said of the job of the majority leader. "Each senator has an independent constituency, has access to the media."

When compared with the Speaker of the House, the Senate majority leader has more meager powers and his party colleagues have much greater prerogatives, so the majority leader's task of promoting the collective partisan interests of his members while not interfering with their individual goal-seeking strategies is more difficult than that of the Speaker. In addition, however, the majority leader faces a dilemma that the Speaker is spared. In the Senate unlike the House, a majority is not sufficient to act; to keep the Senate functioning requires supermajorities and this almost always requires that the majority leader accommodate the minority to some extent. Yet, with the intensification of partisan differences, what his members see as central to the promotion of partisan interests is increasingly likely to be strongly opposed by the minority and thus to work against keeping the Senate functioning as a legislature. Furthermore, in the Senate, a cohesive, organized minority party has available formidable strategies for promoting its partisan interests. Majority party senators expect their leader to thwart such minority party efforts, but doing so is likely to interfere with keeping the Senate functioning.

## Changing Strategies for Pursuing Partisan Advantage

With the increase in partisanship, senators' expectations of what their leaders should do and their expectations of how the leaders should do it has changed. Whether in the majority or in the minority, senators now expect their party leader to promote their collective partisan interests through outside-directed message strategies as well as by internal procedural and legislative strategies. Senators also expect their leaders to carry out all their functions through a highly inclusive and consultative style. In this more partisan era, senators are often willing to be partners in party collective action but they are not willing to be simple followers.

## Message Strategies

The increasing role of the media in American politics contributed greatly to the development of the individualist Senate; senators as individuals found the media available and extremely useful in the pursuit of their goals (Sinclair 1989, chapter 10). By the mid-1980s, senators had come to realize that they needed to be concerned about their party's image and that their leader affected that image; the belief that he would better represent Senate Democrats on television and more effectively promote their issues in the media influenced Senate Democrats' election of George Mitchell to replace Robert C. Byrd as their leader.

National politics have come to be played out much more on the public stage than they used to be, often with audience reactions determining who wins and who loses. In the 1990s, policy battles increasingly came to be fought out in public through public relations wars (Sinclair 1998). Within such an environment, political actors adept at using the media to push their issues to the center of the agenda and to frame the debate to favor their position are greatly advantaged. Consequently, senators' expectations that their leaders effectively promote their issues and burnish their party's image intensified and the message function became an integral party of the Senate party leader's job.

Senate leaders' communications staffs have grown, both parties now have sophisticated television facilities, and the leaders regularly appear on the Sunday talk shows.

Putting forth and promoting a party agenda has become a key component of the Senate parties' message strategies. With Democrats holding the White House, Senate Democrats, House Democrats, and the president have coordinated their efforts in recent years and have agreed upon a joint agenda. The president's State of the Union address has provided the most highly visible forum for publicizing the agenda; but Democrats have staged many other events to highlight their proposals.

It has become customary for the majority party to introduce its top priorities as S.1 through S.5 and the minority to follow with its priorities as S.6 through S.10. In 1999, Republicans concerned about the effect of impeachment on their party image made an especially elaborate effort to promote their agenda with the public. In keeping with the strategy of inclusion, Lott appointed five working groups—each chaired by two senators—on the five top GOP legislative goals: tax cuts, drugs, education reform, restructuring social security, and national defense (Henry 1999). Their charge was to map communications strategy to highlight the Republican positions through press conferences, speeches, town hall meetings, and other events. Once the impeachment trial finished, Senate Republicans launched a sixty-day media blitz that included a number of appearances by Lott at rallies and town hall meetings around the country. Altogether, 150 town meetings were planned, most featuring the Republican senator or senators from the state where they were held. (Gettinger 1999; Doherty 1999).

## Promoting Collective Action within the Party

To successfully promote collective action, Senate leaders with meager powers must persuade rank-and-file senators with a great capacity for acting on their own that it is in their best interest to cooperate and act as part of the party team. With the increase in intraparty ideological homogeneity and interparty polarization, senators came to expect their leaders to pursue partisan objectives more intensely but they themselves also became more willing to work within and through the party. Successful leadership in the individualist Senate demanded an accommodation and service-oriented style. Within the more partisan context, it dictates a highly inclusive style as well. Senate leaders need to consult intensively and broadly and they need to provide their members with opportunities to participate in ways that help these senators as individuals as well as help the party.

To that end, Senate leaders activated and elaborated party organs. The whip systems became more active on both sides of the aisle. Partisan issue task forces, appointed by the leadership, became common. Democrats, who had had a centralized leadership structure, created additional leadership posts.

Leadership staffs, working through various party committees, geared up to provide senators with a variety of useful services. The party policy committees generate and distribute information on issues and legislation through a wide array of publications. The Democratic Policy Committee, for example, produces the *Daily Report*, which reviews recent Senate developments and describes upcoming floor action, briefs on specific issues and pieces of legislation, and fact sheets on Democratic positions and proposals. The Republican Policy Committee prepares a *Legislative Notice* for every major bill awaiting Senate floor action that includes a summary of the bill provisions, related background information and anticipated amendments, and both in-depth research papers and shorter papers on issues and proposals. Both parties run a television information service to alert senators to what is happening on the floor; the text of amendments is, for example, available through that service. The Democratic Technology and Communications Committee contains television studios, extensive video editing capabilities, and facilities for satellite hookups with local television stations that senators can use; the staff helps senators organize media events by doing everything from contacting reporters and selling them the story to reserving the room (Sellers 1999b). The Republican leadership provides similar services for its members through the Republican Conference.

The leaders make use of these media capabilities to convey the party message personally. However, leaders believe that news coverage is more likely if many party members are conveying the same message and are always aware of the imperative of inclusion. So even more effort goes into having senators themselves promote the party message to their constituents and to a wider audience when that is possible. A Republican Conference staffer described the job of the conference chair as "support[ing] the communications effort of the Senate Republican Party, tak[ing] part in promoting their agenda." The job of the staff, he continued, "is to help senators make use of the information that they have to disseminate, the message they want to disseminate and, of course, to encourage them to join in promoting the party message."

The agenda effort is characterized by broad inclusion as well. On both sides of the aisle, the agenda emerges from discussion and interaction among all senators who choose to participate. In the 106th Congress(1999–2000), the Republican Conference by vote formally adopted an agenda.

Inclusion characterizes the leadership style of contemporary Senate leaders across the board. Extensive consultation and broad inclusion are necessary—but by no means sufficient—conditions for success. "Daschle's view of leadership is that of inclusiveness," a senior aide said. "He never wants to surprise people. He wants to make sure they're on board." "[My] job," explained a high-ranking Lott aide, "is to make sure that non-leadership senators' views are heard and that their needs are met . . . openness is a very important part of being a good majority leader."

The senators of each party meet for lunch every Tuesday; Republicans began their party lunches in the mid-1970s and Democrats began theirs in the early 1980s. These meeting are important forums for the discussion of party issues and strategy. "We discuss strategy there," a high-ranking leadership aide explained. "We have a leadership meeting first, and then we make sure everybody is signed off on the general thrust of policy, and we certainly say 'if you have any problems with what we're doing, tell us now.'"

Meetings at the staff level also provide information and feedback. For example, Lott's senior floor staff meets with the committee staff directors every Monday morning "to fill them in on what to expect during the week on the floor." On the Democratic side, various Daschle leadership staffers meet weekly with the legislative directors of Democratic senators, with Senate Democrats' administrative assistants, with their press secretaries, and with the minority staff directors of the committees (Sellers 1999a, 11–12).

Senators are now often willing to be partners in party collective action; they are not willing to be followers. Successful Senate leaders reflect that reality in their style. "[Daschle]'s a person who doesn't free-lance things," explained Majority Whip Harry Reid. "He has his leadership group. He runs things through them. If he has bad ideas they are dropped. If they are good, he takes them to senior members. Then he takes them to the full caucus. But if it doesn't fly, he drops it here" (quoted in Krikorian 1999, A28). "Lott's strength is inclusion," according to Republican Policy Committee Chair Larry Craig; "he brings people together" (quoted in Bresnahan 1998, 34).

In recent years, "bringing people together" within the party has been an especially pressing problem for Republican majority leaders. The 1990s saw an influx of ideologically committed conservatives into the Senate, with many of them being veterans of the highly partisan House. These junior hard-liners are often frustrated with their more moderate senior party colleagues who sometimes defect from party positions.

Moderate Mark Hatfield's (R-Ore.) defection on the constitutional amendment requiring a balanced budget in 1995 first brought their frustration to a head. After the House had approved it, the constitutional amendment failed in the Senate by one vote, with Hatfield, the chairman of the Appropriations Committee, casting the only Republican vote against it. The amendment was a part of the Senate Republicans' agenda and the ideologically driven junior Republicans believed that, on such a crucial vote, a senior committee chair should not be allowed with impunity to vote against the party to which he owed his chairmanship. They proposed stripping Hatfield of his chairmanship but were placated with a reform task force to which three freshmen were appointed.

The provisions proposed by the task force that the Senate Republican Conference adopted included limiting chairs and party leaders (except the top leader) to three terms, requiring a secret ballot vote on committee chairs both in committee and in the conference, and providing for the adoption of a Senate GOP agenda in the conference by a three-quarters vote. The new rules went into effect at the beginning of 1997 and were intended by the junior conservatives to make their senior and often more moderate party colleagues more responsive to the predominantly conservative party membership as a whole.

The rules changes may have had some effect, but senators still pursue individualist strategies and moderate senators are—for policy and reelection reasons—most likely to come into conflict with their party's position when doing so. A Senate majority leader's tools for enforcing party regularity are exceedingly limited and, because he needs those senators' cooperation and votes in the future, he is loath to use what tools he has in a heavy-handed fashion. However, such restraint frustrates junior conservatives. A high-ranking Senate insider explained Lott's problem as well as how he deals with it:

> [Lott] has to ensure that he speaks for the Chafees and the Jeffords, as well as the others in the caucus. He tells critics who say why does he listen to those people, well, would you rather have a Ted Kennedy or a Jim Jeffords as chair of the committee? If we lose people like Chafee and Jeffords, we are going to be in the minority. The practical reality is that he can't ignore these people. But he was quite aware that there is considerable criticism in the caucus.

### Minority Party Strategies

During the 1990s, the minority party in the Senate has become increasingly adept at using the Senate's permissive rules to pursue partisan objectives. Extended debate and loose germaneness rules, which are a considerable weapon for individuals and small groups in the Senate, become truly powerful when employed by an organized partisan minority of considerable size. When procedural strategies are coordinated with a sophisticated public relations strategy that the Senate parties are increasingly capable of orchestrating, the minority can pose a formidable challenge to the majority and greatly complicate the majority leader's already difficult job.

In the 103rd Congress (1993–1994), the Republican Senate minority facing a Democratic president for the first time in over a decade repeatedly used its power under the rules to kill or extract concessions on legislation with majority support. Their first success, the killing of Clinton's stimulus program, provides a good example of how procedural and public relations strategies can be combined to the perpetrators' great political benefit, an example from which Republicans and Democrats learned much. Republicans not only used extended debate to block Senate passage of the bill but engaged in an aggressive campaign to portray the bill as a grotesquely pork-laden waste of money; stories about particularly hard-to-explain projects—"fish maps," for example—appeared in the news across the country. Republicans clearly won the public relations battle and, as a result, they actually gained political advantage from killing legislation they opposed but that a majority of the House and Senate supported.

Democrats as the minority party after 1994 have refined the strategy of combining procedural prerogatives with public relations campaigns to seize agenda control from the majority. The lack of a germaneness requirement for amendments to most bills severely weakens the majority leader's ability to control the floor agenda. If he refuses to bring a bill to the floor, its supporters can offer it as an amendment to most legislation the leader does bring to the floor. The majority leader can make a motion to table the amendment, which is nondebatable. That does, however, require his members to vote on the issue, albeit in a procedural guise, and the leader may want to avoid that. Furthermore, even after the minority's amendment has been tabled, the minority can continue to offer other amendments, including even individual parts of the original amendment, and can block a vote on the underlying bill the majority leader wants to pass. The leader can, of course, file a cloture petition and try to shut off debate, but he needs sixty votes to do so. The minority party can use this tactic to bring its agenda to the floor and, if accompanied with a successful public relations campaign, can gain favorable publicity and sometimes pressure enough majority party members into supporting the bill to pass it.

The fight over managed care in 1999 illustrates this strategy and some of the tactics the majority has developed to respond and thereby illuminates how the contemporary Senate operates. During the 1990s, Americans were increasingly receiving their health care through some sort of managed care plan. As managed care became more pervasive, concerns and complaints that cost control was trumping good medical care also grew and, with them, calls for government regulation. President Clinton in his 1998 State of the Union address had advocated passage of a "patients' bill of rights" regulating managed care plans; but, despite Democratic efforts, no bill came to a vote in the Senate and no legislation was enacted.

In 1999, the president and House and Senate Democratic leaders put patients' bill of rights legislation at the top of their agenda. Congressional Democrats had highlighted it during their 1998 elections campaigns and, in a feat not accomplished since 1934, the president's party had gained House seats in a midterm election. Senate Minority Leader Tom Daschle introduced his party's bill on January 19 as S.6, making it the Senate Democrats' top priority. The president advocated passage during his State of the Union address. On March 3, when Clinton and congressional Democrats held a joint new conference to publicize their agenda for the 106th Congress, the patients' bill of rights was prominently featured.

Because public opinion polls showed increased public demand for action, Republicans also presumed that managed care regulation would be on the congressional agenda. When Majority Leader Trent Lott presented his party's agenda on the floor of the Senate on January 19, he mentioned the issue as one on which action would occur, but it was not among the Republicans' top five priorities, which were embodied in S.1 through S.5. The issue was a difficult one for the Republican Party. With their antiregulatory philosophy of government and their close alliance with business, most congressional Republicans preferred little to no new regulation; yet, for those whose constituents demanded action, doing nothing would be dangerous and, if legislation were to pass, Republicans wanted to both shape it and gain credit with the public. Furthermore, physicians, usually a reliable Republican constituency, were clamoring for action; they believed managed care had taken too many medical decisions away from doctors and put them into the hands of insurance companies.

On January 22, Lott introduced a bill cosponsored by forty-eight Republican senators. A year before he had asked Majority Whip Don Nickles (Okla.) to put together a task force to draft a Republican bill. Despite Republicans as the majority party controlling the committees, Lott resorted to a within party task force, which allowed inclusion of all the key Republican actors, and the exclusion of Democrats. The task force of nine included the chairs of the two committees with jurisdiction, but also Bill Frist (Tenn.), the only doctor in the Senate, moderate Susan Collins (Maine), and conservatives Dan Coats (Ind.), Rick Santorum (Pa.), and Phil Gramm (Tex.). The task force came up with a bill that included some patient protection provisions—but not a right to sue—and "access" provisions, primarily tax breaks aimed at helping the uninsured buy insurance. The bill was referred to the Senate Health, Education, Labor and Pensions (HELP) Committee.

On March 17, HELP met to markup S.326, a managed care bill introduced by its Chairman James A. Jeffords (R-Vt.) and based on the patient protection provisions of the task force bill. Committee Democrats, who believed the Republican bill was much too weak, offered S.6, their bill, as a substitute but it was rejected by a ten to eight party line vote. This set the tenor for the contentious two-day markup; eighteen Democratic amendments were defeated on party line votes before the committee approved the Republican bill on a strict party line vote.

The Democrats' strategy on managed care called for making the issue as visible as possible. Lacking control of both chambers, only strong public opinion could provide the leverage to get their proposal on the congressional agenda and perhaps even pass it. If the public strongly supported the Democrats' patients' bill of rights, Republicans might be pressured into voting for it or at least made to pay an electoral price for killing it. To rouse public opinion, Democrats needed media coverage. Their activities promoting the Democratic agenda had been aimed to garner media attention. So were Democratic reactions to the Senate Republican bill. President Clinton criticized it as falling "far short of the legislation the American people deserve," (Forestel 1999b, 701); Edward M. Kennedy of Massachusetts, ranking Democrat of HELP, called it a "bill of wrongs, not of rights" (702).

Public relations wars are efforts to frame the debate so as to advantage your position. From a policy perspective, Democrats objected to the narrow scope of the Republican bill; it only covered a fraction of people in managed care; and they faulted it for not allowing patients to sue their health care providers when care was denied. Democrats argued that the fear of suits was an important guarantor of good behavior on the part of providers. To simplify and dramatize a complex set of arguments, Democrats honed their message to two basic points: health care decisions should be made by doctors not insurance companies and HMOs, like everyone else, should be held accountable for mistakes they make. When the bill was introduced, Senator Kennedy sounded these themes:

> Mr. President, today, we renew the battle in Congress to enact a strong Patients' Bill of Rights to protect American families from abuses by HMOs and managed care health plans that too often put profits over patients' needs.
>
> Our Patients' Bill of Rights will protect families against the arbitrary and self-serving decisions that can rob average citizens of their savings and their peace of mind, and often their health and their very lives. Doctors and patients should be making medical decisions, not insurance company accountants. Too often, managed care is mismanaged care. (*Congressional Record* January 19, 1999, S366)

Republicans and interest group opponents of managed care regulation responded by trying to frame the debate to their advantage. The Democratic bill, they claimed, would raise costs and make trial lawyers rich without improving health care. The insurance and employer groups opposed to managed care regulations also attempted to shift the debate from patients rights to help, through tax incentives, for the uninsured. Blue Cross Blue Shield had run a series of ads hammering at that point (Foerstel 1999a).

Senator Lott, intending to bring to the floor a package that included the "access" tax breaks, told the Finance Committee, which had jurisdiction over those provisions, to produce legislation. Democrats opposed many of the "access" provisions, convinced they would not help ordinary Americans and were just a give-away to the rich. Furthermore, they saw them as a smoke screen to distract attention away from the core issues of patient protections. Thus, united Republican support was needed on this closely divided committee. However, then-moderate Republican John H. Chafee of Rhode Island would not go along and the committee could not get a majority to report out the bill. Despite the increased partisanship in the Senate, individualism still poses a problem for Senate leaders. Senators have the resources to freelance and many are still willing to do so even in opposition to a high-priority proposal of their own party.

Democrats were eager for Senate floor debate. Republicans, in contrast, were in no hurry. Lott continued to promise floor consideration sometime in the future. The Democratic leadership pushed aggressively for an agreement to bring the legislation to the floor, but bridled at the conditions Lott was demanding.

Given Senate rules, Lott knew he could not simply deny Democrats a vote altogether. But, because the legislation confronted both his members as individuals and the party with political perils, Lott's aim was to kill the Democratic legislation by passing the Republican bill if necessary, and to do so as quietly as possible. "What the Republicans want," explained a high-ranking Democratic aide, "is basically to have a vote on the two versions—the Republican and the Democratic—and then go on and just get it over with, and that would give them the ability to say they voted for one and it would keep much attention from focusing on it." To that end, Lott was insisting Democrats limit themselves to five amendments and, the aide continued, "that he see the amendments before we offer them so he could in effect veto amendments." The Republican leadership wanted to protect its members from politically difficult votes. As Majority Whip Don Nickles later explained, "I don't want our members to go through a lot of votes that can be misconstrued for political purposes," (quoted in Dewar and Grunwald 1999, A8). Furthermore, Lott was demanding that Democrats commit themselves to not bring up the issue again during the remainder of the session.

Lott's conditions were unacceptable to Democrats. After all, as a Democratic leadership staffer said, "We don't have any illusions that we can pass our bill, but we at least want a full debate. We want to be able to define the issues." To do so, Democrats wanted to be free to offer and debate at least twenty amendments.

Extended discussions between Daschle and Lott made no progress and Democrats decided to ratchet up the pressure. According to an aide, Democrats gave Republicans "two weeks notice that June was going to be patients' bill of rights month." Senate Democrats staged a series of "Special Orders" on the floor of the Senate in which senators engaged in a lengthy discussion of the need for and virtues of their bill. The Democrats' aim was to catch the attention not just of the faithful but tiny C-SPAN2 audience but of the news media. Stories about their effort did begin to appear. Daschle put the Republican leadership on notice that starting Monday, June 21, Democrats would offer their patients' bill of rights legislation as an amendment to anything brought to the floor.

Lott countered by bringing up the agriculture appropriations bill; endangering the passage of funding legislation for agricultural programs would be politically tough for Daschle, a farm-state senator. Democrats nevertheless proceeded with their plan and Lott, blasting Democrats for hurting farmers, temporarily withdrew the agriculture bill. The following day, the Senate voted fifty-three to forty-seven to table the Democratic patients' bill of rights amendment. Democrats then threatened to offer their proposal piecemeal as a series of amendments. Their members having to cast a long series of tough votes was exactly what Republicans wanted to avoid so stalemate again ensued.

"It looks like they're acting on behalf of trial lawyers and stepping over the corpses of American farmers," Lott charged, attempting to make the strategy as costly as possible for Democrats (*Washington Post* 1999, A8). Lott also urged Republican farm-state senators to talk to their local media, emphasizing the same point. The Democrats held fast. "We'll get the votes," said Minority Leader Daschle. "It's either that or we'll sit on the Senate floor looking at each other" (A8).

Lott then filed cloture petitions on four appropriations bills. He knew that none were likely to get the necessary sixty votes but believed forcing votes would highlight the Democrats' obstructionism. An aide explained: "The other side has decided to block everything. Essentially, they think the way to win back the Congress is to make us look like a do-nothing Congress, and Lott at least wants to make sure that the media and the Beltway understand that that's what the Democrats are doing, if in fact there is a train wreck on appropriations, its the Dems' fault."

On Monday, June 28, all four cloture motions were defeated on party line votes.

The next day, Lott and Daschle announced they had reached an agreement for debating the patients' bill of rights legislation. The leaders had been negotiating throughout this period and, having determined their relative strengths, had figured out what they could and could not get. Lott took the floor on June 29 to announce the agreement:

> Mr. President, let me say first Senator Daschle and I have labored long and hard to come to an agreement on a unanimous-consent procedure to deal with the Patients' Bill of Rights issue, appropriations bills, and nominations, and it still takes an awful lot of good faith. We have to work together. We have to have some trust. We have to give the benefit of the doubt to the leaders. . . . I ask unanimous consent that the majority leader or his designee, introduce the underlying health care bill and it be placed on the calendar by 12 noon on Thursday, July 8, and the bill become the pending business at 1 P.M. on Monday, July 12, 1999, with a vote occurring on final passage at the close of business on Thursday, July 15, and the bill be subject to the following agreement:

> That the bill be limited to 3 hours of debate, to be equally divided in the usual form, that all amendments in order to the bill be relevant to the subject . . . , and all first-degree amendments be offered in an alternating fashion with Senator Daschle to offer the initial first-degree amendment and all first- and second-degree amendments be limited to 100 minutes each, to be equally divided in the usual form. I further ask consent that second-degree amendments be limited to one second-degree amendment per side, per party, with no motions to commit or recommit in order, or any other act with regard to the amendments in order, and that just prior to third reading of the bill, it be in order for the majority leader, or his designee to offer a final amendment, with no second-degree amendments in order. (*Congressional Record* June 29, 1999, S7811)

Minority Leader Daschle praised the agreement:

> Mr. President, I want to publicly commend the majority leader for the effort he has made over the last several days to find a way to resolve this impasse. I believe this is a win-win . . . I am grateful to him and have, once again, enjoyed the opportunity to resolve what has been a very significant procedural difficulty for us all. . . . I believe this is a good agreement any way one looks at it. It provides us with the opportunity to have a good debate. It provides us with the opportunity to have a series of amendments. It certainly provides us with the focus that we have been looking for with regard to the Patients' Bill of Rights. This is a very good agreement, agreed to, I think, with the direct involvement of a lot of people. So we are grateful. (S7813)

He and other Democrats undertook to make sure informal agreements reached behind closed doors were made part of the record. Thus, Daschle said: "The majority leader mentioned a couple of other matters, one having to do with his desire to work full days. He has assured me we will work 9 to 12 hour days that week we come back because he recognizes the importance of giving this issue a full opportunity for debate. I appreciate his commitment in that regard" (S7813).

"The presumption is that this flexible process will allow a sufficient number of amendments to come to the floor," Democratic Whip Harry Reid reiterated, "that it will not be a process where one or two amendments are brought up and then through a series of extended second-degree amendments delayed?" Lott replied that that would not be possible under the agreement (*Congressional Record*, June 29, 1999, S7813).

Democrats, thus, had obtained a four-day debate on their issue with ground rules that ensured them the opportunity to offer and get votes on most if not all of their amendments. In this case, Democrats wanted the time limits on general debate and on individual amendments so that Republicans could not use procedural means to run out the clock and thereby block a debate and vote on the provisions Democrats wanted to highlight. In return, Republicans got a time certain for the end of the debate and an informal promise from Daschle that, if the issue were indeed fully aired, he would not bring it up again.

Also included in the UCA was a promise to vote on a number of nominations, most notably that of Larry Summers as treasury secretary. In retaliation for the Democrats' tactics, some Republicans had put a hold on the Summers nomination. The adverse reaction of the stock market had, however, made that more of a liability than an asset to Republican bargaining. So Lott was happy to include that in the deal.

As the bill headed to floor debate, the public relations war intensified. Democrats set up near the Senate floor their "Intensive Communication Unit" (ICU)—named to garner media attention. The ICU was staffed by experienced press aides. Democratic senators could walk off the floor and participate in news interviews via rapid satellite feed, radio, or Internet. Although Republicans would have preferred to keep the issue in the background, they too had a "war room" and attempted to get press attention to their perspective, especially to their claim that the Democratic plan would raise costs and thus decrease coverage.

Republicans were aided by a number of influential interest groups with a major stake in the outcome. Since 1998, health plans and business groups had spent millions fighting managed care regulation legislation and they participated aggressively in the 1999 battle, even running television ads. During the first two weeks of July 1999, $1 million was spent on television ads by the Health Benefits Coalition, which includes the Business Roundtable, the National Federation of Independent Business, the U.S. Chamber of Commerce, and other business and industry groups (Kirchhoff 1999). "Make me pay more for health insurance and then expect my vote? Forget it!" a tough looking construction worker said in one frequently run ad.

The American Federation of Labor and Congress of Industrial Organizations (AFL–CIO) and the American Medical Association, both of which supported the Democrats' plan, also ran some ads, though their budgets were considerably smaller. Democrats nevertheless benefited from their broad support and made that an important part of their message strategy. The Democratic bill, said Edward M. Kennedy,

> is supported by a broad and diverse coalition of doctors, nurses, patients, and advocates for children, women, and working families, including the American Medical Association, the Consortium of Citizens with Disabilities, the American Cancer Society, the American Heart Association, the National Alliance for the Mentally Ill, the National Partnership for Women and Families, the National Association of Children's Hospitals, and the AFL–CIO, to name just a few of the more than 180 groups endorsing our bill. (*Congressional Record* January 19, 1999, S366)

Senate rules had prevented Lott from barring the patients' bill of rights issue from ever getting to the floor or from simply disposing of it in one quick vote once on the floor. They did not, however, deprive him of all procedural tools to affect consideration. On July 8, Lott revealed a part of the Republican strategy when he introduced the Democrats' bill to use as the base bill. By making the Democrats' version the bill that would be amended, Lott sought to prevent Democrats from offering the most popular provisions of their measure piecemeal as amendments and forcing Republicans to take a series of hard votes. Pointing out that the Democrats had asked to have their bill made the main vehicle, a Lott spokesman deadpanned, "We offered the Democratic bill to make them defend their own legislation" (quoted in Preston 1999, 38). Democrats responded by introducing the Republican bill as a complete substitute that they could then amend. The two versions were debated simultaneously, with alternate amendments offered to each (Foerstel 1999).

Ordinarily on a major bill, the bill sponsor, usually the committee or subcommittee chair, manages and so plays the most prominent role in floor debate. In this case, Republican strategy called for highlighting senators who would put the most sympathetic and credible face on the Republicans' effort. Only a few weeks before, in the wake of the Columbine High School shootings, Republicans had taken a public drubbing on the Senate floor on gun-control legislation and the fact that their point man was a National Rifle Association board member had contributed to the black eye that debate had given the party. On managed care, having Senators Bill Frist, the only doctor in the Senate, and Susan Collins play prominent roles was intended to counter Democratic claims that the Republicans were insensitive to women's health needs and to the opinions of doctors.

Tactical use of floor amendments constituted the crux of the Republican strategy. The leadership task force chaired by Republican Whip Don Nickles exhaustively surveyed Republican senators on the full range of topics that Democratic amendments addressed (Evans 1999, 15). Using this information, the task force drafted a narrower amendment on the same topic when otherwise the Democratic amendment would put Republicans in a difficult position. Thus, Republicans could vote for the narrower Republican version and against the Democratic version and still argue they had supported the popular position at issue.

Senator Charles S. Robb, a Virginia Democrat facing a tough reelection battle in 2000, led off by offering the Democrats' least controversial amendment; it allowed women to designate an obstetrician or gynecologist as their primary care physician and gave doctors (not the managed care plan) the right to determine the length of the hospital stay after a mastectomy. On a forty-eight to fifty-two vote with only three Republicans defecting, Republicans defeated the amendment. The next day, Republican Olympia Snowe of Maine offered a similar but narrower amendment and it passed on a straight party line vote. That set the tone for the rest of the floor consideration. Democratic amendments were defeated; Republican amendments on similar topics but often with much weaker provisions won. The UCA specified that the majority could offer the last amendment, which could not then be amended. The Republicans combined their patient protection provisions with the tax incentives intended to make health insurance more affordable. The Finance Committee had never managed to get a majority for these "access" provisions, so Lott bypassed the committee. The package passed on a fifty-three to forty-seven vote. The legislation did not allow suits against HMOs and only covered 44 million of the approximately 160 million people in managed care plans. All Democrats voted against it. The Clinton administration blasted the Republican bill and threatened a veto. Although trounced on the Senate floor, Democrats believed that they had won the public relations battle. For both parties, the fight had been as much over party image as over legislation. Although Republicans had managed to provide their members with cover—with an explanation for tough votes, Democrats had managed to force the issue to the floor and, for a short time at least, to the top of the news.

## Majority Counterstrategies and Their Impact

Minority party success in seizing agenda control frustrates and angers majority party senators and they tend to blame their leader. A number of Senate Republicans were unhappy with the UCA Majority Leader Lott worked out on managed care and grumbled that the Democrats had outflanked them. After the gun-control fight in May 1999, Lott was subject to much more strident criticism. In the wake of the Columbine High School shootings, Democrats succeeded in seizing the agenda with gun-control measures. In that case, public pressure was so intense that Lott did not even attempt to prevent the issue from being debated on the floor—a stance for which he was excoriated by a number of his more conservative members.

In public, Lott usually responds philosophically to such criticism. "When you make an agreement like that, people, usually on both sides, are not all that happy," Lott said about the managed care UCA. "I thought it was the best we could get under the circumstances" (quoted in Bresnahan 1999b, 1). His supporters pointed out that Lott had briefed the entire Republican Conference on the agreement and no one objected. Nevertheless, in the current context of policy-polarized parties, the majority leader is under considerable pressure from his own members to be tough vis-à-vis the minority party and to prevent the minority party from seizing the agenda and using the Senate floor to promote their message to the disadvantage of the majority.

To counter minority party efforts, majority leaders use a variety of strategies. They now more frequently attempt to impose cloture early since postcloture amendments must be germane (Thorson and Nitschke 1999). On campaign finance reform in the 105th Congress (1997–1998), Majority Leader Lott responded to the Democrats' strategy with a variety of hardball tactics. Lott brought the bill to the floor with no prior notice to its supporters, thus catching them unprepared. He then "filled the amendment tree"; that is, he used the majority leader's prerogative of first recognition to offer an amendment Democrats considered antilabor and strongly opposed and then to offer enough other second-degree amendments that his amendment could not be further amended. His purpose was to prevent the Democrats from amending his amendment and thus to force them to filibuster. Stalemate ensued; the bill was on the floor for several days but neither side could muster the votes to impose cloture. Lott then pulled the bill. This was, of course, the outcome he had hoped for.

The bill's proponents were furious and still had plenty of ammunition to continue the battle. Democrats started blocking everything except appropriations bills by threatening to offer the McCain-Feingold campaign finance bill as a nongermane amendment, and the Senate ground to a halt. Finally, Lott gave in and made a deal; he promised a full debate on campaign finance the following year, including an up-or-down vote on McCain-Feingold. Republicans eventually succeeded in preventing passage of the bill but at a considerable price in bad publicity.

Robert C. Byrd had attempted the same tactic of filling the amendment tree—this time with friendly amendments—in the 103rd Congress (1993–1994) to protect President Clinton's stimulus program from hostile amendments. In the end, that bill was killed by a filibuster and Republican rage at Byrd's tactics may have contributed to that outcome. Lott appears to be using the tactic considerably more than his predecessors. On three occasions in 1999, Lott attempted to protect Republican bills from Democratic amendments—some relevant amendments as well as other clearly nongermane amendments—by using that procedural strategy. On the Y2K Act, the social security lockbox bill, and the Ed-Flex Act, Lott used his right of first recognition to fill the amendment tree and then immediately filed a cloture motion which, if successful, would have required that all amendments had to meet a strict germaneness test. In some cases, Lott offered to open the amendment tree but only for amendments that Republican leaders found acceptable.

Senate Democrats have reacted with outrage—and with cohesion—to these tactics. They have charged the majority leader with abusing his position and attempting to muzzle the minority ("Senator Lott's Record of Shutting Down the Senate to Silence Democrats," typescript, n.d. [summer 1999]). During Senate debate on July 26, 1999, Democrats vented their anger. "We are even being precluded from offering amendments in order to have our positions considered; is that not correct?" Senator Paul S. Sarbanes (D-Md.) asked in a colloquy with the minority whip. "That is absolutely true," replied Senator Harry Reid (D-Nev.). "For example, on the issue of the lockbox, cloture has been filed three to five times. We have never uttered a single word in a debate about that issue. We have never had the opportunity to offer a single amendment. We agree with the lockbox concept, but does it have to be theirs? Can't we try to change it a little bit?" (*Congressional Record* July 26, 1999, S9199) Lott was trying to prevent any debate on controversial issues, charged Tom Harkin (D-Iowa): "It has been common now for the majority to take the position that we do not have any regular debate on controversial subjects" (S9178). Such criticism was not limited to the more liberal and more partisan Democrats. "The minority is being placed under the gag rule," the venerable Robert C. Byrd concurred. "It is being laid down here: You will do it our way or we will jerk the bill down. You have to do it our way. You have to limit your amendments to 5 or 6 or 8 or 10—no more. That is not in this Senate rule book. That is not in this Constitution. And it is not in the best interests of the American people that the Senate is being run that way" (S9188).

Lott responded that what he was doing was not unprecedented. "I didn't invent that procedure [of filling the amendment tree]. Other Senators who have been majority leader certainly have used that." He justified its use, saying, "That is a very legitimate tactic or process which can be used, one that should not be used all the time, and one that has been used relatively rarely, but it certainly is a legitimate thing the majority leader can do to focus debate and to get debate concluded in a reasonable period of time" (*Congressional Record* July 26, 1999, S9202). In response to charges that he was trying to set up a Senate analogue to the House Rules Committee, Lott responded, "There is no desire at all to set up a Rules Committee in the House of Representatives sense, but there is a desire by this majority leader, as by every majority leader, to find a way to move the process and the legislation through the Senate" (S9202).

Democrats countered that the time constraint argument was only a smoke screen. Leading the charge, Senator Harkin of Iowa said:

> the argument of limited time is often suggested as a reason—we do not have all
> this time—but that is clearly a veil that hides nothing. . . . How many days . . .

have we spent on the floor with nobody here, quorum call after quorum call, simply because the majority leader does not want to have a measure on the floor to which we can add our amendments and openly debate them? (*Congressional Record* July 26, 1999, S9178)

Democrats further argued that the Senate was never meant to be an efficient legislation processing machine. "The Senate is a very inconvenient place and not a very effective or efficient place in the way it disposes of legislation. But that happens to be the way George Washington and Thomas Jefferson and Ben Franklin and Mason and Madison anticipated this place should work," Byron Dorgan (D-N.Dak.) asserted (*Congressional Record* July 26, 1999, S9174). "It doesn't hurt to talk at length about issues," contended Harry Reid. "It is good for the country to talk about issues. It is good for the body politic" (S9171).

Democrats have reacted with more than outrage; they have responded by maintaining high cohesion on cloture votes. Even Democratic supporters of the legislation at issue have refused to vote for cloture when Republicans attempted to shut out Democrats with these procedural tactics. Thus, Senator Ron Wyden (D-Ore.), cosponsor of the Ed-Flex bill, stuck with his party and voted against cutting off debate on that bill. As a result of Democratic cohesion, the tactic seldom works in preventing Democrats from getting votes on their major amendments. On the Ed-Flex bill, Republicans were eventually forced to work out a UCA that allowed Democrats to offer, debate, and get a vote on their amendments that incorporated the Democratic education agenda. When the majority employs these tactics, the result is most often gridlock, with no legislative work accomplished on the Senate floor until an accommodation is reached. As Republican Policy Committee Chairman Larry Craig of Idaho explained, "Inevitably, anybody who wants to get a vote on the floor of the United States Senate will get it if they're persistent" (Bresnahan 1999b, 1).

## THE DILEMMA OF MAJORITY PARTY LEADERSHIP IN THE SENATE

In the current context of policy-polarized parties, the Senate majority leader walks a fine line and successful majority party leadership is a sometime thing. The ideologically driven conservatives who now make up a majority of his membership push Lott to pursue hardball partisan tactics and to avoid ideological compromise. However, that approach is hard to carry out successfully within the party and nearly impossible to implement successfully in the Senate as a whole. A majority leader who does not cooperate with the minority leader and accommodate the minority party to some considerable extent is one who cannot keep the Senate functioning. And if the legislative process in the Senate breaks down, all senators are dissatisfied. Senators want to gain partisan advantage on the big issues but they also want, for both reelection and policy reasons, to pass bills. This dilemma is more acute for the majority leader since majority status means his members expect greater partisan advantage and he gets more blame if the Senate is mired in gridlock. However, the minority leader is also subject to partially conflicting expectations from his members. They too want both to garner partisan advantage and to pass legislation.

Their common dilemma gives the two leaders a strong incentive to work together. If the two leaders do not work together closely on a daily and sometimes hourly basis, the Senate will cease to function and both leaders will have failed to live up to their members' expectations. But both leaders are also subject to their members' expectation that they pursue partisan advantage and this impels them to use strategies that push the Senate to—and sometimes over—the brink of gridlock. In an era of both individualism and intense partisanship, Senate leadership—especially Senate majority party leadership—is an uncommonly tricky enterprise.

## NOTE

In addition to the references cited here, this paper is based on interviews conducted by the author. All unattributed quotes are from those interviews.

## CHAPTER FIVE

# Senate Leaders, Minority Voices: From Dirksen to Daschle

## BURDETT LOOMIS

Senate leadership. As a concept it remains more than a bit fuzzy. If we are to believe floor leaders and scholars, the entire notion of "Senate leadership" is at least oxymoronic, or more likely a simple contradiction in terms (Davidson 1985). Indeed, of all major leadership positions in the Congress, the majority and minority floor leader jobs were among the last to become institutionalized (Baker and Davidson 1991). Although these positions—especially that of majority leader—had been clearly established by the 1920s and 1930s, they grew in prominence during the 1950s as three great senators, Robert Taft (R-Ohio), Lyndon Johnson (D-Tex.), and Everett Dirksen (R-Ill.) took up the reins of party leadership (Baker and Davidson 1991). Moreover, the floor leadership structures had developed to the point that Donald R. Matthews (1960) could draw distinctions between the Senate parties as of the late 1950s.

Nevertheless, Senate leadership remained a highly personal element of a highly personal institution. Especially as practiced by Taft, Johnson, and Dirksen (and less positively by William Knowland of California), leaders played both inside and outside roles in the textbook Senate of powerful committee chairmen and a dominant Conservative Coalition (Sundquist 1968; Shepsle 1989). However large Taft and Johnson loom in congressional history, it is Dirksen who may well have had the most influence on the ways that Senate floor leaders operated in succeeding decades. Although a singular figure, Dirksen understood that a Senate leader needed to work effectively with a variety of distinct constituencies, from his fellow GOP senators to the president to the press.

This chapter does not address party leadership in general.[1] Rather, it focuses on the evolution of the minority leader position in the context of a Senate that

92 BURDETT LOOMIS

transformed itself from a collegial body in the 1950s to an intensely partisan, thoroughly individualistic chamber of the 1980s and 1990s (and beyond, in all likelihood) (Ripley 1969; Sinclair 1989). As with presidents, any examination of Senate party leaders suffers from a small number problem, to the point that between 1959 and 2000 there have been fewer minority leaders (six) than presidents (nine). Well-defended generalizations may be hard to come by, as both the Senate and its context have changed substantially over the past forty years. Still, some trends do emerge. Minority leaders generally receive *less* media coverage today than they did thirty years ago, yet they may rely *more* on the press to set the policy agenda. The importance of fund-raising and campaigning has risen steadily during this time. And the relationships between presidents and minority leaders have grown more distant. In addition, the use of the filibuster—a most important tool for the minority—has changed substantially over these years.

In the end, the central question about minority leaders remains: How (and how much) can they influence policy outcomes? Given that much of what they do is difficult to pin down (e.g., determining Bob Dole's impact in the deal-making process), this chapter will proceed first to discuss the various constituencies and then lay out the changing context for relationships with different constituencies. The context of leadership has changed over time, and this chapter will examine the leadership environments for Dirksen, Hugh Scott (R-Pa.), Howard Baker (R-Tenn.), Robert Byrd (D-W.Va.), Bob Dole (R-Kans.), and Tom Daschle (D-S. Dak.). Drawing on examples from all the leaders, but disproportionately from Dirksen and Daschle, this chapter will flesh out how and why *voice* has become more important than *influence* in defining the essence of the contemporary minority leader. To the extent that the crafting of political positions comes to dominate the leader's attention, the potential for conventional influence may wane further, as posturing for electioneering purposes overwhelms the goal of influencing policy outcomes.

Complicating all of this is the likelihood that a minority leader will serve with a president of his own party—and thus know that a presidential veto (real or threatened) can move the majority toward compromise. Articulating a strong position and not budging early in the proceedings can lead to ultimate policy impact, given the president's support. Likewise, the leverage of the filibuster means that voice and influence can become intertwined when the minority leader can hold his troops together on procedural votes (Binder and Smith 1997; Sinclair 1999d).

## MINORITY LEADERS AND THEIR CONSTITUENCIES: THE "MAN OF ALL WORK"

Describing his role as floor leader, Everett Dirksen concluded that he "is supposed to . . . keep himself informed on all matters within the domain of the

Senate relating to legislation and governmental matters and to keep the members of his party informed likewise. In other words, he is a "man of all work" (Dirksen 1961). The notion of "all work" has changed and expanded since Dirksen's day; the leadership is somewhat more collective, although this varies by individual, and its responsibilities have become more oriented toward elections and capturing the majority. Still, the minority leader must address the demands and expectations of multiple constituents (see fig. 5.1).

Demands on floor leaders come from myriad sources, and few can be completely ignored. Still, some are more important than others, and some can be given relatively short shrift. For example, home-state constituents may be content with less overall attention, anticipating that their interests will be served by their senator's leadership stature. Among these leaders, only Byrd consistently and conspicuously placed his home-state citizens as a first-rank constituency, to the point that he ultimately chose to serve as Appropriations Committee chair rather than majority leader in 1989.

The linkages between leaders and constituencies can all vary in strength. Even the most essential bond—that between the two floor leaders—changes from leadership pair to leadership pair (Byrd-Baker/Byrd-Dole) and can evolve within a relationship between two leaders (Trent Lott and Daschle). Over time, floor leaders have generated closer ties with an increasing number of constituencies, which has the effect of making their work more difficult. In particular, the floor leaders have come to rely on their ties with elements outside the Senate to

**FIGURE 5.1   The Constituencies of the Minority Floor Leader**

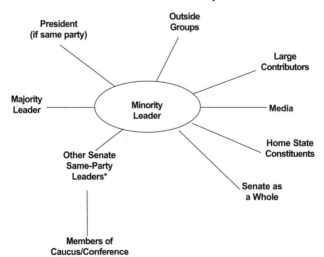

*Both party leadership and top committee slots

enhance their leadership within the chamber. Thus, a leader will form a political action committee (PAC) in order to raise funds to distribute to senatorial candidates, to say nothing of hitting the campaign trail as a fund-raiser.

Conversely, in the mid-1960s Everett Dirksen regarded Lyndon Johnson as his primary constituent, to the extent that it raised serious questions among members of his own party, who had elected him to the leadership position, but did not constitute a continuing check on his preferences and behavior. Since Dirksen's tenure, no minority (or majority) leader has enjoyed such a strong personal and political relationship with a president. Perhaps the most difficult situation comes under divided government, when a minority leader *must* regard the president of his own party as a major constituent, despite the personal, political, and policy differences that separate them (e.g., Dole and George Bush).

## CONSTITUENCIES AND SENATE CONTEXTS

Although their constituencies have remained relatively constant over the past forty years, the Senate context has changed substantially. Staffing levels and resources have increased greatly, and the Conservative Coalition has mostly expired, largely due to the changing regional/partisan composition of the chamber. Most dramatically, the Senate has become more partisan and more individualistic (Sinclair 1999d; Ornstein, Mann, and Peabody 1993; Smith 1993), a combination that has changed the nature of congressional leadership and probably made it more problematic.

The transformation of the Senate did not occur in one fell swoop, but two distinct eras do take shape within the 1959–2000 period—1959–1980 and 1981–2000. The 1980 break point makes sense in several ways: (1) Republicans won control of one house (the Senate) for the first time since the 1952 election; (2) Ronald Reagan won the presidency and demonstrated a great talent for setting the policy agenda; and (3) many scholars see the postreform era in Congress as beginning at about this time (Davidson 1992). Moreover, three important dimensions of the Congress—parties, structures, and budgets—come together to present a substantially different context for leadership by the 1980s.

### Party Majorities and Partisanship

When Republicans won forty-two seats in 1968, Everett Dirksen finally "commanded" a minority of more than thirty-six members. Throughout the 1960s, as he had helped write civil rights laws and offered support for the Vietnam buildup, the ranks of Republican senators had fluctuated between thirty-two and thirty-six. In contrast, Bob Dole's minorities averaged in the mid-forties, as have those of Byrd and Daschle. Well before the House became highly competitive in the early 1990s, the Senate had settled into a pattern of narrow partisan majorities, as shown in table 5.1.

Not only did partisan voting patterns change, but the partisan behavior of minority leaders changed as well—and dramatically so. Between 1959 and 1980, Minority Leaders Dirksen, Scott, and Baker compiled an average partisan support score of 60.3, which fell well below the overall Republican minority's score of 74.2. With their small band of fellow partisans and a relatively weak Republican conference, the leaders could seek to work with the majority to shape policy outcomes. But after 1980, things changed substantially. In the next ten congresses, just once (Dole in 1987–1988) did the minority leader register a *lower* party loyalty score than that of the party as a whole. On average, the leader's average score of 85 was (a) much higher than that of the previous period and (b) almost five points higher than that of all minority party senators. With heightened overall partisanship and the continuing chance to win back the chamber, minority leaders consistently took more partisan positions than their followers, at least on this measure. Although Senators Byrd, Dole, and Daschle have taken clear partisan positions, they do not fall outside the party mainstream. Rather, their leadership role may well have led them to act in a more partisan manner than they would have otherwise.[2]

### Divided Government and Filibusters

Shrinking partisan majorities in the Senate were matched by the growth of divided government at the national level. Minority leaders often had to find ways to support their party's president, even though they did not control their chamber. Being in the minority but not in the opposition creates any number of problems for a floor leader, who must simultaneously represent the administration

**TABLE 5.1 SENATE PARTY BALANCE, PARTY UNITY, PARTY SUPPORT SCORES, AND THE MINORITY LEADER, 1959–1999**

| Period | Average Size of Minority | Party Unity Votes (% of All Votes) | Average Minority Party Support Score | Average Minority Leader Party Supplemental Score |
|---|---|---|---|---|
| 1959–1980 | 37.5 | 39.4 | 74.2 | 60.3 |
| 1981–1999 | 45.3 | 50.1 | 80.3 | 85 |

Source: Data drawn from *Congressional Quarterly Weekly Reports*, 1959–1999; Norman J. Ornstein, Thomas E. Mann, and Michael J. Malbin, *Vital Statistics on Congress, 1997–1998* (Washington, D.C.: Congressional Quarterly Inc., 1998).

and act as the head of the opposition within the Senate. In many ways, Bob Dole found it much easier to act as the minority leader in 1993–1994, in Clinton's first term, than he had in the previous six years with Reagan and Bush. Indeed, Dole spent much of his first term as minority leader in an unsuccessful attempt to win the GOP presidential nomination, then had to serve with his former adversary for four years. When the minority leader gloated that he had been "turned loose" in 1992 by Clinton's electoral triumph, his sentiments were easy to understand. One illustration of this new, focused energy against a unified Democratic administration came in the attention Dole obtained from the television networks. In 1991–1992 he appeared a mere forty-two times on the network news shows; in the next two-year period, with a Democratic administration to oppose, he appeared 328 times (see table 5.3). This figure far surpassed any two-year total of any other minority leader during the 1959–1999 period. Being both in the minority and the opposition made a real difference.

If divided government shaped the context of minority leaders' choices from outside the Senate, the filibuster shaped the internal context of Senate politics. Over the course of the last forty years, the use of the filibuster has risen sharply, as Sarah A. Binder and Steven S. Smith (1997), among others, have noted. Although filibusters began their marked increase in the 1970s, the rise continued through the 1980s and escalated in the 1990s. Filibusters have become part of the ordinary landscape of senatorial politics; Barbara Sinclair (1999d) notes that of the major measures that could have been subject to a filibuster in recent years, more than half were. With forty-five-plus senators in the minority, the forty-one votes required to block cloture are well within the grasp of a Senate that has grown steadily more partisan in its voting patterns. Binder and Smith conclude that "Polarized conflict between the two parties, especially in the 1980s, certainly encouraged the minority party to exploit its parliamentary rights" (1997, 18). This trend has continued, as illustrated in table 5.2.

In the end, filibusters become routine tools in interparty battles, rather than special weapons, to be employed only on occasion. And minority leaders know that on many issues the number of votes required to prevail is forty-one, not fifty or fifty-one. This tool is double-edged, however, in that it gives the caucus/conference leverage over the leader, as much as it provides the leader with a tactical tool. Indeed, the leader may not want to use a filibuster, but will have his hand forced if his colleagues seek his backing for such an action.

## BUDGETARY POLITICS AND THE GROWTH OF OMNIBUS APPROPRIATIONS

If 1980–1981 represents a break point on various partisan and structural dimensions, these years also mark a sea change in budgeting and appropriations. In

### TABLE 5.2 DIVIDED GOVERNMENT AND FILIBUSTER ACTIVITY, 1959–2000

| Period | Div. Govt. (% of years) | Div. Govt. with President of Minority Senate Party (%) | Filibusters per Congress[a] | Cloture Votes per Congress | Successful Cloture Votes per Congress |
|---|---|---|---|---|---|
| 1959–1980 | 45 | 45 | 7.9 | 13.8 | 4.7 |
| 1981–2000 | 90 | 60 | 23.8 | 38.8 | 11.7 |

*Source:* Data drawn from Barbara Sinclair, "Individualism, Partisanship, and Cooperation in the Senate," paper presented at the Robert J. Dole Institute for Public Service and Public Policy Conference on Civility and Deliberation in the U.S. Senate, Washington, D.C., July 16, 1999.
[a]Filibuster figures, 1961–1998.

1980, reconciliation procedures, which "require Congress to change revenues and spending to the level set in the budget resolution," went into effect for the first time, thus profoundly altering the context of spending politics (Thurber 1997, 326). Originally intended to strengthen Congress, reconciliation "was captured by the White House in 1981 and used to achieve President Reagan's objectives" (Oleszek 1996, 73). Walter J. Oleszek notes that "reconciliation can be used by either branch or party provided they have the votes to implement their objectives" and that "reconciliation's proven effectiveness in compelling fiscal retrenchment has made it an important and regular part of the budget process" (1996, 73–74). For a minority leader with a president of his own party, this means that maintaining a strong relationship is crucial, in that the chief executive can likely bargain more effectively with the Senate majority than can a minority in a process where budget rules deny the use of the filibuster.

From 1980–1981 on, budget and appropriations politics increasingly came to dominate the business of the Congress. One of the unintended consequences of the fiscalization of policy has been the frequency with which so-called omnibus measures—budget agreements (e.g., 1993), continuing resolutions (e.g., 1995–1996), and final spending bills—have become regular features of the legislative process (Krutz forthcoming). With hundreds of billions of dollars on the table and ideological polarization growing, omnibus spending/budget measures "made it possible to wrap unpopular spending cuts and sometimes tax increases into one big package—and get a single vote on the package as a whole" (Sinclair 1997, 94). Although minority leaders were granted a seat at the table for the intense negotiations that transpired over the myriad provisions of these bills, they were often at the mercy of the (same-party) president and their individual members, who could object to an essential unanimous consent agreement on their own. Again, leaders had to treat the president and their colleagues as favored constituents.

Along with partisan and structural changes, the evolution of the
budget/appropriation process meant that the legislative context for minority
leadership was altered substantially by the 1980s. All these changes meant that
leaders had less control over negotiations and policy compromises than they had
enjoyed in the 1960s and 1970s. Moreover, all of these changes moved leaders
toward more "position-taking" behavior and less emphasis on compromise and,
especially, deliberation. With the 1986 decision to televise Senate proceedings,
leaders became more visible and, arguably, less capable of making deals that
might anger their supporters, in and out of the chamber. More and more, leading the Senate minority (and majority) seemed to require the outside skills of
campaigning and issue presentation, rather than the inside skills of negotiation.

## LEADERSHIP AS VOICE: COMMUNICATION AND CAMPAIGNS

If there is less running room for Senate leaders in reaching the kinds of deals that
typified the Dirksen, and to a lesser extent, Scott and Baker years, floor leaders
may well turn to other venues to change the agenda, to enhance their majorities,
and to influence outcomes. Increasingly, they have adopted campaign and media
strategies to accomplish what deliberation and compromise cannot. The poster
boy for this approach to legislative leadership is Newt Gingrich, but he represents a broad trend that has affected both chambers and both parties. For example, Senator George Mitchell (D-Maine) won a surprisingly easy victory as
Democratic floor leader in 1988 in large part because he offered his colleagues
an attractive face for the media. And Bob Dole demonstrated the numerous pos-
sibilities for solidifying his leadership by raising funds for fellow Republicans,
incumbents, and challengers alike. Of course, playing to the media and raising
campaign funds have long existed as leadership tools. Dirksen was certainly a
master at the former and competent at the latter (in an era of minimal reporting
on fund-raising activities). Still, these outside paths to influence within the
Senate have probably grown in importance over the past forty years. In terms of
press attention, however, the irony is that the dominant national media have covered Senate leaders less and less over time (Sinclair 1989, 64). This has meant
that legislative leaders have had to become more inventive and more collective in
their attempts to gain national attention for their ideas.

### Minority Leaders and the Media

The role of the news media in covering Congress has evolved over the past
forty years, as the mix of adversarial and symbiotic relationships between
reporters and legislators has increasingly tilted toward the adversarial, especially
in the wake of Watergate. As Timothy E. Cook (1997 and 1999) points out,

however, most coverage is "negotiated" as both sets of participants have long-term interests to protect. Party leaders represent key negotiators, even though each senator ordinarily can set the terms for his or her own exposure. Cook concludes that (1) "Political agendas are increasingly reactive to news agendas, and policies *have* to be crafted with news values in mind" and (2) "Political processes are sped up under the media spotlight" (1999, 29, emphasis mine). The implications of these two trends are daunting; Cook argues, "news coverage pushes for a quick elite response, thereby favoring the most available alternative . . . [and] the news media favor an interpretation of the legislative process that focuses more on it as a dramatic game . . . and less on it as a crucial and sober process of decision" (1999, 23). Of course, the ways in which legislators present their views surely affect the possibility that deliberation can flow from disagreements. And in an age of position taking, that may be unlikely.

Without question, the print side of the national media pays less attention to Congress today than it did thirty or forty years ago, and the decline for Senate leaders has been linear and without regard for individual personality (Smith 1993, 283). Again, the context of congressional leadership has changed substantially (see table 5.3). The evidence on television coverage for all congressional leaders is less clear in that several recent leaders (Mitchell, Thomas P. "Tip" O'Neill, and Gingrich, among others) have received substantial coverage (285).[3]

Moreover, the proliferation of news/talk outlets has allowed for more attention to leaders, but each individual appearance is surely worth less (e.g., conversing on late-night CNBC with Tim Russert or Chris Matthews). Most striking perhaps is the steady decline in the *New York Times*'s reporting that focuses on the Senate minority leader. Everett Dirksen averaged a citation in the *Times* approximately *once every two days* for his entire tenure as floor leader; in his first two congresses, as leader, Tom Daschle was mentioned less than *once every two weeks*.

On the other hand, references in *Congressional Quarterly Weekly Reports* (*CQWR*) have remained relatively consistent over the past four decades, although there is some variation among the leaders and, on occasion, within the tenure of individual minority leaders. What is clear from the *CQWR* data is the continuing importance of variation between the leaders within the same legislative era. Robert Byrd averaged fifty-nine mentions per year during his tenure as minority leader with a president of the opposing party; Bob Dole, in a similar situation for two years (1993–1994) averaged 140 citation annually. Even with a president of the same party (1987–1992), Dole received 119 mentions per year, or twice Byrd's rate. Byrd's style kept him on the Senate floor for long hours, while Dole was more comfortable in working with large numbers of Senate groupings to move various pieces of legislation toward passage. Moreover, as a once and future presidential candidate, Dole felt more comfortable with the press than did the more reserved, more scholarly Byrd.

## TABLE 5.3 NATIONAL NEWS COVERAGE OF MINORITY LEADERS, 1959–1999

| | New York Times Mentions/Year | Congressional Quarterly Weekly *Reports* Mentions/Year | *Network TV* Appearances/Year |
|---|---|---|---|
| **Dirksen** | | | |
| 1959 | 138 | 91 | na |
| 1960 | 147 | 77 | na |
| 1961 | 181 | 86 | na |
| 1962 | 185 | 97 | na |
| 1963 | 132 | 93 | na |
| 1964 | 180 | 96 | na |
| 1965 | 215 | 139 | na |
| 1966 | 210 | 160 | na |
| 1967 | 195 | 107 | na |
| 1968 | 165 | 65 | 37 |
| 1969 | 187 | 78 | 69 |
| **Scott** | | | |
| 1970 | 155 | 94 | 64 |
| 1971 | 194 | 104 | 59 |
| 1972 | 196 | 61 | 54 |
| 1973 | 151 | 56 | 78 |
| 1974 | 104[a] | 52 | 94 |
| 1975 | 129 | 39 | 60 |
| 1976 | 77 | 26 | 27 |
| **Baker** | | | |
| 1977 | 96 | 42 | 81 |
| 1978 | 90 | 61 | 62 |
| 1979 | 86 | 43 | 112 |
| 1980 | 53 | 63 | 95 |
| **Byrd** | | | |
| 1981 | 44 | 41 | 85 |
| 1982 | 29 | 58 | 35 |
| 1983 | 31 | 44 | 32 |
| 1984 | 16 | 27 | 16 |
| 1985 | 21 | 79 | 32 |
| 1986 | 24 | 104 | 58 |
| **Dole** | | | |
| 1987 | 65 | 103 | 31 |
| 1988 | 45 | 82 | 62 |
| 1989 | 28 | 120 | 28 |
| 1990 | 47 | 140 | 52 |
| 1991 | 24 | 130 | 23 |
| 1992 | 47 | 140 | 52 |
| 1993 | 82 | 126 | 133 |
| 1994 | 109 | 155 | 195 |
| **Daschle** | | | |
| 1995 | 22 | 102 | 47 |
| 1996 | 16 | 82 | 34 |
| 1997 | 20 | 51 | 24 |
| 1998 | 19 | 71 | 39 |
| 1999 | na | 98 | 50 |

*Sources:* Data drawn from indexes of the *New York Times, Congressional Quarterly Weekly Reports,* and the Vanderbilt television archives. References do not include presidential campaign mentions.
[a]Watergate/Nixon events are excluded.

The network news appearance data are similar to the *CQWR* data, in that there is no clear trend over time. Perhaps the most telling numbers relate to Tom Daschle, whose forty-one appearances per year fall below even Byrd's average of forty-three. As we shall see, this is ironic for a legislator whose leadership is built, in part, upon the idea of giving voice to Democratic policy ideas. At the same time, Daschle's *CQWR* visibility is roughly equivalent to that of Scott, Baker, and Byrd; the inside role of the leader remains more of a constant than that of achieving outside visibility.

Only Byrd and Dole move from the majority leader's position to that of minority leader and both serve during the first term of a new president from the opposing party. In many ways, this latter circumstance offered these leaders the chance to win substantial publicity. Although Byrd took some modest advantage of the opportunity, Dole clearly stepped up his public presence in the absence of a GOP president. During Reagan's first year in office, Byrd received more attention from the *Times* and television networks than at any other time as minority leader, but his *CQWR* score actually fell well below his six-year mean. With President Bill Clinton as foil (and presidential ambitions spurring him on), Dole achieved record levels of visibility on all three measures. In the days before the Gingrich speakership, Dole possessed the most powerful and familiar voice of opposition in Washington. He doubled his average number of mentions in the *Times* (from 42.6 to 95.5) and quadrupled his average network coverage (from 41 mentions per year to 164). In short, changes in context lead to differing emphases on constituencies. At the same time, both secular trends (e.g., the decline of coverage in the national print press) and the personal styles of majority leaders (e.g., Dirksen versus Byrd) remain important in shaping the legislator's relationships with sets of constituents.

### The Minority Leader in Electoral Politics

With the Senate changing hands in 1980, 1986, and 1994 and party margins hovering within five seats of a majority for both parties, contemporary minority leaders can easily envision themselves becoming majority leaders in the next congress. Close margins and divided government also lead to an emphasis on position taking, in which victory in the next election is a more important consideration than producing a deal that may not completely satisfy one's constituents.

More specifically, the minority leader, like any other party leader in Congress, plays a major role in determining who gets party backing in at least five different, though related, ways: (1) contributions from the party's Senate campaign committee; (2) contributions (often soft money) from other party units; (3) funds from friendly interest groups, whose PACs may well seek counsel from the party leader; (4) direct contributions from the minority leader's own PAC; and (5) the direction of funds from other senators' campaigns and PACs

to other, more competitive, campaigns. No party leader can completely dominate this process, but their combination of position, information, and influence
can enhance their strength within the conference/caucus.

In 1976, party expenditures for senatorial campaigns stood at a meager
$118,000 for both parties; by 1980 that figure stood at $6,567,000, with minority party Republicans spending more than 80 percent of the total on their road
to recapturing the chamber. By 1992, the total came to more than $28 million,
although it has declined in recent years (Ornstein, Mann, and Malbin 1998,
106–7). With all these funds, legislative leaders can exert great leverage by directing funds (however informally) to given races.

Circumstances are much the same with PACs, whose numbers increased to
more than four thousand by the early 1980s and whose level of
contributions/expenditures rose to more than $200 million by the mid-1990s.
Again, party leaders play a major role in directing these funds, even without any
formal coordination. There is a certain rationality for a Dole or a Daschle to
spend time currying favor with PAC managers and party officials who control
millions of dollars in campaign funds. Likewise, taking positions that may lead
to electoral advantage rather than policy deals makes sense in an era of slender
majorities.

In addition, as more and more individual senators have established their own
PACs, party leaders feel pressured to establish their own. In 1984 and 1986,
Minority Leader Byrd made $107,000 and $171,000, respectively, in contribu-
tions for Democratic Senate candidates. Bob Dole contributed more than $1.5
million over the 1988 through 1994 election cycles to help elect a Republican
Senate, and his Campaign America PAC spent $820,000 in 1996 to help keep
the Senate in Republican hands. Minority Leader Daschle did not form his own
PAC until the 1999–2000 cycle, but he began with a bang; he collected $1.3
million at a Washington fund-raiser and followed that with a foray into Silicon
Valley (with sixteen other Democrats) to raise funds from new political sources
as well as to establish links to the technology community (Henry 1999;
Krikorian 1999).

In sum, Senate floor leaders have increasingly come to treat funding
sources—within the party, among interest groups and lobbyists, or direct mail
targets—as important constituents. To the extent that party margins remain
tight in the Senate (and Congress as a whole), leaders will act within the confines
of the two-year electoral cycle. Individual senators may still get some respite during the first years of a six-year term, but a party leader who wants to win (or
protest) the majority must focus on the short-term of electoral politics and the
attendant fund-raising. The politics of position taking thus gets one more substantial boost.

## Dirksen and Daschle:
## Minority Leaders, Voice, and Influence

Inclusion—that has a lot to do with the cohesion we've been able to acquire. It all comes down to our caucus feeling the need, having the opportunity, for inclusion. Democratic senators really need to be able to hear what is the current set of circumstances and they need to be able to express themselves. Minority Leader Tom Daschle, 1999. (Quoted in Newlin Carney 1997, 2361)

Well, [Dirksen] saw it as leader of the Republican party . . . and as leader of the Senate who owed a responsibility to the President, to the party at the same time—which created a sort of ambivalence on occasion—but he saw it as a matter of serving his colleagues and leading the party in a position and discharging a responsibility to the presidency—those three things mixed together. Republican Senator, 1960s. (Quoted in Torcom 1973, 331)

At either end of the forty years of minority leadership examined here, Everett Dirksen and Tom Daschle both have operated within the opportunities afforded them and the limits imposed upon them by the sets of constituencies to whom they must respond. Dirksen and Daschle (to date) both served only in the minority, but Daschle could hope to become majority leader, whereas Dirksen could realistically see no light at the end of that tunnel. But Dirksen did have true friends in the White House and enough southern Democrats with whom he could sometimes make common cause (and sometimes oppose, as on civil rights). In many ways, Dirksen had more room to maneuver than has Daschle in his years as minority leader.

Indeed, Dirksen gained a measure of strength from what should have been his greatest liability—the size of his minority. With an average of thirty-four to thirty-five Republicans during the Kennedy-Johnson years, Dirksen needed to work with the majority and the president if he wanted to have any influence. Moreover, Dirksen found it easy to give significant committee roles to most GOP senators, in that anyone who wished to participate actively could do so. At the same time, he centralized the party leadership, based on his strong ties to Democratic leaders and president.

In a Democratic era, Dirksen reminded the electorate that there was a Republican party beyond the unstable image of Barry Goldwater and that there were other policy perspectives beyond those of the president, at a time when the "imperial presidency" was near its apex. When considering Dirksen's "voice," we must literally hear it, and regardless of his position, he is speaking for himself. As a *Time* cover story described it:

He speaks, and the words emerge in a soft, sepulchral baritone. They undulate in measured phrased, expire in breathless wisps. He fills his lungs and blows word-rings like smoke. The sentences curl upward . . . Now he conjures moods of mirth, now of sorrow. He rolls his bright blue eyes heavenward. In funereal tones, he paraphrases the Bible and church bells peal. "Motherhood," he whispers, and grown men weep. "The flag," he bugles, and everybody salutes. (*Time* 1962, 27)[4]

Dirksen's performances (for that is what they were, replete with detailed notes for speeches and many floor statements) were important, but not central. The rhetoric often overwhelmed the substance of his remarks. Still, Dirksen contributed to the evolution of the floor leader position by maintaining a high profile. One of the criteria for selecting floor leaders has become the ability to present one's self as an attractive, articulate public figure.

Dirksen did regularly turn on the partisan rhetoric, as in the weekly "Ev and Charlie [Halleck]" show when the two minority leaders would hold forth with their views on contemporary politics. But being the individual that he was, he did not necessarily speak for the Republican forces in the Senate; this was especially true after the elections of 1966 and 1968, with the election of several independent-minded new Republican senators. Dirksen's relations with an independent-minded senator like Charles Percy (R-Ill.) were consistently rocky. The minority leader correctly understood that, if senators started to cut their own deals, his leverage with the Democratic leadership, the southern Democrats, and the White House would be severely limited.

In the end, Dirksen did pay close attention to his core constituents—his fellow Republican senators—but he knew that in terms of influence his most important relationships were with Democrats at both ends of Pennsylvania Avenue.

Tom Daschle's most important relationships are almost certainly with his major set of constituents—the other forty-four Democrats in the U.S. Senate. After winning the minority leader position by a one-vote margin over Chris Dodd (D-Conn.), Daschle has earned the support of the caucus by listening to its members and forging a group that has proven to be extremely cohesive, witnessed both by its 85 percent party unity score over the 1995–1999 period and by its support of President Clinton in unanimously opposing the two articles of impeachment. Despite a host of fiscal constraints and potential partisan land mines, Daschle has established a strong working relationship with Majority Leader Lott (Newlin Carney 1997). But Daschle does possess the filibuster weapon, so his ties to Lott are conditioned by the capacity of the Democrats to stop the Senate's business and take a firm position that may well turn into an advantageous issue. Although he may not be as electorally oriented as Speaker-in-waiting Richard A. ("Dick") Gephardt, Daschle is often willing to press for political advantage, rather than striving to cut a compromise deal that may well unravel at some other stage of the legislative process. In this context, voice may be more important than influence.

But Daschle's voice is nothing like Dirksen's. He conducts a partisan chorus rather than performing as a soloist. This becomes apparent in the finding on media coverage; Daschle simply does relatively well in carrying the Democrats' tune as a party spokesperson. Even if the data (see table 5.3) underestimate his impact, the Democratic voice must come from a host of singers. And that is precisely what Daschle has orchestrated. As Daschle puts it, "Without unity, we really can't make ourselves heard. *When you have multi-voices, you have no voice*" (Newlin Carney 1997, 2362).

Daschle's homey strategy seems to be working. In a pair of papers, Patrick J. Sellers (1999b and 2000) (a former congressional fellow in Daschle's office) finds that party leaders tend to select issues that will resonate among their fellow partisans in the Senate. Thus, "even when forced to discuss macroeconomics and taxes, the Minority Leader tried to link those issues to health, education, and the environment. By structuring the caucus message in this manner, [Daschle] created a message with greater benefits for his followers" (1999b, 13).

The leader's emphasis on a coordinated message will work only if his fellow partisans join in the chorus or, more likely, blend the core message with their own perspectives and the related issues of their home-state constituents. In addition, Sellers (2000, 18) finds that message development and promotion can generate larger amounts and more positive coverage in the national media. In fact, the *New York Times*, the very outlet that has mentioned Daschle so little, appears to cover the Democrats' issues more thoroughly in the wake of their emphasis, although the causal relationships remain tenuous. Still, as Tip O'Neill famously observed, "There is no limit to what you can accomplish if you don't care who gets credit for it" (O'Neill 1987, 275). Daschle's corporate message strategy may well herald an era of position taking, in which the message may trump policy, all in the interest of capturing the chamber.

For both Dirksen and Daschle, and those who served between them, the position of minority leader remains highly constrained, often frustrating, but rarely uninteresting. Dirksen did not have numbers, but he had the day-to-day hope of influencing policies; Daschle has more troops, with perhaps less influence. Both have important constituents in the White House, although Dirksen's strong personal ties to Lyndon Johnson far outweigh Daschle's marriage of convenience to Bill Clinton. To lead is to choose, and for Senate minority leaders the choices are often severely constrained. Yet Dirksen influenced more policy than anyone could have reasonably expected, and on occasion Daschle has managed to move the agenda without a solo voice. Such accomplishments must satisfy the minority leader, "the man of all work."

## NOTES

Many thanks to Heather Hoy and Dakota Loomis for providing me with valuable research assistance on this project.

1. Any number of articles and books have addressed the nature of contemporary party leadership—with emphasis, understandably, on the majority. These include Barbara Sinclair's chapter in this book, as well as her "The Sixty-Vote Senate: Strategies, Process and Outcomes" (1999c), among others.

2. The overall position of the leaders within the party has been accorded substantial study, but these data are adequate to demonstrate a real change between the two periods.

3. Smith shows the Vanderbilt television archives as listing considerably more appearances by Senator Dole during the 1985–1990 period than do my calculations.

4. There is no credit to an author, but Dirksen's biographer, Neil MacNeil, wrote the article.

## CHAPTER SIX

# Message Politics
# and Senate Procedure

## C. LAWRENCE EVANS AND WALTER J. OLESZEK

A well-known adage of congressional politics is that disputes about procedure are in reality usually disputes over policy. The rules and procedures utilized by lawmakers determine which alternatives are considered in committee and on the floor, the order and timing of consideration, the modes through which different lawmakers can participate in decision making, and other factors that shape the content of legislation. Not surprisingly, the academic literature is replete with examples of procedural maneuvering aimed at influencing policy outcomes within Congress.

However, in recent years procedural wrangling on Capitol Hill has often been driven by the broader partisan-electoral context of legislative deliberation. Congressional Republicans and Democrats increasingly have sought to structure floor action to publicize partisan messages—the issues, themes, and policy symbols that legislators believe will generate a positive response toward their party among voters (see chapter five by Burdett Loomis). The intensity of this message-driven procedural infighting has been particularly marked in the Senate, where the majority party's control over the agenda is weaker than it is on the House side.

The purpose of this chapter is to explore the procedural consequences of message politics in the contemporary Senate, and the implications for the role of party in the chamber. The first section is about the nuts and bolts of message politics. It examines how an issue or proposal gets included in a party's message, and outlines how major items considered by the Senate during 1999 related to the Republican and Democratic messages. The next section is an analysis of the consequences of message politics for key aspects of Senate procedure and practice. We end with a brief conclusion.

## Party Messages in the Senate

"We need your help to communicate this important message outside-the-belt-way and we urge you to use the materials enclosed in this packet to promote the 'Lock Box' proposal," wrote Republican Senators Paul Coverdell of Georgia, secretary of the Republican Conference, and Connie Mack of Florida, the GOP Conference chair. The message book, provided to Republican members just before the July 4 recess in 1999, was part of an effort to coordinate the themes and policy stances that GOP lawmakers would emphasize during meetings with constituents. Among other points, the message book recommended that Republican lawmakers assert that, "Democrats want to spend the surplus on other federal programs. Americans deserve a sound Social Security system—not IOUs signed by Bill Clinton that will have to be paid by our children and grandchildren." Majority Leader Trent Lott (R-Miss.) also scheduled periodic roll call votes on the lockbox initiative to help focus public attention on the issue.

### Emergence of an Organized Message Process

One indicator of the rise of message politics in the Senate is the changing character of "morning business," which is the period at the start of each new legislative day. Long used by senators to make brief speeches on miscellaneous topics, by the 1990s it was routinely employed for coordinated partisan message sending.

We sampled the first five-day period of Senate business during June of each odd-numbered year to determine the length of time devoted to morning business and the average time constraints placed on individual speakers.[1] Table 6.1 suggests that the amount of morning business per day has increased somewhat since the 1970s, especially during the majority leadership of Trent Lott. The time constraints placed on individual speakers have become less restrictive. The rise of message politics is particularly clear when we examine the content of the speeches. In our June samples, morning business was not used for organized party message sending until 1991, when a team of GOP senators heralded their party's commitment to the missile defense system. By the mid-1990s, such coordinated party speeches were commonplace.

By most accounts, the Senate has emulated the House in meshing campaign strategies with internal legislative tactics. Television was a factor here. The House went first in providing gavel-to-gavel coverage of floor proceedings in 1979; a full seven years before the Senate followed suit. One rationale for televising the Senate was the growing visibility of House members relative to senators. The rise to power of Representative Newt Gingrich (R-Ga.) occurred in part because of his skill in exploiting televised floor proceedings. Former Speaker Thomas P. "Tip" O'Neill (D-Mass.) once observed, "as far as [Gingrich and his allies] were concerned, the House was . . . a sound stage from which to reach the people at home" (1987, 354).

## TABLE 6.1 TRENDS IN MORNING BUSINESS: FIRST FIVE LEGISLATIVE DAYS IN JUNE, 1977–1999

| Year | Limit on Morning Business (in minutes) | Average Speaker Allotment (in minutes) |
|---|---|---|
| 1977 | 22.50 | 1.40 |
| 1979 | 23.75 | 5.00 |
| 1981 | 63.00 | 6.57 |
| 1983 | 58.40 | 8.14 |
| 1985 | 40.00 | 5.00 |
| 1987 | 31.00 | 5.00 |
| 1989 | 44.00 | 5.00 |
| 1991 | 69.00 | 6.67 |
| 1993 | 51.00 | 5.00 |
| 1995 | 49.60 | 12.30 |
| 1997 | 86.00 | 8.33 |
| 1999 | 81.00 | 10.00 |

*Source: Congressional Record*, selected volumes.

Among House Democrats, Richard Gephardt of Missouri took the lead in establishing an organized "message team" for his caucus, shortly after becoming majority leader in 1989. By the early 1990s, Gephardt's group was routinely putting out a "message of the day," which fellow House Democrats were encouraged to articulate repeatedly to the media and anyone else who would listen.

Interestingly, many of the House members who worked closely with Gingrich and Gephardt on message efforts in that chamber were elected to the Senate during the 1990s. In the 106th Congress (1999–2000), for instance, twenty-six GOP senators are former House members, while twenty Senate Democrats formally served in the chamber. Like their House brethren, GOP senators since the early 1990s have regularly reserved blocks of floor time to draw more public attention to their agenda and attack the other party. Craig Thomas (R-Wyo.) provides a good example of a GOP House member who brought his experience with message politics to the Senate. In the early 1990s, Thomas was a member of the House Republican "theme team." When he began his Senate service in 1995, he organized the other ten GOP freshmen into a "Freshmen Focus" group that regularly took to the floor to heighten public awareness of the Republican agenda.

In the current Senate, Republican members typically orchestrate their message efforts via small working groups with issue-specific assignments. This approach was developed by Republican Conference secretary Paul Coverdell, who first brought the idea to Lott and then sold it to the full conference. In the 106th Congress, the Republicans formed working groups on health (chaired by Majority Whip Don Nickles, Okla.), social security (chaired by Rick Santorum, Pa., and Craig Thomas), defense (chaired by Jon Kyl, Ariz., and Olympia Snowe, Maine), drugs and crime (chaired by Spencer Abraham, Mich., and Mike DeWine, Ohio), and education (chaired by Bill Frist, Tenn.). A GOP leadership aide explained:

> We don't have a theme team selling the message. Craig Thomas is responsible for getting people to the floor to speak during dead times. We always have a communications component on major items. We give offices information, talking points. Coverdell is aggressive on that, working with J. C. Watts [GOP Conference chair in the House]. (Authors' interview, December 1999)

In contrast, Senate Democrats organize a single message team that operates across different issue areas. The practice began when Tom Daschle of South Dakota became minority leader during the 104th Congress (1995–1996).

## Message Selection

How does a policy item become a message issue? In important research, Patrick J. Sellers (1999a) explores how Senate leaders formulate party messages and coordinate media efforts around these issues. According to Sellers, message items tend to be issues where (1) rank-and-file lawmakers within a party are relatively homogeneous in their preferences; and (2) the party "owns the issue in the eyes of the general public" (1999a, 4).

The emphasis on intraparty preference homogeneity is a straightforward extension of the concept of "conditional party government," first advanced by David W. Rohde (1991) and applied to the Republican House in two papers by John Aldrich and Rohde (1995 and 1996). If preferences within both parties on an issue are homogeneous, but the views of Republicans and Democrats diverge, then the issue becomes a potential message item for both parties. Alternatively, if preferences within one party are homogeneous but the other party is divided, the item is a potential message item only for the unified caucus. And when preferences in a policy area are heterogeneous within both parties, each one finds it "difficult to claim a single position and record, which by extension undermines their efforts to win public support" (Sellers 1999a, 4).

According to Sellers (1999a), a party must also "own an issue" for it to be a viable message item. This reference to issue ownership is from John R. Petrocik (1996), who argues that voters tend to view one political party (or candidate) as better able to handle the problems associated with certain issue areas. The concept is familiar to observers of polling trends. For instance, a Greenberg-Quinlan poll conducted in October 1999 asked respondents whether, overall, they thought the Democrats or Republicans would "do a better job . . . with early health and learning for your children." Fifty-seven percent responded that Democrats would do somewhat or much better, while just 20 percent felt that the Republicans would do a better job.[2] According to these data, Democrats own the issue area.

Based on Petrocik's work, and his own analysis of survey data and the roll call record, Sellers (1999a) asserts that the broad areas of health, education, and environment are owned by Democrats. Defense he characterizes as owned by the GOP. Social welfare, macroeconomics, labor, immigration, civil rights, and civil liberties are issues with divided ownership.

Intraparty preference homogeneity and public attitudes about issue ownership certainly matter. However, leaders can increase party loyalty on a measure by first transforming it into a message vote. And the policy areas that Sellers and Petrocik associate with one or both parties tend to be broad. Often, discrete policy proposals can be crafted within these categories that resonate with favorable public perceptions about either political party. Indeed, devising such proposals, and mobilizing party support behind them, is an important source of leadership influence in the Senate (Evans 1999; Sellers 1999a).

Consider the case of education policy during the 106th Congress. As mentioned, Democrats have traditionally polled well on these issues. But GOP senators embraced proposals to increase the discretion of states in deciding how to spend federal education resources—the so-called "Ed-Flex" and "Super Ed-Flex" initiatives. A Republican leadership aide observed that, "Republicans are becoming more comfortable on education, more confident that they can talk about education and win [by] appealing to suburban swing voters. We saw it in [Missouri Republican Senator Christopher S. "Kit"] Bond's race in 1998. . . . People stood up in the conference and said, 'we can do this.' " Interestingly, the staffer noted that the value of Ed-Flex as a Republican message issue derived in part from its bipartisan support: "Democrats couldn't really attack us on the merits. Only Kennedy and Wellstone were noes" (Authors' interview, December 1999).

Senators and staff rely on a range of informational cues to gauge which issue areas will resonate favorably for them with the public. They consider public opinion data, especially the large national polls that regularly ask questions about the public's priorities or which party will do a better job handling different issues. The leadership offices and policy committees generally lack the resources necessary to regularly do the polling themselves. But the national committees poll fairly often and regularly share the results with their fellow partisans on Capitol Hill

A number of other information sources are useful for message formulation. Included are member communications and discussions with their constituents;

press and media reports; party "theme team" and caucus meetings; meetings with House counterparts; and discussions with lobbyists and other elites. Individual senators develop their own views about what the party's message should be, and these preferences are considered during the weekly caucus and conference meetings conducted by each Senate party, the weekly policy and message committee meetings, and informal conversations between members and staff. Thus, the formation of the message is poll-influenced, but not poll-driven. The polling that is conducted is often aimed at finding symbols, themes, and language that are useful for selling the items a congressional party has already decided to include in its message agenda.

We spoke with top Senate leadership aides (from each party) with primary responsibility for formulating and selling the messages for his or her side of the aisle. During these interviews, we asked the aides to evaluate the relevance to the GOP and Democratic messages of thirty major items considered in some way on the Senate floor in 1999 (the first session of the 106th Congress). The staffers' responses were averaged and the items were divided into categories of high-, medium-, and low-message relevance. The results are summarized in table 6.2.[3]

Notice that twenty-one of the thirty floor items (70 percent) are rated as "highly relevant" to the messages of one or both parties. One reason is that we sought to include on the list as many message items as possible. But the table also reflects the pervasiveness of message politics and the intense partisanship of the current Senate. Interestingly, the largest cell is for items highly relevant to both party messages.

Also noteworthy is the relative success of the minority party in bringing its message priorities to the floor. Of the items in table 6.2, Republicans and Democrats both had a "message advantage" on nine issues.[4] Five items are rated high for the Democrats and low for the GOP, while just three (missile defense, the social security lockbox, and military pay) are high Republican and low Democrat.

Contrary to the assertions of some pundits, the Democrats did not control the Senate floor agenda in 1999. Republicans were also successful at maintaining their unity and deriving at least a degree of message value from certain traditionally Democratic areas such as managed heath care reform. But table 6.2 also indicates that the minority party was able to secure floor action on its issues, reflecting the strategic skill of Democratic leaders and the relatively limited agenda powers available to the Senate majority party.

The importance of framing and other leadership tactics is also apparent in table 6.2. Consider education policy, which is often characterized as a Democratic issue. Four of the items relate to education: teacher hiring, after school programs, Ed-Flex, and the Individuals with Disabilities Education Act (IDEA). The first

## TABLE 6.2 RELEVANCE OF SENATE FLOOR ITEMS TO PARTY "MESSAGES," 106TH CONGRESS, 1ST SESSION

| Democrats High | Democrats Medium | Democrats Low |
|---|---|---|
| | **GOP High** | |
| Clinton Impeachment | Ed-Flex | Missile Defense |
| Kosovo Involvement | Tax Reduction | Social Security Lockbox |
| Juvenile Justice | Partial-birth Abortions | Military Pay Hike |
| Managed Health Care | Bankruptcy Reform | |
| Confirmation of | IDEA (unfunded mandates) | |
|    Judge Ronnie White | | |
| Nuclear Test Ban Treaty | | |
| | **GOP Medium** | |
| Gun Control | Financial Services Overhaul | Reorganize Energy |
| Farm Assistance | Y2K Liability | Department |
| | Africa Trade/CBI | |
| | Medicare Reimbursements | |
| | **GOP Low** | |
| Teacher Hiring | Steel Import Quotas | Appropriations Caps |
| After School Programs | Dairy Compact | Judicial Confirmations |
| *Roe v. Wade* | |    in General |
| Minimum Wage | | |
| Campaign Finance Reform | | |

*Source:* Interviews with Senate leadership staff.

two are Democratic priorities with little relevance to the Republican message. As mentioned, GOP leaders countered with the Ed-Flex bill.

The IDEA item was also part of the GOP arsenal on education issues. This proposal would increase federal funding for IDEA, first passed during the Nixon administration. Under existing law, state and local governments are required to provide disabled students with the resources necessary to receive a public education. However, the federal government has provided only a portion of the funding necessary to cover these costs, creating an unfunded federal mandate on state and local governments. Along with education flexibility, clamping down on unfunded mandates is a key GOP priority. Senate Republicans countered the Democratic teacher hiring proposal with amendments to allocate the money instead to funding IDEA. They sought to shift the focus from the Democratic to the Republican message—and perhaps force Democrats to cast a vote that Republicans could portray as unfriendly to disabled kids.

## PROCEDURAL CONSEQUENCES OF MESSAGE POLITICS

Senators use a wide range of procedures and tactics to highlight and advance their party messages in the legislative process. But certain rules and tactics are especially relevant here. Consider Senate action on juvenile justice reform during 1999. Just weeks after the April 1999 shootings at Columbine High School, Senate Democrats conducted a news conference rife with charts, props, and expressions of outrage about firearms and juvenile violence. They unveiled new gun-control proposals, including mandatory background checks before weapons could be sold at gun shows. Democrats initially sought to add these proposals as amendments to a year 2000 (Y2K) bill protecting computer companies from lawsuits. So Majority Leader Lott scheduled floor action on a languishing juvenile justice bill, and indicated that Democrats would be able to offer certain gun-control proposals as amendments to that vehicle. Several procedures played a prominent role in the ensuing parliamentary tangle.

- Senate Rule XIV enables members to place newly introduced legislation directly on the Senate calendar, effectively bypassing committee action. In January 1999, Judiciary chairman Orrin Hatch (R-Utah) used this procedure to place the juvenile justice measure directly on the calendar of the full chamber. He wanted to avoid a lengthy committee review that might restrict Lott's ability to call the measure up on the floor.

- During the first three days of debate on juvenile justice, the Senate considered fifteen amendments from each party, but Democrats had many additional proposals to offer. A frustrated Lott urged his colleagues to accept a unanimous consent agreement (UCA) designed to "allow for a list of amendments to be locked in and [establish a] passage time for this vital piece of legislation." Minority Leader Daschle indicated that Democrats could not accept a time certain on final passage. Lott characterized the resulting UCA as "a pathetic accomplishment" (*Congressional Record*, May 14, 1999, S5329).

- As mentioned, Democrats initially attempted to hold the Y2K measure hostage in exchange for opportunities to offer gun-control proposals on the floor. Lott responded by filing for cloture on aspects of the Y2K bill. When his attempts to achieve a comprehensive UCA on juvenile justice failed, he startled Democrats by asking for cloture on the motion to proceed on Y2K. If accepted, this would have pulled the juvenile justice bill from the floor.

- At another point, Lott attempted to block consideration of Democratic gun amendments by "filling the amendment tree."[5] Daschle described this as a tactic "that the [majority] leader can use to offer multiple amendments and thereby fill all of the available amendment slots that a bill has under Senate rules, precluding any Senator from offering an amendment" (*Congressional Record*, October 28, 1999, S13365). In the end, Democrats were able to force action on their main gun-control amendments, including one that passed when Vice President Gore cast a dramatic tie-breaking vote.

Thus, the juvenile justice bill directs our attention to four aspects of Senate procedure for understanding message politics—Rule XIV, the strategic use of cloture, filling the amendment tree, and heightened difficulties in achieving unanimous consent. We consider each in turn.

## Rule XIV

As mentioned, Senate Rule XIV enables individual lawmakers to circumvent committee consideration and place a bill or joint resolution directly on the calendar. According to the rule, all measures introduced in the Senate are to be read twice on different legislative days prior to their reference to committee. Typically, these readings are waived by unanimous consent and the parliamentarian refers the legislation to the appropriate panel. On occasion, a member will strategically raise an objection to the second reading, in which case the bill is placed on the full Senate calendar for possible floor action.

Rule XIV is not invoked for the vast majority of measures, but it can be a useful tactic when senators want to bypass committee. There might be insufficient time for a lengthy committee review. Perhaps there is concern that a bill will get stymied in committee. Or the majority leader may want the flexibility to call a measure up whenever he deems appropriate.

Rule XIV is particularly useful on message items. Party leaders usually want to maximize their control over the contents of such proposals, and they may be reluctant to delegate drafting responsibilities to a committee with minority party representation or an independent-minded chairman. Skipping committee enhances a leader's discretion over timing, which can be critical on message issues.

Senate insiders point out that use of Rule XIV increased markedly during the 1990s, and that it is disproportionately associated with message issues. We conducted a systematic search of the *Congressional Record,* looking for signs of Rule XIV usage during the decade. We also examined the content of Rule XIV measures during the first session of the 106th Congress.[6]

Figure 6.1 indicates that the number of Rule XIV measures has indeed increased over time, especially during the Lott years.[7] Prior to 1994, the tactic was used (on average) less than five times per year. Beginning in 1994 (the last year of Democratic Senate control) and continuing throughout the decade, the number of Rule XIV measures rose significantly, reaching a peak of thirty-seven in 1999.

Table 6.3 provides summary information about the substantive content of Rule XIV bills and resolutions during 1999. (Here, we separate out issues in the "high relevance" categories of table 6.2.) Not surprisingly, the Rule XIV tactic is mostly used by members of the majority party. The minority lacks the formal agenda privileges (such as preferential recognition rights) necessary to fully exploit the rule. As we shall see, they have other tactics for bringing their message items to the floor.

**FIGURE 6.1    Rule XIV Measures**

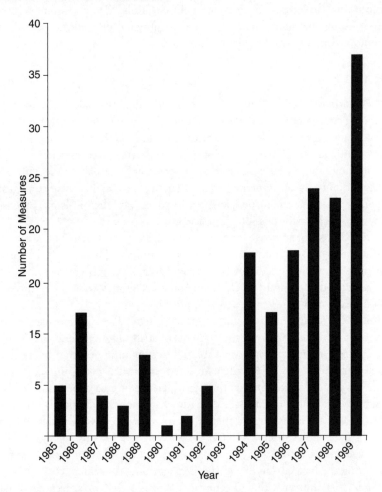

In addition, Rule XIV does appear to be a message-oriented tactic. Only a small percentage of the two thousand bills and resolutions introduced in the Senate during 1999 were message items. But of the thirty-three Rule XIV measures introduced by Republicans, sixteen were highly relevant to the GOP message. Three of the four Rule XIV bills sponsored by Democrats were in the "high-message" category for that party. Indeed, most of the high-message priorities for Republicans included in table 6.2 are also on the list of Rule XIV bills. And three of the most prominent message bills considered during 1999 (juvenile justice reform, managed health care, and partial-birth abortions) were actually brought to the floor via the Rule XIV process.[8]

# TABLE 6.3 SUBJECT MATTER OF RULE XIV MEASURES, 1999

## Republican Proposals
### High Relevance to Party Message

| | |
|---|---|
| S. 1692 | Partial-birth Abortion |
| S. 1606 | Bankruptcy Reform |
| H.R. 1218 | Abortion |
| S. 609 | Juvenile Crime and Drugs |
| S.J.Res. 13 | Social Security Lockbox—Constitutional Amendment |
| H.R. 350 | Unfunded Mandates |
| S. 508 | Restrict Military Operations in Serbia-Montenegro |
| S. 269 | Missile Defense |
| S. 270 | Military Pay Hike |
| S. 271 | Ed-Flex |
| S. 254 | Juvenile Justice |
| S. 40 | Abortion |
| S. 41 | Abortion |
| S. 42 | Family Planning/Abortion |
| S. 44 | Juvenile Crime and Drugs |
| H.R. 350 | Unfunded Mandates |

### Other

| | |
|---|---|
| S.J.Res. 37 | Panama Canal |
| H.R. 1883 | Resource Transfers to Iran |
| S. 1770 | Research and Development Tax Credit Extension |
| S. 1771 | Foreign Sanctions (Agriculture) |
| H.R. 17 | Foreign Sanctions (Agriculture) |
| S.J.Res. 33 | Clinton Policy on FALN Terrorists |
| S. 1427 | Special Counsels |
| S.J.Res. 26 | Unit Citation for U.S. Indianapolis |
| S.J.Res. 22 | Dairy Compact |
| S. 767 | Tax Extension for Military Personnel |
| S. 755 | Ethical Standards for Federal Prosecutors |
| H.R. 975 | Steel Imports |
| S. 508 | Banking Regulation |
| H.R. 99 | FAA Reauthorization |
| S. 43 | School Prayer |
| S. 45 | Limit Extension of Title 7 |
| S. 40 | Affirmative Action |

## Democratic Proposals
### High Relevance to Party Message

| | |
|---|---|
| S. 1832 | Minimum Wage |
| S. 1256 | Patients Bill of Rights |
| S. 564 | Teacher Hiring |

### Other

| | |
|---|---|
| S. 754 | Federal Building Designation in North Carolina |

## Cloture

In recent years, senators have grown more willing to engage in filibusters and other dilatory tactics, and there has been an accompanying rise in cloture motions filed to bring debate to a close. Barbara Sinclair (1999c) argues that the result is a "Sixty-vote Senate." Passing major or controversial legislation increasingly requires that cloture be invoked, which in turn requires a supermajority of at least sixty votes.

A related trend is for the majority leader to file for cloture early and often on a measure to require that all amendments be germane to the pending legislation. The Senate has no general germaneness rule, but it does operate with strict germaneness requirements after cloture has been invoked. In the 106th Congress, Senator Lott occasionally filed for cloture on the first day of a measure's consideration, then took up other matters, only to return to the bill when cloture "ripened" (two days later) to see if sixty senators would vote to invoke Rule XXII. Meanwhile, no senator could offer and debate any amendments to the clotured measure.

For purposes of tractability, we focus on the strategic use of cloture during 1999. Over the year, cloture motions were filed on forty-three separate occasions. Eleven of these motions were successfully invoked, thereby cutting off debate on the underlying matter. Majority Leader Lott filed all but three of the motions for cloture; Democratic leaders sponsored the others. The source of the motions and the relative difficulty of securing sixty votes reflect the high levels of conflict on these bills and the narrow GOP majority. Throughout the year, party loyalty was very high on cloture votes.

Table 6.4 reproduces the message categories of table 6.2, and also denotes which of the items were affected by *contested* cloture motions (five or more no votes). An item is in bold if (1) a motion for cloture was directly filed on that bill or amendment; or (2) a motion was filed on another measure, but the clear intention was to affect chamber consideration of the item in bold. Recall that one of the cloture motions on the Y2K liability bill was partially motivated by Lott's desire to keep gun control off the floor. Cloture was filed on Y2K, but the main target was the debate about guns. In table 6.4, the number of contested cloture motions per item is included in parentheses. Over the year, cloture votes also occurred on three issues not included on our list. These measures are listed at the bottom of the table.

Although cloture motions were filed for items in all of the cells of table 6.4, there are differences in the strategic role of cloture across the various cells. For one, cloture attempts on message issues were seldom successful. Of the seven contested motions that were actually invoked (i.e., they received sixty or more votes), only two touched even tangentially on a message issue. On July 28, by a bipartisan vote of seventy-seven to twenty-two, the Senate accepted a Lott cloture motion aimed at bringing the juvenile justice bill to conference committee with the House. A number of Republicans voted no (against Lott) because the Senate-passed bill included a Democratic gun-control provision. On November 2, also

## TABLE 6.4 CLOTURE AND THE PARTY MESSAGE, 1999

| Democrats High | Democrats Medium | Democrats Low |
|---|---|---|
| **GOP High** | | |
| Clinton Impeachment | Ed-Flex (4) | Missile Defense |
| Kosovo Involvement | Tax Reduction | Social Security |
| Juvenile Justice | Partial-birth Abortions | Lockbox (5) |
| Managed Health Care | Bankruptcy Reform | Military Pay Hike |
| Confirmation of | IDEA (unfunded mandates) | |
|     Judge Ronnie White | | |
| Nuclear Test Ban Treaty | | |
| **GOP Medium** | | |
| Gun Control | Financial Services Overhaul | Reorganize Energy |
| Farm Assistance | Y2K Liability (2) | Department (1) |
| | Africa Trade/CBI (3) | |
| | Medicare Reimbursements | |
| **GOP Low** | | |
| Teacher Hiring (4) | Steel Import Quotas (1) | Appropriations Caps |
| After School Programs | Dairy Compact (3) | Judicial Confirmations |
| *Roe v. Wade* | | in General (1) |
| Minimum Wage (2) | | |
| Campaign Finance Reform (2) | | |

Other Contested Cloture Attempts
    Steal, Oil, and Gas Loan Guarantee
    Transportation Appropriations
    Interior Appropriations

by a bipartisan vote, the Senate adopted cloture on an amendment to the Africa trade bill. This motion was tied up in the procedural politics of minimum wage, a Democratic message priority. However, the other five examples where cloture was successfully invoked did not relate to message issues.

The goals behind cloture also vary somewhat across the different cells of table 6.4, depending on whether an item is (1) important to both party messages, (2) mostly important to the Democratic party message, or (3) mostly important to the GOP party message.

Consider the strategic context of managed health care, which eventually became a message item for both Senate parties (upper left cell of table 6.4). In early 1999, the issue was a message priority for Democrats, but of little relevance to GOP message plans. Throughout the spring and summer, the minority party focused on securing floor time for its patients' bill of rights, including ample opportunity to offer amendments. The Republicans moved managed care legislation through committee, but sought to put off floor action until after the appropriations process was completed. In response, Democratic leaders shut down the Senate for a full week in June, filibustering GOP attempts to bring a succession of spending measures to the floor. In a two-day period, Lott filed five cloture motions aimed at breaking the logjam. Four of the motions lost on near party line votes, and the fifth fell without a roll call.

By summer 1999, the Republicans had come to believe that they could compete on managed health care reform. (The staff interviews for this study were conducted after floor action; as a result, managed care was ranked as a message priority for both parties.) The June parliamentary tangle resulted from the inability of Republican and Democratic leaders to come up with a procedural accord for structuring the amendment process. Thus, cloture was not filed to clamp down on unrelated or nongermane message amendments. Both parties had a menu of proposals relevant to the health care debate. The procedural jockeying mostly concerned the number of amendments to be made in order for each side, the quantity of time to be allocated for debate, and the content of the vehicle for amendment.

Now move to the upper right cell of table 6.4 and consider the strategic context on the social security lockbox, a GOP message priority of little interest to Democrats. On this matter, cloture primarily functioned as a tool for producing a roll call record that could be used for purposes of position taking. Over the year, Republicans repeatedly brought versions of their lockbox measure to the floor to counter Democratic charges that GOP tax reduction proposals would dip into the social security trust fund.

When the lockbox was before the full Senate, Lott usually manipulated the parliamentary context to restrict the ability of Democrats to offer amendments aimed at providing them with cover. Close observers of the Senate perceived that the GOP was all but inviting Democrats to filibuster, which they did. Lott responded by repeatedly filing cloture motions, with an eye toward producing a roll call record that his party could use to portray Democrats as insufficiently committed to protecting social security.[9] When an issue is a message priority for the majority party, but not for the minority, cloture can be used to force a vote and put senators on record.

Next, consider the lower left cell of table 6.4, which is for items important to the Democratic but not the GOP message. Here, the main challenge for the minority party is to secure some form of floor consideration. Notice that cloture motions were especially prevalent in this cell of the table. Two of the cloture motions were test votes on campaign finance reform. During the summer of 1999, Republican leaders reacted to Democratic demands for action by scheduling a vote to follow the August recess. Unlike most of the legislative agenda, the underlying measure in this instance was Democratic. The GOP responded by fil-ibustering. Democratic leaders filled cloture by attempting to bring the legisla-tion to a vote, but were unsuccessful.

On teacher hiring, after school programs, and the minimum wage, the strate-gic dynamic was very different. Here, Democratic leaders lacked the outside polit-ical support necessary to bring the issues to the floor as freestanding measures, and instead sought to offer them as amendments to Republican priorities. On mini-mum wage, Edward Kennedy (D-Mass.) offered his proposal as an amendment to a range of measures, including the Y2K bill and bankruptcy reform. Lott coun-tered by filing for cloture on the underlying bills. If he had succeeded, debate on the measures (postcloture) would have proceeded under a germaneness restriction, effectively precluding Kennedy from offering a minimum-wage amendment.

The cloture votes relevant to teacher hiring and after school programs took place early in the year on the Republicans' Ed-Flex bill. As on minimum wage, the Republicans viewed the Democratic proposals as nongermane to the underlying matter. During negotiations over the UCA for Ed-Flex, they sought to keep the Democrats from offering these items as amendments. The minority party filibus-tered the underlying bill, and Lott repeatedly attempted cloture. In the end, Lott lacked the votes necessary to succeed with this strategy, and he eventually accepted a UCA that allowed Democrats to offer their main message amendments.

## Filling the Tree

A related procedural tactic concerns the strategic manipulation of the floor amendment process, also known as "filling the tree." In the Senate, the nuts and bolts of tree filling are complex, but the underlying intuition is straightforward.[10] Consider an amending scenario in which the majority leader wants to offer an amendment to a piece of legislation, but would like to keep Democrats from offering an alternative. Under normal circumstances, such a proposal might be in order as a second degree, or perfecting amendment. But the majority leader could block the offering of such an amendment himself by offering a second-degree proposal to his own amendment, effectively filling the amendment tree.

On a number of occasions during the 106th Congress, Lott responded to nongermane message amendments from the minority party by filling in the amendment tree and blocking these proposals from floor consideration. Democrats claimed that Lott was attempting to make the Senate operate like the House, with its tighter rules for debating and amending legislation. "There is nothing deliberative about the Senate today," declared Daschle. Senator Lott wants to "make this a legislative assembly line. You take something up, you vote it up or down, and you move it along." Daschle added, "We haven't been able to pass any-thing where the majority leader has filled the tree until he has torn the tree down" (*Congressional Record*, October 28, 1999, S13366). It was particularly galling to

Democrats when Lott asked to see proposed Democratic amendments in advance to determine whether they should even be offered to a specific measure. "But what our Republican colleagues continue to insist upon is that they act as an ad hoc rules committee," Daschle remarked. "They want to approve our amendments first. And only then will they allow our amendments to be considered once they have been given their approval" (quoted in Bresnahan 1999a, 28). Lott answered Daschle's complaints: "We're not saying we have to see all their amendments. The [informal] rule around here is you give notice of amendments" (28).

There were instances after the tree was filled when the majority leader announced his willingness to withdraw the last amendment so senators could offer their amendments. But he further stipulated that any Democratic amendment must be relevant to the subject matter of the bill—reducing opportunities for the minority party to use the amending opportunity to push unrelated message items. This is a "deal" that the Democrats regularly turned down. Instead, they looked for other legislative vehicles to attach their policy priorities, including must-pass measures such as appropriations bills.

Compared to other Senate leaders, how often did Lott actually fill the tree during the first session of the 106th Congress? Table 6.5 presents a list of comprehensive "tree filling" attempts since 1985. Clearly, the tactic predates the Lott majority leadership. And Lott resorted to fully filling the tree on only a few occasions during the 106th Congress. Interestingly, Minority Leader Daschle himself filled in the amendment tree on campaign finance reform to preclude amendments that might have blurred the Democratic message.

Table 6.5 also indicates that the measures evoking the amendment tree strategy are disproportionately likely to be message matters. For example, Lott filled the tree on Ed-Flex to constrain the ability of Democrats to offer their teacher hiring amendment. He filled in the tree on Y2K to keep a Democratic gun-control proposal off the floor. Tree filling was also a regular feature of Senate consideration of the social security lockbox proposal, a core component of the majority's message. On the Africa trade bill, Lott filled the tree to block a Democratic amendment dealing with the minimum wage. And as mentioned, Democrats filled the tree on campaign finance reform, a key part of their message agenda. Notice that cloture and tree filling are complementary strategies for the majority party. Both are aimed at protecting majority party message proposals from competing minority initiatives, and at keeping the minority party's message off the floor.

If a Senate leader is primarily interested in building a coalition behind a bill and passing it, then filling the tree is a counterproductive strategy. The usual impact of the tactic is to alienate other senators (typically members of the minority party) and create incentives for them to engage in dilatory tactics. Instead, filling the tree is useful when final passage and credit claiming are less important than framing and position taking. The tactics can be employed to avoid certain politically difficult

## TABLE 6.5 FILLING THE AMENDMENT TREE, 1985–1999

| Date | Issue (Member) |
|------|----------------|
| 1999 | Ed-Flex |
|      | Social Security Lockbox (4 occasions, Lott) |
|      | Y2K (Lott) |
|      | African Growth Act (Lott) |
|      | Campaign Finance Reform (Daschle) |
| 1998 | Campaign Finance Reform (Lott) |
| 1997 | Campaign Finance Reform (Lott) |
|      | Transportation Funding (Lott) |
| 1996 | Minimum Wage (2 occasions, Dole) |
|      | White House Travel Office (Dole) |
|      | Term Limits (Thompson) |
| 1994 | Whitewater (3 occasions, Mitchell) |
| 1993 | Economic Stimulus (Byrd) |
|      | Gays in the Military (Mitchell-Doyle) |
| 1992 | Balanced Budget Amendment (Byrd) |
| 1988 | Campaign Finance Reform (Byrd) |
| 1985 | Budget Resolution (Dole) |

*Source: Congressional Record,* selected volumes.

roll call votes, and to shape how the votes that do occur are covered by the media, portrayed in campaigns, and perceived by the general public.

### Unanimous Consent Agreements

Rule XIV, cloture, filling the tree—all three strategies relate to the increased difficulties that Senate leaders face in devising UCAs on message issues. The contemporary Senate relies on UCAs to constrain the array of permissible amendments, limit the time available for considering individual items, and set a time certain for final passage.

There seldom is sufficient consensus about the process to develop a comprehensive UCA that encompasses the entire floor process on a measure (Smith and Flathman 1989; Evans and Oleszek 1999). For most major bills, floor action begins with a partial accord that serves to bring the legislation to the floor and begin the amending process. As members work their way through the amendments, the majority leader attempts to strike piecemeal agreements that set limits on these amendments. The leadership usually seeks consensus on a comprehensive list of amendments that members will offer. As the amendment process continues, the majority leader may attempt to devise a schedule for completing the process and voting on final passage. Thus, on most major bills, floor action is structured by a number of UCAs, rather than one comprehensive agreement forged at the beginning of the process.

Message politics makes this entire process more complicated, difficult, and unpredictable. It raises the political stakes in UCA bargaining. When senators disagree about policy, there usually is a degree of middle ground and the possibility of compromise. The bargaining game is positive-sum. However, there is little room for cooperation in the broader game of electoral competition between the two political parties. When Democrats pick up Senate seats, the number of Republicans in the chamber falls by an equal amount. The game of message politics (which concerns electoral gain) is often zero-sum. Within this context, it is more difficult to achieve consensus about the terms of legislative debate.

The emphasis on position taking and managing the message also makes the unanimous consent process less predictable. As mentioned, the minority party often uses nongermane amendments and surprise tactics to bring its message priorities to the floor. Consider the sequence of strategies that led to the defeat of the Comprehensive Test Ban Treaty (CTBT) in October 1999. In prior years, the Senate had ratified international treaties with a bipartisan coalition of Democrats and internationally minded Republicans. But passage of these items also required systematic lobbying efforts by the administration and significant modifications aimed at building support among Republicans. On the CTBT, the coalition-building efforts of the administration were sporadic at best. For two years, the treaty languished in committee.

Then, in early October 1999, a group of Democrats took to the floor and lambasted Lott for not bringing up the treaty—even though the likelihood of passage was uncertain at best (see chapter two by Roger H. Davidson). The Democrats were led by Caucus Chairman Byron Dorgan(D-N.Dak.), a leader on party message efforts, and Foreign Relations Committee ranking member Joseph Biden (D-Del.). Lott and other Republican leaders perceived that the Democrats were trying to exploit the test ban issue for message purposes. The majority leader called the Democratic bluff, and proposed a UCA for the measure that scheduled twenty-two hours of debate and a vote. Daschle and other Democratic leaders (who were on record as demanding floor action) were unable to reject the proposed UCA, even though the treaty lacked the votes to win.

At this point, President Clinton and other administration officials spearheaded a lobbying campaign aimed at putting off the vote. According to Senate rules, overriding a UCA requires unanimous consent, and conservative Republicans promised to object to any changes here. They viewed the test ban vote as a potential embarrassment for Democrats, and thus a message opportunity for the GOP. Lott devised a strategy for putting off the vote without changing the UCA, but conservatives objected to that tactic as well. In the end, the treaty was rejected on a vote of forty-eight to fifty-one, with only four Republican senators breaking party ranks to vote yes (all Democrats voted in favor of the treaty). Interestingly, in the days before the roll call, sixty-two senators signed on to a letter proposing that the vote be postponed until the 107th Congress (2001–2002). But message strategies on both sides of the aisle had pushed the chamber into a procedural corner, and the roll call occurred anyway.

Similar dynamics were at work on a number of major issues considered by the Senate during the 106th Congress. GOP and Democratic leaders had substantial difficulties forging procedural accords via the unanimous consent process, in part because of the zero-sum character of message politics. Lott often attempted to proceed with the legislation anyway, and Democrats responded with dilatory tactics, leading to cloture attempts by the majority leader. In a related scenario, the majority leader might bring the underlying bill to the floor, and then attempt to clamp down on the amendment process by invoking cloture and filling the amendment tree. On a number of occasions, he used Rule XIV to bypass committee, thereby enhancing his tactical flexibility vis-à-vis committee chairs and the minority party. Increasingly, the procedural context of floor deliberation is shaped by the partisan rhythms of message politics.

## Conclusion

The increased emphasis on party messages on Capitol Hill has affected the public utterances and media strategies of members of Congress. But for contemporary legislators, coordinating the message also means stage-managing legislative deliberations within the House and Senate.

Congressional scholars and media observers have traditionally viewed procedural disputes from the perspective of the internal legislative game. But the increasingly sophisticated communications strategies employed by current members of Congress make it difficult to separate intrachamber procedural matters from the broader partisan-electoral context. Members seek to structure floor action to dramatize proposals that reflect their own party messages, and to restrict the ability of the opposition party to advance its own message via roll calls and amendments. This trend is particularly apparent in the Senate, with its open-ended amendment process, unwieldy membership, and broad distribution of power.

Thus, there are important procedural features to message management in the Senate. In this chapter, we have highlighted some specific trends. The use of Rule XIV to bypass committee and place items directly on the floor calendar is closely related to the relevance of a bill to the majority party's message. The strategic use of cloture and attempts to manipulate the floor amendment process by "filling the tree" are also procedural features of message politics. Within such a message-driven partisan environment, the Senate's traditional practice of unanimous consent has grown increasingly complicated and less predictable. The result is a Senate that is highly responsive to the short-term communications strategies of the two political parties, but perhaps less responsive to the pragmatic policy needs of the country as a whole.

## NOTES

1. We excluded the important, but unusually long presentations about Senate history that were periodically delivered by Senator Robert Byrd, D-W.Va..

2. Remaining respondents answered "both," "neither," "don't know," or refused to answer the question.

3. Items were selected for inclusion based on a large number of interviews conducted by C. Lawrence Evans with Senate chiefs of staff and the amount of coverage in the *Congressional Quarterly Weekly Report*. Appropriations and budget measures were excluded. Overall, we sought to include all probable message items on the list, as well as a few likely nonmessage items for purposes of contrast. Thus, the list is intentionally message-oriented, and not representative of the entire population of issues considered by the full Senate.

4. A message advantage for a party on an issue is obtained if the issue is rated as more relevant to that party's message.

5. The tactic was used when Democrats attempted to offer gun-control proposals to the Y2K bill.

6. To identify instances in which senators made strategic use of Rule XIV, we conducted a computer search of the *Congressional Record* using Lexus-Nexus. We focused on the key words and phrases that parliamentary experts associate with the tactic.

7. The Rule XIV tactic can only be used for bills and joint resolutions, and not for Senate resolutions and concurrent resolutions.

8. Notice that certain bills placed on the "other" list for the GOP could also be reasonably construed as message items, especially the proposals dealing with FALN terrorists, research and development tax credits, school prayer, and affirmative action. We have adopted a high threshold for categorizing a Rule XIV measure as a message item.

9. Within the context of the broader parliamentary deal on managed health care reform, Lott was able to successfully invoke cloture on a lockbox proposal on July 1 by a ninety-nine to one vote. In this one case, the proposal was not offered in a way that precluded Democratic "cover" amendments.

10. There actually are four different amendment trees (referred to as charts) in the rules of the Senate. Each chart is designed to accommodate the different purposes or distinctions among amendments (which are motions) to the pending question. Chart 1 permits a maximum of three amendments if offered in a certain order and it is used when a senator offers a motion to insert (or add) language to the pending matter. Chart 2 allows five amendments

and deals with a motion to strike (or delete) language. Chart 3 also authorizes five amendments, but it addresses amendments that strike and insert (replace completely what is in a section of the bill with something else). Finally, Chart 4 also deals with a motion to strike and insert, but the kind of amendment it regulates is a substitute for the entire bill rather than the smaller-scale Chart 3 change. Depending on the order in which amendments are offered, Chart 4 actually permits anywhere from seven to eleven amendments that could be pending simultaneously. In short, the specific tactics necessary to "fill in the tree" will vary depending on the amendment scenario. In addition, completely filling the tree on a bill involves filling in a separate tree for the motion to recommit the measure back to committee with amendatory instructions.

# PART THREE

## Senate Reform in Historical Perspective

## CHAPTER SEVEN

# Twentieth-century Senate Reform: The View from the Inside

## DONALD A. RITCHIE

Throughout the twentieth century, repeated efforts took place to reform the U.S. Senate, both constitutionally and internally. At the dawn of the century, progressive reformers and muckraking journalists targeted the Senate as a "millionaires' club," more representative of corporate interests than of the people. This drumbeat of protest led in 1913 to ratification of a constitutional amendment for direct election of senators. During the next two decades, additional complaints arose about the lame-duck sessions that regularly occurred at the end of each Congress, leaving the Senate prone to filibusters that bottled up legislation. Reformers aimed to solve this problem with another constitutional amendment, which in 1933 advanced the opening of Congress each year up to January. By the 1940s, members of both houses of Congress found fault with its antiquated structure, overlapping committee jurisdictions, and inadequate staff. These complaints resulted in the Legislative Reorganization Act of 1946, which streamlined the committee system and established the first professional staff. By the 1970s came a further wave of reform that created minority staffs for committees, expanded senators' personal staffs, opened committee hearings to the "sunshine" of publicity, and reduced the number of votes needed to invoke cloture on filibusters from two-thirds to three-fifths. An extension of sunshine occurred when first the House and later the Senate opened their floor debates to television coverage. The viewing public did not always like what it saw, and Congress ended the century under another barrage of criticism, voiced loudly on radio talk shows, which resulted in yet another constitutional amendment in 1992 to regulate congressional pay increases, and in the Congressional Accountability

131

Act of 1995, which required that Congress live up to the laws and regulations it inflicted on the rest of society.

The century's finale makes an appropriate occasion to ask how these many reforms actually changed the Senate. In recent years, scholars have devoted much attention to the "transformation" of the Senate, and to the continuing problems with its structure and procedures (Sinclair 1989; Binder and Smith 1997; Lee and Oppenheimer 1999). Rather than survey these scholarly analyses, or offer additional statistical data—recognizing that the Senate is not as readily quantifiable as the House of Representatives—this work instead offers a more impressionistic assessment of the various reforms drawn from the personal observations of Senate staff members whose careers spanned significant portions of the century. While they were professionally anonymous through most of their service on Capitol Hill, after they retired they contributed insights grounded in decades of personal experience. All the interviews cited are part of a series of life-review oral histories that the Senate Historical Office has been conducting since 1976. The interviews are open for research at the Library of Congress, the National Archives, on microfiche, and in some cases on the Senate's website: www.senate.gov (Ritchie 1982).

Leading the list of senatorial reform was a fundamental change in the method of selecting senators. Since the Seventeenth Amendment shifted senatorial elections from state legislatures to popular vote by the people, scholars have pondered whether direct election made any difference in who was elected or in how they operated as senators. The progressives promoted direct election based upon a conviction that the people would rally to the cause of better government. It came as a great disappointment, therefore, when the people went to the polls for the first time in 1914 and reelected every incumbent who was running. That a senator as reactionary as Pennsylvania's Republican Boise Penrose could defeat so prominent a reformer as Gifford Pinchot was profoundly demoralizing to the progressive movement. Apparently, the voters saw little difference between their own interests and the corporate interests that senators supported. Initially, at least, there appeared little difference in senators following direct election. One study detected that the proportion of lawyers declined slightly—although it remains debatable whether that was any deterrent (Daynes 1971; Crowley 1989; Crook and Hibbing 1997).

Floyd M. Riddick, the Senate's parliamentarian-emeritus told how his predecessor, Charles Watkins, who had worked for the Senate since 1904, described the direct election of senators as the greatest mistake ever made in American government: "He used to say that the senators previous to that were much greater scholars and students than they are today; that they're now politicians." Riddick, who came to Capitol Hill as a political science student in the 1930s, and who for many years published an annual review of the congressional sessions in the

*American Political Science Review*, agreed with Watkins's assessment and noted the change in senators during his own forty years on the Hill. The first senators he encountered had been reserved and imperious, speaking only to God and their constituents. Over the years, Riddick lamented that the atmosphere changed until senators seemed hardly any different than the representatives (Riddick Oral History).

Other staff also attested to a change in the types of senators elected during the course of their service, but they attributed this more to television than to any constitutional amendment. Beginning in the 1950s, they watched the news media dramatically change the ways senators campaigned for office. Stewart E. McClure, who joined the staff of Democratic Senator Guy Gillette of Iowa in 1949 and retired as staff director of the Senate Labor, Education, and Public Welfare Committee in 1973, argued that the political system had worked best when senators rose through the ranks, from local office and state legislature, to election to the House and perhaps as governor, before they arrived in the Senate as seasoned legislators in their fifties and early sixties. Television, he complained, brought in a new crop of senators elected by "their looks," and their public exposure on television, or by virtue of their renown in a field other than legislation, such as movie actors and astronauts "who know nothing about the Senate and public policy." McClure conceded that television provided some leavening, in the sense that senators now came from many different backgrounds and were not all lawyers or all practicing politicians, some never having held any office before entering the Senate; but he considered too many of them "really green," and that they took "quite a time to find out where they are" (McClure Oral History, 275).

Echoing McClure's comments, Rein J. Vander Zee, who ran the Senate Democratic Cloakroom in the early 1960s, commented that under the old party system senators had risen through the "crucible" of local politics. "And by the time they bubbled up to the top—let's face it, they were the Harry Trumans, they were tried and tested. If they were foul balls, chances are they would have been eliminated long before they got to that level. And nowadays with the TV set, they send the foul balls straight to you" (Vander Zee Oral History, 90). Roy L. McGhee, who started as the United Press reporter on Capitol Hill before becoming superintendent of the Periodical Press Gallery in 1973, also blamed television for reducing political campaigns and governance to a few seconds of quotation on the evening news broadcast. Senators' staffs had to struggle to find a colorful quote, and rehearse the senator on when to say it, in what context, and what venue, "so that it will have the sound bite impact" (McGhee Oral History, 121). Not everyone shared this bleak assessment, however. Darrell St. Claire, whose Senate years extended from 1933 to 1977, thought television exposure had lifted the overall quality of the senators. "I think you have a man [now] who has to know a hell of a lot more about everything than his predecessors of the '30s did," he judged (St. Claire Oral History, 229).

What they were describing, of course, were changes in the larger political system that affected the recruitment, campaign strategies, and election of candidates at all levels of government, not just the U.S. Senate. Their interviews reflected a certain nostalgia that is inherent in most reminiscences. Political giants of the past always tend to stand taller than those who currently occupy their seats. This was best put by Ruth Young Watt, chief clerk of the Permanent Subcommittee on Investigations. When she came to the Senate in 1947, at the age of thirty-two, she was young and the senators were old. When she retired in 1979, she was old and the senators were young. "They seem like babies today!" (Watt Oral History, 298–99)

In assessing the impact of constitutional amendments on senators, the list of reforms needs to include the Nineteenth Amendment, since giving women the right to vote also brought them into public office. Although the larger House of Representatives has always moved in advance of the Senate in the diversity of its membership, women added to the blend in the Senate as early as 1922. The Senate debated for two days on whether to seat Rebecca Felton, whom the governor of Georgia had appointed in a symbolic act to fill a brief vacancy in the Senate. She thanked the gentlemen for giving a lady a seat and then delivered a brief speech encouraging other women to follow her. Until 1992 there were never more than two women senators at the same time. At the century's end there were nine women senators serving together, and swinging doors near the Senate chamber marked "Senators Only" no longer lead just to the men's room (Byrd 1991).

In 1933, another constitutional amendment changed the congressional calendar by moving the start of a new session from December up to the January. Most observers agreed that doing away with the long interregnum between the election and the beginning of a new Congress, and of a new presidency, was essential for a modern government. The old lame-duck sessions had rarely been productive. Congress readjusted its annual schedule and settled into a pattern by which it met for about six months each year, working six days a week. Until the 1960s, it was commonplace for Senate offices to be open on Saturday mornings. What changed the Senate schedule the most, said the staff, was not the Twentieth Amendment but the transcontinental jet, which allowed even senators from the West Coast to go home over the weekend. After 1958, the Senate and House steadily truncated their schedules, trying to avoid votes on Mondays and Fridays to accommodate members' travel schedules. With senators away every weekend, the Saturday morning schedule faded away, and along with it much of the Saturday night socializing. Senators found less time and fewer opportunities to build the kinds of personal bonds that facilitate legislative harmony (Baker 1980).

A sympathetic response came from Pat M. Holt, who came to the Senate Foreign Relations staff in 1950 and retired as its staff director in 1977. "It used to be that a senator from California or even Texas would get on a train in January and spend three to five days coming to Washington, and then get on a train again in June or July and go back home," Holt recalled. "Now the poor devil is expected to get on an airplane Friday afternoon, make a speech in Los Angeles that night, make two or three other speeches, and come back to Washington on Sunday." He further judged that the Tuesday-to-Thursday schedule had "a desultory enervating effect on Senate debate. The Senate used to have some really very good unscheduled debates on the spur of the moment, and that doesn't happen anymore" (Holt Oral History, 301–2).

Many of the interviewed staff members had been part of the first generation of professional staff assembled under the Legislative Reorganization Act of 1946. In retrospect, it is remarkable that the Senate managed to cope with the turmoil of the Depression, the New Deal, and the Second World War with its antique committee system and scant staff support. The lack of a professional staff required Congress to depend on the executive branch to draft legislation and even to write speeches for the floor managers (Ritchie 1991, 136–37).

When the Legislative Reorganization Act went into effect at the start of the Eightieth Congress (1947–1949), the Senate claimed a total of 590 employees, which included 232 committee staff members. Francis O. Wilcox, who became the first staff director of the Foreign Relations Committee under the new law, was amazed that the committee had gone through the Second World War with a staff of "two and a half," which consisted of a chief clerk, who taught half-time at the University of Maryland; an assistant clerk, who took dictation, typed, ran a stenotype machine, and generally took care of the office; and a secretary who spent half her time with the committee and the other half in the chairman's senatorial office. "Now, you can see, at that point there could be no adversarial relationship between the two branches of government, because most of the professional work clearly had to be done in the Department of State or in the government somewhere," said Wilcox.

> Speeches had to be written there; committee reports to the Senate were prepared by the executive branch; there was no mechanism really by which the Senate could act independently, or could bring to bear the kind of helpful advice and counsel that a professional staff could bring. This meant that the Senate committee turned customarily to the executive branch for help. It wasn't until we had created the professional staff that the Senate was in a position to develop an independent judgment of its own, based on its own sources of information.

The change occurred just in time. During the Eightieth Congress, the new professional staff would deal with a flood of Cold War–related legislation. "We had

a whole host of important issues before the Senate and the House that constituted the base, the pillars for our postwar international relationships," Wilcox
recalled (Wilcox Oral History, 35–36).

The Reorganization Act of 1946 streamlined the committee system and
established professional staffs for committees and for individual senators. Its
sponsors envisioned a nonpartisan professional staff, and to a remarkable degree
got one. How was it possible to create a nonpartisan staff for a partisan institution? For Francis Wilcox, who as chief foreign policy specialist for the Legislative
Reference Service had accompanied the congressional delegation to the San
Francisco conference that founded the United Nations in 1945, it was a matter
of winning the confidence of senators in the delegation from both parties. When
the Reorganization Act passed, and Republicans won the majority in the 1946
congressional elections, the outgoing Foreign Relations Committee Chairman
Tom Connally, a Texas Democrat, asked Wilcox to become the committee's first
staff director. "I think I can talk Old Van into it," said Connally, referring to the
ranking Republican, Arthur Vandenberg, who would succeed him as chairman.
But before Connally spoke with Vandenberg, the Michigan Republican called to
offer Wilcox the job himself. "This meant," said Wilcox, "that Senator Connally
was under the impression that he had gotten me the job, and I was therefore his
man; and Senator Vandenberg had asked me, regardless of what Senator
Connally had said or done after the event. So . . . I was more or less welcomed
by both the Senate committee leaders, which put me in a very good position"
(Wilcox Oral History, 25–26).

Having worked with George Galloway at the Legislative Reference Service,
Wilcox understood the intent of the reorganization. "We exchanged views about
executive-legislative relations, and about the organization of the committee," he
commented. "We did not think it was necessary to have a large staff. We got
along reasonably well—despite the heavy legislative burden—with four top professional staff people." Like others from that generation, Wilcox regretted the
later staff expansion, which departed from an integral aspect of the original
reform, "namely the capacity of staff members, and their willingness to serve
both Democrats and Republicans with equal ability and interest" (Wilcox Oral
History, 38–39).

Carl M. Marcy, whom Wilcox appointed to the staff from out of the State
Department, agreed that the staff "tried to serve all the members of the
Committee with equal attention. After all, they were senators and we didn't
think very much about whether they were Republicans or Democrats—at least I
didn't. As you know, at that time the concept of a bipartisan or nonpartisan
approach to foreign policy was pretty well accepted by the Committee members.
That was reflected in the staff. I think Francis, for example, was probably a
Republican, but I'm not sure. He never made a point of it. I called myself an

Independent, but I did tend to be more oriented toward the Democratic side" (Marcy Oral Interview, 45).

Another committee staff member of that era, Pat Holt, offered as an example of its nonpartisan nature a controversial coffee agreement, which broke the committee's usual bipartisan approach to foreign policy issues. "The committee had a minority view, which was something that didn't happen very often then," he commented.

> I was the guy who was handling the coffee agreement and I wrote both the committee report and the minority views. During consideration of the coffee agreement, Senator [Karl] Mundt . . . called up and said he wanted to talk to the minority staff man, and I said there wasn't one. That surprised him a little bit, and he said, "Well, I want to oppose the coffee agreement, and where can I get some help." And I said, "From me." He sounded a little skeptical about that but asked me to come around and see him, and I did, and gave him the case against the coffee agreement, and wrote a speech for him, I guess. He later said . . . that he was very satisfied, to his surprise.

Having been a reporter before he joined the staff, Holt considered this "a perfectly straight forward exercise of the kind one finds in academia or in the better journalism." He simply stated the reasons for ratifying the coffee agreement, and then stated the reasons for not doing it. In fact, it was sometimes much easier to criticize something than to defend it, even if you had written it yourself. "One of the things that was always insisted upon in the '50s and '60s was that members of the staff ought not themselves to become emotionally involved in issues that were before the committee, that we were supposed to be detached, dispassionate, objective," Holt reflected. "Well, as the emotional content of issues mounted, primarily in the first instance over Vietnam, this became increasingly difficult to do, even for them" (Holt Oral History, 278–82).

Bipartisanship and a nonpartisan staff lasted as long as it suited both parties' purposes. No civil service has ever existed on Capitol Hill, and the professional staff has always worked at the pleasure of the majority. When the majority changed, as it did four times during the decade after 1946, the staff collectively held its breath and waited to see how the incoming majority would treat them. Pat Holt recalled some of that trepidation: "I remember the first meeting the Foreign Relations Committee had after the Republicans took over in '53. They ran all the staff out of the room. We were sitting there in that back room in the Capitol, and geez it seemed like it was going on interminably. Somebody said, 'I haven't been so nervous since my Ph.D. orals.' " After waiting in suspense, one of the staff members finally dared to crack the door and look into the committee room. "And hell they had all gone," said Holt, "which is typical of senators, you know, they'd never think to tell somebody waiting on them that they're through; they just walk out the damn door." Francis Wilcox ran the new chairman, Alexander Wiley, down and asked what he planned to do. "Oh, yes, we're not going to make any changes in the staff," said Wiley, who simply added his own administrative assistant to the committee staff. Wiley reassured the staff that they had done a good job and he intended to keep it that way. Carl Marcy noted that even adding that single personal staff member caused "a bit of hassling, a tug-of-war within the staff between Wilcox, who was scrupulously nonpartisan, and Wiley's AA, who was an outspoken Republican, and who later caused consternation among the members of the committee" when he delivered some partisan speeches (Holt Oral History, 46).

In addition to committee staffs, the Legislative Reorganization Act of 1946 authorized senators and representatives to appoint an administrative assistant. Many senators had no idea what to do with an administrative assistant. Guy Gillette, an Iowa Democrat who had been defeated for reelection to the Senate in 1944 and again elected in 1948, found that during the interim between his terms Congress had created this new position. This put Gillette in a quandary, since he already had a good executive secretary and a staff of "four or five girls" who handled his constituent correspondence and committee paperwork (there were as yet no legislative assistants). What could this new administrative assistant do when there was nothing for him to administer? Finally, Gillette decided that he could use "an idea man." He hired Stuart McClure and gave him a desk in the anteroom to the Agriculture Committee. There McClure spent his mornings reading the *Congressional Record* and his afternoons listening to debates in the Senate chamber. After a while he started writing speeches, until the senator gradually developed some confidence in him. "As time went on and I found my feet I became in effect the administrative assistant." McClure noted that some of the senators used the job as a sinecure for their top political advisers, who had gotten them elected. Some assigned them to do research and speech writing, as was McClure's experience. Only in a few of the larger states, with larger staff, did the first administrative assistants actually administer their offices (McClure Oral History, 12–16, 43).

Other reforms of the institution went unheralded. The expansion of senators' personal and committee staffs reduced their need for other patronage positions, which at one time accounted for all of the clerical jobs, doormen, elevator operators, and Capitol police. During the 1960s, the Senate organization quietly switched from patronage to professional staff. Darrell St. Claire, who had staffed the Democratic Patronage Committee under its long-time chairman, Senator Carl Hayden, recalled that when he started a change in party meant a change in nearly all jobs in the Capitol, along the lines of the nineteenth-century slogan: "to the victor belongs the spoils." Senator Hayden parceled out the jobs, by assigning each senator "say a policeman, a doorman, and an elevator operator," adding up to a certain dollar amount in salaries. Partly because the Democrats retained control of the Senate for so long, and because senators began to have more staff positions within their own offices, the patronage system began to fade. When Mike Mansfield of Montana became majority leader in 1961, an estimated 30 percent of the jobs around the Senate were still assigned by patronage. Mansfield decided to make himself the patronage committee, and since he had no formal program for appointment of Senate personnel, he simply let patronage wither away. Francis R. Valeo, whom Mansfield appointed as secretary of the Senate, and St. Claire, by then the assistant secretary, "conveniently lost the lists" of what jobs were supposed to be patronage. It was a mark of their success that the next time the Senate underwent a change in party control in 1980, very few changes in the professional staff took place (St. Claire Oral History, 9–10, 70–76; Valeo Oral History, 471–73).

For several decades after the Second World War, the Senate remained a relatively small, close-knit organization, for which the term "club" fit snugly. This was the institution that William S. White described in *Citadel: The Story of the U.S. Senate* (1957), and Donald R. Matthews observed while writing *U.S. Senators and Their World* (1960). Until 1958, the entire Senate operated out of half of the Capitol Building and one Senate Office Building. Within these close confines, the staff all ate in one dining room and got to know most of their counterparts in other senators' offices and other committee staffs. Remarkably, the Senate still paid its staff in cash, requiring them to line up at the Disbursing Office twice a month for their pay envelopes. Senate Disbursing Office accountants still worked in the Bob Cratchit school of green eyeshades and arm bands, sitting on high stools, and keeping their account books in pen-and-ink. None of the operations were mechanized, and Senate officials remained deeply suspicious of computers. When Frank Valeo became secretary of the Senate in 1966, he discovered that aside from the Senate the only agency of the federal government still paying in cash was an army outpost in Alaska where they used silver dollars. When he raised the issue of installing computers and paying by check and direct deposit, the disbursing clerk replied, "Oh, that's impossible under the Senate system" (Ridgely Oral History, 449, 478). It took an elaborate three-year conversion in which computers were phased in while the clerks continued their pen-and-ink ledgers until the Senate stopped payment in cash in 1971. That change fortuitously facilitated the vast expansion of the Senate staff that began with the Legislative Reorganization Act of 1970.

The 1970 reorganization permitted the appointment of minority staff for the committees, and allowed each senator one staff member per each committee assignment, which in the words of Stuart McClure transformed the Senate into "a metropolis out of what has been a small barnyard." Contrary to previous reform efforts designed to streamline the institution, the new reform stimulated rapid growth until by the end of the century the Senate had more than four thousand employees, of whom a thousand staffed the committees. "Every year it would get bigger," Ruth Watt marveled. Committees kept adding more sub-committees, and more staff. The days when "everybody knew everyone in the building" disappeared. The staff explosion caused construction of a third Senate Office Building in 1982. Some staffs grew so large that it became hard to learn the names of everyone who worked for your committee, or your senator, let alone to make regular contact with your counterparts in other offices. Stuart McClure described walking by the Labor Committee one afternoon, after he had retired as staff director. "They were having a staff meeting," he said. "There were twenty-five guys and girls sitting around a table. A staff meeting! It was a mob." He recognized that senators needed more assistance, but he feared that the enlarged staff would generate "an enormous amount of make-work . . . think up new amendments and new laws and keep their senators busy, busy, busy, so they can justify their own jobs." Rather than expediting the legislative process, the veterans believed that the swollen staff had made the Senate an even more unwieldy institution. "It was always designed to not do anything, to prevent rash action," said McClure, "but boy, I think it's just become almost unmovable in some respects" (McClure Oral History, 294–98; see also Ornstein, Mann, and Malbin 1998).

Frank Valeo labeled Senate Resolution 60, which further reformed Senate practices in 1975, "really a very bad piece of legislation" because the enormous growth in the staff had transferred more power away from the committees and the party structure to the individual senators. By assigning every senator one staff member for every committee, the reform broke up "the concept of a professional committee staff quite apart from politics. The net result was that every committee staff then began to be split between Democratic and Republican designees." Chairmen lost control of their committees. "The more they added staff," Valeo observed, "the less time they had to do anything" (Valeo Oral History, 633, 644). The creation of minority staffs for committees also implied that the nonpartisan professional staff was in fact the committee majority's staff. This was not universally apparent until the parties changed in 1980 for the first time in twenty-six years. This time, the new majority caused a complete overhaul of the committee staff, with minority staff moving into the majority, and formerly nonpartisan professional staff moving into retirement.

Senior staff members also regretted the sunshine reform adopted in 1975, which required committees to do their work in public, and particularly brought bill markup sessions out from behind closed doors. Reformers reasoned that the public's business needed to be conducted openly where the press and the public could observe. But that meant conducting more business in the presence of executive branch officials and lobbyists. Pat Holt recalled that when he joined the Foreign Relations Committee administration, officials had routinely sat in on committee meetings. "When I first came up there, somebody from the executive branch was always present when they marked up a bill and would argue with them about why a particular amendment ought not to got in there and that kind of thing." As bipartisanship broke down in the 1960s, the committee excluded all executive branch personnel from markup sessions. But in the 1970s, the sunshine rules meant that they were right back there again, although as Holt noted, this time "the executive branch did not speak up as much as it once did" (Holt Oral History, 38).

For Roy L. Elson, who served as a young administrative assistant to the elderly chairman of the Senate Appropriations Committee, Carl Hayden, sunshine blundered by opening markup sessions to lobbyists. This made it more difficult for senators to craft the compromises needed to reach consensus. "You don't find the public there, it's the lobbyists," Elson complained. "You can hardly get in for falling over the lobbyists. You're not able to go into executive session, particularly in a mark-up, where in the art of politics is the compromise, or the working out of these difficulties and complicated subjects, where you can have this give-and-take and make the argument, where a lot of things *were* decided in the old days." What sunshine had forced, in his opinion, was for members to meet quietly ahead of time in little groups or over the phone, to decide on what they were doing to do. "Then the rest is a damn show." No senator could count on getting everything he wanted, or everything he had promised to lobbyists. But it became harder to agree to a compromise even though it was less than what the lobbyists wanted. "But so many times a member ends up looking at one of the lobbyists sitting there and he's afraid to [compromise] . . . because they'll end up telling him, 'this is the bottom line, we can't go beyond this.' " As a result, said Elson, the deal was too often lost. "In an executive session you could work out those things" (Elson Oral History, 285).

The senator generally given the credit for changing the U.S. Senate most was the unassuming Mike Mansfield. Becoming Democratic majority leader immediately after the hard-driving Lyndon Johnson, Mansfield began a process of decentralization, turning responsibility back from the leadership to the committees and to the individual senators. Not every staff member appreciated Mansfield's own leadership, which at times seemed too lackadaisical to push legislation along forcefully. Jerry T. Verkler, who directed the Interior Committee under the chairmanship of Henry "Scoop" Jackson, thought that the change in leadership style under Mansfield "helped send the Senate into disarray in a real sense," and made the Senate "a harder place to work and get something done." Verkler accused Senator Mansfield of "bending over backwards to accommodate all of the one-hundred prima donnas" (Verkler Oral History, 113, 167). Yet he acknowledged that Mansfield's emphasis on small "d" democracy gave a larger role to junior senators and facilitated the extraordinary burst of legislation during the 1960s. Mansfield also set the pattern for future majority leaders, from both parties (Ritchie 1991; Baker 1998).

Some staff members also attributed the alterations in the structure and functioning of the Senate to the increased role of political scientists. "A lot of them became members of committee staffs," Frank Valeo noted. "Some of them were at the Library [of Congress]. A lot of them came in as professional consultants . . . or just as volunteers." He considered political scientists "the main sources of this revolution" in the way the Senate operated. Staff members also attributed these changes to the loss of faith in the presidency that occurred during the Vietnam War and Watergate scandal. Scholars who had focused on the presidency as the solution to all government problems suddenly began turning to Congress. "There was a great flow to the Capitol of the kind of people who would normally not even have thought of going to Congress with any idea or any belief or complaint," Valeo recalled. Previously, they would automatically have thought in terms of the executive branch, but "because the Senate played this rather unique role of counterfoil for an executive branch and a president sort of gone wild . . . they came to the Senate as a last hope, almost in desperation" (Valeo Oral History, 654–55; Marcy Oral History).

The pace of Senate reform accelerated in the 1970s with another restructuring of the committee system, which again revised jurisdictions and reduced the number of standing committees. With this revision, Congress jettisoned most of the joint committees that the Legislative Reorganization Act of 1946 had promoted as a means of expediting business. In the mid-1970s, a Commission on the Reorganization of the Senate looked into the eccentric divisions of responsibilities in the Senate's administrative structure and recommended a consolidation of virtually all Senate staff functions under the secretary of the Senate. Needless to say, this did not sit well with the sergeant at arms, without whose cooperation the proposals languished. Twenty years later, another sergeant at arms came across the commission report and reviewed its organizational proposals more positively, offering some wholesale revisions in the organizational flow charts. Once again, however, the weight of tradition restrained any wholesale change (Valeo Oral History, 504; Casey Oral History, 86, 94, 165).

Political scientists who studied the Senate were more successful in convincing the parties to reconfigure their policy committees. The policy committee had originated during the discussions leading up to the Legislative Reorganization Act of 1946. Since House Speaker Sam Rayburn objected to any infringement on his powers, he blocked inclusion of the policy committees in the reorganization bill. The Senate simply created its own by inserting them in a supplemental appropriations bill. During the next half century the Republican and Democratic Policy Committees evolved quite differently, reflecting the different traditions of the two parties. Republicans divided leadership, electing a separate policy committee chair; while Democrats consolidated party leadership posts in their floor leader. Essentially, the policy committees served as small advisory councils to the leadership, and staff operated as "think tanks" (Ritchie 1997, 86–87). As a result of reforms in the 1970s, Republicans restructured their policy committee to consist entirely of ranking members of chairs of the standing committees. On paper, this made for a powerful committee. In reality, it was too cumbersome to convene. Kelly D. Johnston, who served as staff director of the Republican Policy Committee in the 1990s, confirmed that "The Policy Committee never truly meets. It's really a tool of the chairman and some degree of the staff based on what the members want" (Johnston Oral History, 47, 59).

Whenever they were asked to cite what had changed the Senate the most, rather than any institutional reforms, the staff invariable responded: television. Beyond its impact on campaigning and candidates, television subtly affected the internal activities of the Senate. As early as the 1950s, staff directors found it much easier to establish a quorum when television was present. Ruth Watt described Bobby Kennedy as chief counsel of the McClellan committee calling senators to report: "We're going to have television today" (Watt Oral History, 303). Carl Marcy recalled that the senators would call him to find out if Foreign Relations Committee hearings would be televised, and he would explain that the decision lay with the networks rather than the committees (Marcy Oral History, 109–11). Perhaps Marcy was being coy. His colleague Pat Holt recalled that Marcy used to encourage television coverage by talking with network representatives in advance and asking: "Would you be interested in televising it if we had a hearing with these witnesses on this day." This helped promote the committee's agenda and educate the public, but it also ensured the staff director "a good turnout" of the senators (Holt Oral History, 204).

Many of the staff were dubious of the value of televising Senate debates. From his perspective in the Periodical Press Gallery, Roy McGhee felt certain that television in the chamber would lead only to more partisan posturing (McGhee Oral History, 121). Darrell St. Claire, who handled senatorial travel arrangements to meetings of the International Parliamentary Union, recalled warnings from other delegates whose parliaments were being televised. Once the cameras went in, he recalled a member of the Israeli parliament telling him, "they never go out" (St. Claire Oral History, 629–30). Frank Valeo, who arranged for the first television cameras to be installed in the Senate chamber in 1974, in anticipation of an impeachment trial of President Nixon, shared these reservations, fearing both that senators would play to the cameras, and that the networks would excerpt only moments of humor or drama (Valeo Oral History, 629–30, 642–43). But while some worried that television would diminish the Senate's dignity, others believed it would serve as a boost for democracy. Former Senate Sergeant at Arms F. Nordy Hoffman noted that once citizens began

watching Congress on C-SPAN, their reaction time to issues became much
speedier than in the days when they waited to read the news in the papers. "This
way they just look at it and make up their minds right now," which accounted
for mounting constituent mail in every senator's office (Hoffman Oral History,
253–57).

As sergeant at arms in the late 1970s, Hoffmann shouldered the responsibly
for bringing computers into the senatorial offices. Initially, he encountered stub-
born resistance. Many senators and most of the staff, he found,

> had a feeling that the computers were going to replace the people who were
> working in the offices. . . . Well, that was never intended. It was just to be an aid
> to help them do a better job and quicker. It took a long time to get this across. I
> remember I went around personally to all the one hundred senators' offices. I
> walked in and asked them to show me where the computer was. I would say
> ninety percent of the people that took me back there, I had to climb over boxes
> to get where it was. It was hidden. They weren't using it.

Several years passed before the staff became accustomed to working with computers, and today they are addicted to them. An ever increasing percent of constituent correspondence these days is via e-mail and every senator posts a home
page. During the presidential impeachment trial in 1999, the Senate's e-mail system crashed when the volume increased from seventy thousand messages a day
to over a half million (Hoffman Oral History, 206).

The last legislative reform of the century occurred shortly after the
Republicans returned to the majority in both houses for the first time in forty
years. The new majority acted quickly to pass the Congressional Accountability
Act of 1995, which is already making itself felt on Capitol Hill. The
Accountability Act had strong bipartisan support (Democrats had tried to pass a
version of it the previous Congress) and reflected deep public suspicion of a legislature more interested in perks and special privilege than in serving the public
interests. The act essentially subjects Congress to most (although not all) of the
laws that govern the rest of the nation. It is not certain that members realized the
full implications of this reform and its effect on a two-hundred-year-old institution. When Kelly Johnston, the first secretary of the Senate to administer these
new provisions, began briefing senators on its affects, the common reaction he
got was: "I can't believe what we passed!" (Johnston Oral History, 79–81) The
Accountability Act opened the Capitol and the Congress to labor issues under
the Fair Labor Standards Act, Occupational Health and Safety Act, and the
Family and Medical Leave Act. Johnston noted that many senators and their top
staff took the attitude that "no one is going to sue me," but he had to explain
that unless they complied with the new law they could indeed be sued in federal
court (Johnston Oral History, 79–81). They had to devise an overtime system,
face efforts to unionize the Capitol police and cafeteria workers and other serv-

ice staff, and puzzle over whether unions could bargain for government wages. The Accountability Act required the Senate to establish new mechanisms to deal with such human relations issues as sexual harassment. The act also eliminated the last vestiges of patronage. "You can't do patronage under the Accountability Act," explained Gregory S. Casey, who as sergeant at arms from 1996 to 1998 was responsible for implementing much of the law. "You cannot hire someone at a different salary than somebody else doing the same work in a 'nonpolitical' job and pay them a different amount of money" (Casey Oral History, 88, 112).

From the foregoing litany of reform, even in such abbreviated form, it seems clear that the Senate as an institution underwent great change during the twentieth century. One can see this physically while standing in the Capitol Plaza. A century ago, the entire Congress, the Supreme Court, and Library of Congress were consolidated within the Capitol Building. Today the plaza is ringed by massive marble buildings housing the Library of Congress, the Supreme Court, and the vastly expanded Senate and House staffs. Inside, the Senate now meets more frequently, passes more legislation, and handles bills that are thicker and more complex than anything that earlier senators encountered. For all these physical changes, rules revisions, and constitutional amendments, however, the Senate in 2000 remains very similar to the Senate in 1900. Remarkably, the Senate made it through the twentieth century with all of its powers intact. While the reformers in Britain, back in 1910, stripped their House of Lords of the power of the purse and the ability to delay legislation indefinitely, American reformers of the same era were content to change the method of election and allow the voters to purify the system. As a result, the U.S. Senate remains a uniquely powerful "upper body" among national legislatures (Sinclair 1998).

From the perspective of the Senate staff, the greatest changes were organic and societal rather than constitutional. A century of change in communication, transportation, political style, leadership, and the complexity of modern government had the greatest impact on the venerable institution, while much of the more formal tinkering failed to budge it. The many efforts to reduce filibusters seemed to have resulted in far more filibusters than ever before—if one counts failed cloture motions as a measure of filibusters. Without much revision of the formal rules of the Senate, the institution wound up at the end of the century with a powerful party leadership structure that had not existed a hundred years earlier. In 1900 there was no majority leader. Today, it would be hard to imagine the Senate functioning without one. The Senate has grown more open and accountable, but no less powerful. It is also more democratic and less aristocratic than the authors of the Constitution most likely envisioned. Yet it still carries out James Madison's original intention that it act as a "necessary fence" against sudden shifts in public opinion and the frenzies of the moment. After the congressional turnover in 1994, the newly elected members of the House of

Representatives rushed to enact their sweeping legislative program in their first hundred days in office so swiftly that House speaker Newt Gingrich compared their accomplishment to the First Hundred Days of the New Deal. But then the Senate proceeded to deliberate and the pace slowed down as parts of the program were delayed, defeated, or scaled back. One angry representative howled that "the Senate is the enemy!" Speaker Gingrich, however, replied that the last time he looked at the Constitution, the Senate was still there. And he was right (*Washington Post* 1996).

## CHAPTER EIGHT

# Twentieth-century Senate Reform:
# Three Views from the Outside

## RICHARD A. BAKER

What is the U.S. Senate? Is it faithful to the vision of the Constitution's framers? Does it serve the needs of modern America? While thoughtful people have posed these and related questions for more than two centuries, this line of inquiry took on a special intensity, as well as a greater sophistication, during the opening decades of the twentieth century.

Two developments coincided early in the century to promote this acceleration. The first was the nation's rise to world-power status, through the experience of the Spanish-American War and the First World War. The resulting enhancement of presidential authority pressured the Senate as never before. Its constitutional structure and methods of doing business, conceived in the eighteenth century and appropriate to the challenges of the nineteenth century, appeared hopelessly out of date to a growing legion of critics at the dawn of the twentieth century. This increased pressure for institutional examination and reform contributed to—and benefited from—the concurrent rise of political science as an organized academic discipline.

In the final quarter of the nineteenth century, two pioneers shaped graduate-level study in the fields of political science and history. John W. Burgess established Columbia University's political science graduate program in 1880—"the first graduate faculty of the political and social sciences in the United States"—and created the *Political Science Quarterly* to offer a showcase for promising new scholarship in that field (Hoxie et al. 1955). At Johns Hopkins University, which opened in 1876 as the nation's first educational institution devoted to advanced study and research, Herbert Baxter Adams developed path-breaking seminars in history and political science. In 1883, the year Woodrow Wilson entered the

147

university's doctoral program in political science, Adams established the *Johns Hopkins Studies in Historical and Political Science* as a vehicle for publication of doctoral dissertations in both fields (Somit and Tanenhaus 1982). (A student of Adams, Wilson completed his dissertation in 1884 and published it the following year under the title *Congressional Government*.[1])

Adams at Johns Hopkins and Burgess at Columbia emphasized the importance of applying scholarly research techniques and findings to an understanding of public policy issues and the operation of American political institutions. Both men stressed the importance of historical study, in Burgess's words, "to find the origin, follow the growth and learn the meaning of our legal, political, and economic principles and institutions" (Burgess 1883, 188; Adams 1887). Adams was instrumental in founding the American Historical Association in 1884 and Burgess played a similar role for the American Political Science Association in 1903. Active at a time of reawakened interest in the history and operations of the Senate, Adams and Burgess shaped several generations of history-sensitive political scientists and thereby shaped Senate-related scholarship well into the first half of the twentieth century.

This chapter examines the contributions of George H. Haynes, Lindsay Rogers, and George B. Galloway, three important early twentieth-century Senate political scientists who came under the influence of Adams and Burgess, to determine what attracted them to the Senate, what they considered as its fundamental role, and what reforms they proposed. What can be concluded from their experience about the challenges facing those who seek, from the detached perspective of outside observers, to understand and describe this most subtle and conservative political institution?

Born in the latter half of the nineteenth century, Haynes, Rogers, and Galloway had much in common. Haynes and Rogers earned their political science doctorates at Johns Hopkins. Galloway took his from another pioneering institution, Washington's Robert Brookings Graduate School of Economics and Government, whose faculty included graduates of both Columbia and Johns Hopkins. Both Haynes and Rogers pursued traditional and stable academic careers. For a half century, from 1887 to 1937, Haynes taught at Worcester Polytechnic Institute in Worcester, Massachusetts; Rogers made Columbia University his home from 1920 to 1959. Galloway spent much of his professional life with institutions closely related to academia, including the American Political Science Association and the Library of Congress. Each of these three men, by the twentieth century's midpoint, had produced a major book on the Senate.

In these works, Rogers, Haynes, and Galloway set the twentieth-century foundation for Senate institutional evaluation. Each engaged the institution with the fresh perspective of an outside analyst to articulate his view of the essential

Senate and its susceptibility to reform. The following account summarizes their reform views from the perspective of Rogers's *The American Senate* (1926), Haynes's *The Senate of the United States* (1938), and Galloway's *Congress at the Crossroads* (1946).

## LINDSAY ROGERS, 1891–1970

Lindsay Rogers wrote like a first-rate journalist and thought like an eminent political scientist. Born in Baltimore in 1891, he received his bachelors degree in 1912 from Johns Hopkins University. He then worked as a newspaper reporter while studying for a Johns Hopkins political science doctorate. As a journalist, he covered the arrival of the *Carpathia*, which bore the survivors of the *Titanic* disaster, and William Jennings Bryan's activities at the 1912 Democratic National Convention. By 1916, he had earned a Johns Hopkins Ph.D. and a University of Maryland LL.B. He taught at the University of Virginia from 1915 to 1920 and lectured for a year at Harvard University. In 1920, Rogers moved from the orbit of Herbert Baxter Adams at Johns Hopkins to that of John Burgess when he joined the Columbia University faculty. He taught in Columbia's Department of Public Law and Jurisprudence for the next four decades and, in 1929, was selected as the first Burgess Professor of Political Science. He also served, for most of his tenure at that university, as associate editor of the *Political Science Quarterly*, founded in 1886 by Burgess (Hoxie et al. 1955, 270–71).

To expand his base of governmental experience, Rogers took time away from the classroom to serve on various boards and commissions, and traveled extensively overseas to study parliaments and international administrative bodies. From 1924 to 1926, he worked as secretary to the New York governor's Advisory Commission on the Cloak, Suit, and Shirt Industry. In 1928, Governor Al Smith appointed him to lead a commission investigating charges of fraud in the state Bureau of Workmen's Compensation. His report on that project attracted the attention of the state's next governor, Franklin Roosevelt, and led to Rogers's appointment as deputy administrator of the National Recovery Administration, at the start of the New Deal. Later, during the Second World War, Rogers served as senior assistant director general of the International Labor Office (Hoxie et al. 1955, 118). His breadth of interests is evident in the titles of his major books, which include *The Postal Power of Congress: A Study in Constitutional Expression* (1916), *America's Case against Germany* (1917), *The American Senate* (1926), *Crisis Government* (1934), and *The Pollsters: Public Opinion, Politics, and Democratic Leadership* (1949). He also wrote widely for newspapers, magazines, and scholarly journals. In the 1950s, he regularly contributed to the *New York Times*, writing editorials, book reviews, and features for that paper's "Topics of the Times" and "Speaking of Books" columns. Rogers died in 1970 (*New York Times* 1970, 30; Rogers 1926, xxviii–xxix).

## Cloture

Rogers prepared *The American Senate* at a time of intense controversy over the Senate tradition of unlimited debate. This controversy pervades his book, which he jokingly explained was composed with "complete partiality and a bad temper" (1926, ix). In March 1917, facing a war emergency, President Woodrow Wilson issued his immortal blast against the exercise of that tradition by filibustering senators. "The Senate of the United States is the only legislative body in the world which cannot act when its majority is ready for action. A little group of willful men, representing no opinion but their own, have rendered the great Government of the United States helpless and contemptible" (Link 1983, 320). Four days later, the Senate yielded to the force of events and added a cloture provision to its Rule XXII. This change permitted two-thirds of the senators present and voting to close debate on a pending measure, with each senator given the option of speaking on that measure for up to one hour (Haynes 1938, 402–5).

From 1917 until *The American Senate* appeared in 1926, the Senate closed debate under Rule XXII only twice. The new cloture rule's infrequent use strengthened Rogers's confidence that the tradition of unlimited debate remained firmly in place, except in times of dire national emergency.

Rogers's interest in the Senate grew from his studies at Johns Hopkins and his first book on Congress's use of its postal power. In 1923, he observed that of all governmental institutions, only the Senate was capable of conducting serious investigations into the scandals that were beginning to break around Warren Harding's presidential administration. Unlike the House of Representatives, where leaders of the Republican majority had the power to block embarrassing investigations of their party's presidential administration, Senate Republicans, also in the majority, enjoyed no such authority, because the Senate required a supermajority of two-thirds to cut off a filibuster. They knew, Rogers wrote, that "Senator Thomas J. Walsh of Montana and other Democrats could hold up important business [through the filibuster]; hence they had to consent to the thoroughgoing inquiry that was demanded." He then asked, rhetorically, whether the threatened filibuster—despite its delay of pressing legislative proceedings—was in the public interest. His answer: "it is sufficient to remark that three out of ten cabinet members were permitted or pressed to resign, and that there were several indictments and two suicides" (Rogers 1959, 22).

The issue gained additional public attention in March 1925, when incoming Vice President Charles Dawes took advantage of the traditionally ceremonial vice presidential inaugural ceremony in the Senate Chamber to deliver a blistering attack on a small band of progressive Republican senators who had been filibustering end-of-session legislation. Dawes urged the Senate to revise Rule XXII to allow for majority cloture. The existing rule, he thundered, "at times enables Senators to consume in oratory those last precious minutes of a session needed for momentous decisions," thereby placing great power in the hands of a few senators. Unless Rule XXII were liberalized, it would "lessen the effectiveness, prestige, and dignity of the United States Senate." Dawes's unexpected diatribe infuriated senators of all philosophical leanings, who believed that the chamber's rules were none of the vice president's business (Hatfield et al. 1997, 363–64).

Lindsay Rogers fundamentally disagreed with Dawes. In his memorably stated view, the "undemocratic, usurping Senate is the indispensable check and balance in the American system, and only complete freedom of debate allows it to play this role." "Adopt closure [cloture] in the Senate," he argued, "and the character of the American Government will be profoundly changed." The Senate owed its greatness to its unique ability to "exert supervision over the executive." That function, he argued, would be impossible if the Senate significantly limited its debate (Rogers 1968, ix, 186–88).

Today, we remember Rogers's *The American Senate* principally for its arguments against cloture by simple majority. His intention, however, was to present a book-length essay—in 250 pages—on the Senate in its institutional entirety. After an opening chapter on the founding fathers' plans for the Senate, Rogers adopted a topical structure with chapters on the Senate's executive and legislative functions, its investigating role, its ability to serve as a check on presidential "propaganda," and as a "forum of the nation and critic of the executive."

### Committee Investigations

For Rogers, the filibuster's major value was as a weapon in the hands of a minority seeking to initiate committee investigations of questionable executive branch conduct (Rogers 1968, 191, 202). Forty-two years after the *American Senate* first appeared, Rogers altered his views on congressional investigations in a reprint edition of this work. "I still believe," he explained, "that the Senate should be able to investigate and even on occasion to conduct inquisitions, but I think that, *save when pending legislation is the subject matter*, the duty of inquiring should be handed over to a more efficient piece of governmental machinery"—a special investigating commission created by Congress and appointed by the president. Perhaps his experience later in the 1920s as a labor fraud investigator caused him to rethink the views he expressed in his book earlier in that decade. He charged that as "inquisitors, Congressmen have been fumbling and the reason is that they have been amateurs attempting jobs that required professionals." He reasoned that even the most talented senatorial inquisitors lack the time and attention span to do the job effectively (xx–xxi, xxiv–xxx).

## Concentration of Influence

In 1921, the Senate eliminated most of its "sinecure" committees—those that existed principally to provide their chairmen a clerk and an office. It also imposed reforms to limit the practice in which a handful of the most senior senators dominated conference committee proceedings. For the 105 conference committees appointed during the Sixty-fifth Congress (1917–1919) to reconcile differences in Senate-and-House-passed versions of legislation, five senators greatly expanded their own influence by securing places on eighty-two of them. Anticipating reforms of the 1970s, the Senate provided that no member could chair more than one of the body's ten major committees and could not sit on more than two of those panels. Rogers applauded these reforms and noted approvingly, regarding conference committees, that one of the Senate's great strengths grew from its ability to dominate the House of Representatives in these panels (1968, 109).

## Workload

Following his belief that senators should delegate to outside bodies major investigations for which they lacked the time and expertise, Rogers lamented that members of both houses spent too much time on minor matters that would best be left to executive agencies, or to state and local governments. In the following two sprightly drafted sentences, he laid out the issue.

> An astonishing proportion of the time of Congress is spent in authorizing the construction of bridges, changing the names of steamers, permitting the coinage of silver pieces to commemorate various anniversaries, sanctioning monuments and memorials, regulating minor Indian affairs, paying private claims against the government, authorizing conveyance, sale, or transfer of public lands, and regulating military and naval property. It is difficult to believe that these picayune matters—to say nothing of the private legislation which is by all odds the chief interest of many members—merit the collective wisdom of 531 statesmen who draw substantial salaries, enjoy extensive perquisites, meet in a magnificent building for the greater part of the year, and publish their emendations on this petty business to the extent of millions of words. (1968, 104–5)

## Direct Elections

Although the Seventeenth Amendment's provisions for direct popular election of senators had been in effect for only a decade when the *American Senate* appeared, Rogers believed he could already detect their impact—and he was not sure he liked it. Suspecting that long-serving senators would have more difficulty gaining reelection at the hands of the vastly expanded electorate, he feared this would deprive the nation of their greater fund of expertise, which allowed the

Senate to polish and perfect measures following their passage by the House of Representatives. The writings of George Haynes significantly shaped his views on this subject (Rogers 1968, 20, 111–16).

## Treaties

Rogers set aside his admiration for the Senate's inherent moderating and restraining influences when he considered its role in reviewing treaties. Writing within a few years of the Senate's rejection of the Treaty of Versailles, he borrowed the words of Secretary of State John Hay to label the Senate's treaty powers an "irreparable mistake" by the Constitution's framers (1968, 78–79, 250–52). Rogers believed that the vagueness of the Senate's advice and consent powers invited unconstitutional behavior. "Its impregnable position and its sense of power lead to assertions of authority that are unwise politically and improper constitutionally. . . . [P]owerful in respect to treaties, the Senate desires to make a pretense of being powerful in respect to American foreign policy in general." From this perspective, Rogers acknowledged, "unrestricted debate is an evil" (80, 84, 87). Although confident that the Constitution would never be amended to diminish the Senate's treaty powers, he nonetheless wished that treaty approvals could be handled, like general legislation, by both houses of Congress (251).

## "Report and Question Period"

As an admirer of the British Parliament, Rogers urged that the Senate adopt arrangements requiring executive agency heads to regularly come before its members to report their activities and permit member questions. This, he believed, would offer the collateral benefit of enlivening Senate proceedings and avoiding the customary disillusionment of gallery visitors who observe only a single senator addressing empty desks (Rogers 1968, 254).

## Assessment

*The American Senate* is about more—and less—than the American Senate. It is neither tightly structured nor carefully disciplined. Rogers's frequent and extended excursions to the Senate—related current events and comparisons with other legislative bodies—suggest a book quickly drafted, with an undercurrent of good humor, a splash of irony, but little "bad temper." Several of his reform suggestions—delegation of investigations and sharing treaty powers with the House—now seem naïve and unrealistic. Yet, aside from its frequent digressions, the book's remaining text appears as fresh and vital today as it did three-quarters of a century ago.

Robert Luce, an incumbent House member and contemporary authority on legislative procedures, took Rogers to task for his opinion that the U. S. House of

Representatives was "the most ineffective lower chamber in the world" and commented on the difficulties of observing the Senate from the outside. Using as an example Rogers's misreading of statistics on the number of Senate amendments to House appropriations bills, Luce chided, "Had he taken part in the work he would have known that many of these amendments were merely corrections of typographical or clerical errors. . . . This may illustrate how difficult it is to deal accurately with legislative processes from the outside. The result may be as futile as an attempt to discern the character of a man through his photograph" (1927, 178–79).

## GEORGE H. HAYNES, 1866–1947

The 1938 publication of George Haynes's two-volume *Senate of the United States* instantly made him the nation's leading academic authority on that institution. Reviewers routinely ranked his work with Charles Warren's monumental three-volume *The Supreme Court in United States History* (1928), published fifteen years earlier. While others had produced major studies examining individual areas of Senate activity, and while Lindsay Rogers had created an extended essay on the institution in defense of unlimited debate, Haynes was the first to attempt a comprehensive history. His thorough documentation and detailed index made the volumes a handy and satisfying reference work for several generations of scholars, journalists, and general readers.

Born in Sturbridge, Massachusetts, in 1866, George Haynes graduated from Amherst College in 1887 and immediately took a teaching post in modern languages and mathematics at Worcester Polytechnic Institute, not far from his central Massachusetts hometown. After three years of teaching, he traveled south to Baltimore to begin doctoral studies in political science at Johns Hopkins University. (In this, he preceded Lindsay Rogers by two decades.) Receiving his doctorate in 1893, Haynes returned to Worcester with the rank of professor in economics and government, and remained at that institution until his retirement in 1937 ("Seventy Years" 1999).

Haynes followed a circuitous road from his graduate training to his landmark study of the U.S. Senate. In 1894, his Johns Hopkins mentor Herbert Baxter Adams acknowledged the young scholar's promise by publishing Haynes's doctoral dissertation, "Representation and Suffrage in Massachusetts, 1620–1691" in his *Johns Hopkins University Studies in Historical and Political Science* (Haynes 1894). Haynes then shifted his interest in the Massachusetts legislature ahead two centuries to the year 1855, to examine what happened when the Know Nothing Party won nearly all that body's seats. The American Historical Association, reflecting Herbert Adams's influence, recognized the quality of Haynes's scholarship by including the resulting article in its annual proceedings for 1896 (Haynes 1896, 175–87).

By 1900, Haynes had broadened his focus from Massachusetts to state legislatures in general (Haynes 1900, 204–35). His study "Representation in State Legislatures" (1900) caused him to examine the role of those bodies in electing U.S. senators. He recognized that the increasing number of deadlocks over hotly contested Senate vacancies kept them from addressing matters of more immediate concern to their constituencies. Consequently, his interest in divesting state legislatures of this constitutional burden grew from his desire to reform these institutions rather than from "optimistic assurance that the personnel or efficiency of the Senate would be notably improved by popular election" (Haynes 1914, 231).

The Worcester professor's *The Election of Senators* appeared in 1906, just as novelist David Graham Phillips was serving up his sensationalized "Treason of the Senate" series in William Randolph Hearst's *Cosmopolitan* magazine (Haynes 1906). While both accounts focused on opportunities for corruption under the indirect election system, Haynes's more sober study began with the view that public opinion, in practice, strongly influenced selection of the Senate's membership. At that time, at least one-third of the states allowed their voters, by various methods developed over the previous decade, to indicate support for likely Senate candidates in advance of formal state legislative balloting. As Haynes later described the evolving process, "The people pressed the button; the members of the State Legislature did the rest" (1924, 252). But, Haynes concluded, the symbolism behind the electoral process counted for as much as the process itself. "Whether the Senate be regarded as the sheet anchor of the Republic in the troubled seas of democracy, or as the stronghold of corporate interests—as the country's only safeguard, or as its chief menace—the question becomes one of paramount [symbolic] importance: how do men come to membership in this overpowering body?" (1906, vii–viii).

With the Seventeenth Amendment's ratification in 1913, Haynes reiterated his belief that the Senate "is not to be 'reformed'—so far as reform is necessary—by a mere change in the mode of election," but he hoped "that it will be less easy for certain types of men, who have brought reproach upon the Senate," to be elected. The "reactionary" should disappear and the state boss "may find the voters at large less docile in his support than have been members of the Legislature whom he has helped to office" (1914, 231, 233). He cautioned—as did Lindsay Rogers—that popular election could accelerate an already evident and disturbing trend away from the type of senator suited to "deliberate—perhaps too deliberate—study of what is wise to do" to those who were younger and less experienced, but who displayed a vote-winning "aptitude for getting things done. . . . [F]or the future, it is going to be harder for a Senator of manly independence to hold a course which does not square with the opinion of the day; for his chance of re-election will be largely determined not by whether his acts have been wise, but by whether they have been popular" (232–33).

Over the three decades that followed publication of his 1906 *Election of Senators,* Haynes broadened his knowledge of Senate procedures and processes. His *Senate of the United States* appeared in 1938, on the eve of the Senate's 150th anniversary. A combination of that coincidental anniversary and the author's unbridled determination to see a thirty-year project through to completion eventually overcame difficulties in finding a publisher for so large a work. He explained his volumes' size and his publisher's reluctance by noting that, unlike the other branches, the Senate lacked "a certain unity of scope. . . . The Senate's tremendous powers, . . . are not merely legislative, but executive, judicial, and investigative as well. To organize such diverse material in a coordinated survey cannot fail to be a task forbidding in prospect and difficult in process" (1938, vii).

Following Lindsay Rogers's model, he devoted his first two chapters to the Senate's founding period; then he switched to a topical format, with the next eighteen chapters addressing such subjects as the Senate's specific constitutional powers, its rules and officers, its committees and major investigations, its elections and its leadership, and its relations with the House of Representatives and the president. A final chapter summarized his views on the ever-changing Senate. Here is a resume of Haynes's reform comments.

## Size

Contrary to Lindsay Rogers, who saw the Senate's relatively small size as its strength, George Haynes believed the Senate was too large and too publicly accountable through direct election to perform its constitutional responsibilities effectively. He blamed the nation's territorial growth for what he perceived to be the body's diminished influence. The addition of each state materially "lessened the Senate's fitness for exercising those distinctive powers from which its preeminence has largely been derived." He quoted Madison's warning on this score: "The use of the Senate is to consist in its proceeding with more coolness, with more system, and with more wisdom than the popular branch. Enlarge their numbers and you communicate to them the vices which they are meant to correct. . . . Their weight should be in inverse ratio to their number." Haynes concluded that "no constitutional convention of the present day would for a moment consider the assigning of [the Senate's executive and judicial] powers to a popularly elected legislative body of nearly one hundred members" (1938, 1038). He offered no reform suggestion.

## Malapportionment

As population ratios between large and small states widened dramatically, Haynes considered the equal representation of states in the Senate to be "steadily becoming more preposterous." He reported, sympathetically but without optimism, contemporary proposals of political scientists to shift the Senate's basis of representation to occupational groups, "governmental units," or "blocks of population." Yet, he acknowledged that in the "character, ability, and statesmanship of their Senators the small states have often excelled the states of largest populations and thus exercised a stronger and more beneficial influence" (1938, 1038–40, 1055).

## Members' Characteristics

George Haynes must have been among the first of congressional scholars to collect "data sets" on members of the Senate. He began this activity at the start of the twentieth century by preparing his 1906 *Election of Senators*. He gathered information on senators' age distribution, educational levels, governmental and business experience, military service, wealth, and length of Senate service. His goal was to learn "what were the apparent 'qualifications' which had made them the most 'available' candidates for choice by state legislatures." He updated that survey in 1910, and again in 1913, for the last Senate to have all of its members formally elected by state legislatures. He then reviewed the situation in 1923, ten years after the amendment's ratification, and again in 1933. For that latter year, Haynes concluded that senators were slightly older, marginally better educated, more likely to have been lawyers, and—regrettably—less legislatively experienced than in the years prior to the Seventeenth Amendment's implementation (1938, 1043).

## Direct Election

Based on his member surveys, Haynes "emphatically disclaim[ed] the implication that the adoption of the Seventeenth Amendment has been the sole or dominant cause of contrasts or apparently new trends." All he could report with certainty was that it ended "the blurring of issues in the election of members of the [state] legislatures, and to the prolonged deadlocks which often distracted and delayed, if they did not actually prevent, the doing of the essential tasks of lawmaking and providing the means for carrying on the state governments." He added,

> No intelligent man who had actual knowledge of the election of Senators by state legislatures would wish to see a return to a method which proved itself subject to the grave abuses which led to its abandonment. Popular election has eliminated some of the worst features of the earlier method, but it has developed serious defects of its own which need frank recognition and correction. (1938, 1043, 1070, 1073)

## Campaign Financing

Foreshadowing the late-twentieth-century crisis in campaign financing, Haynes acknowledged that "Popular election of Senators has proved immensely more costly than was anticipated by either its advocates or opponents." He calculated that the direct primary and popular election of senators "doubled and tripled the length of the campaign, and tripled and quadrupled the cost and scandals connected with electing Senators." Citing contemporary campaign spending scandals, Haynes acknowledged "it is very difficult . . . to formulate logical and adequate restrictions as to the size of campaign contributions, or the sources from which they may be received, or the objects for which they may legally be expended" (1938, 1074–76). Finding a solution proved as elusive in the 1930s as it has in our times.

In another example of a reform proposal that failed to find a permanent application, Haynes noted with some enthusiasm a plan tested in Oregon for the 1934 primaries. Under that plan, the state published an official "educational campaign pamphlet" for each of the two major parties. Both pamphlets contained statements of up to four pages in which candidates for party nominations, for a small fee, set forth their qualifications for the desired office. For that same fee, any person could submit a four-page statement opposing a candidate. Haynes observed, "In this form of publicity, at minimum expense, all the candidates, rich and poor, stand more nearly upon the same plane" (1938, 1074–76).

Additional costs of the direct primary system included "an absurd multiplication of candidacies, often of the most preposterous quality, yet throwing the whole campaign into turmoil and uncertainty, which may result in a grab-bag choice of Senator." He also decried the

> vulgarizing of the candidates' campaign methods. . . . [P]resent-day primary campaigning is largely a cheap bidding for notoriety, carried to the extreme when candidates with circus stunts and screaming "sound-motors" tour their own states and come to the chivalric aid of like-minded colleagues in other states. . . . [I]t is hard for a Senator to hold himself steadily to the cool-headed and conscientious performance of his duties as "a Senator of the United States" while such roistering campaigning for his seat is in progress in his own state. (1938, 1078, 1082)

## Decline in Senate Prestige

Perhaps Haynes reflected the common tendency of Senate observers to favorably compare the institution's imperfectly remembered past—its "golden ages"—with their direct impressions of more recent times as he deplored the Senate's loss of prestige over the twenty years since the Seventeenth Amendment's ratification.[2] "There has been no period in our history when there was more need for the cool and courageous exercise of the Senate's distinctive powers of revision and amendment, of confirmation and ratification, and of investigation, than in the years since the people took into their own hands the direct election of Senators." He found three explanations for the perceived decline. First, as Woodrow Wilson—who preceded him in his Johns Hopkins doctoral studies by a decade—once observed, if the conditions of public service "starve statesmen and foster demagogues, the Senate itself will be full of the latter kind, simply because there are no others available." Second, a senator's "tasks in recent years have become much more difficult and complicated." And, finally, the senator's "work must now be done amid incessant distractions necessary in maintaining satisfactory contacts with his constituents, that his days may be long in the seat which they gave him" (Haynes 1938, 1071–73).

## Assessment

Reviewers generally agreed that Haynes had fashioned a masterful synthesis of the Senate's institutional operations, although he devoted little attention to party organization and floor leadership (Berdahl 1939, 298). Writing in the *Harvard Law Review*, Florida Senator Claude Pepper observed that both volumes "literally bristle with indications of Mr. Haynes' intimate knowledge and understanding of the Senate, its precedents, its personnel, the world, physical and political, in which it has had its being" (1939, 1026–27). But many political scientists criticized him for his lack of analysis. Harold J. Laski saw it as "a supplement to rather than a corrective of Professor Lindsay Rogers vivid volume," and concluded that "[a]s a commentary, the latter still holds the field" (Laski 1939, 384; Dangerfield 1940, 374–75). Rogers examined Haynes's volumes and concluded that he "limits himself to expounding and does not bother to exhort" but he praised Haynes for a work that "[d]espite its scope and its excessively factual character, . . . is not dull. Mr. Haynes has a feel for the humorous and the picturesque. He has filtered the facts through a sympathetic and trained intelligence" (Rogers 1939, 19). Rogers added, "Mr. Haynes (and many observers agree with him) cannot see that the character of the Senate has changed greatly [since 1913]. Scandals there have been in connection with campaign expenditures. Demagogues are certainly no less numerous. Whether the level of ability has risen and fidelity to the national interest has increased are wide open questions" (Rogers 1939, 19).

A close examination of this work reveals that Haynes harbored a deep ambivalence about the Senate. His long association with the topic, particularly against the backdrop of its role while he was composing this work in the 1930s, bred sentiments closer to contempt than admiration. His prescriptions for institutional reform flowed from a decidedly unsympathetic pen.

## GEORGE B. GALLOWAY, 1898–1967

At the August 6, 1967, memorial services for George Galloway at Washington's Cosmos Club, Oklahoma's Democratic Senator A. S. Mike Monroney observed, "Few men—and perhaps no man outside of the Congress itself—had as much to do as did George Galloway in inspiring and perfecting the various steps and stages in improving the Congress and its machinery to carry on the difficult tasks of the last half of this 20th Century" (*Congressional Record*, September 19, 1967, 25944).

Born in Brooklyn, New York, in 1898, Galloway earned a bachelor's degree from Wesleyan University, a master's from Washington University in St. Louis, and, in 1926, a doctorate in political science from the short-lived (1924–1929) Robert Brookings Graduate School in Washington, D.C. Although he focused his graduate work on the study of Congress, he shifted his attention over the following fifteen years to public policy issues, first at Editorial Research Reports and then at the National Economic and Social Planning Association, which he cofounded. From 1933 to 1935, he served as a deputy administrator of the National Recovery Administration—a post Lindsay Rogers also held for a short time in 1933.

In January 1941, George Galloway returned to the study of Congress when the American Political Science Association—true to the interests of its founder John Burgess—established a permanent committee to evaluate the effectiveness of Congress and appointed him chairman. (Within two months, the *Political Science Quarterly* published an article by its editor, Lindsay Rogers, calling for a significant increase in the level of professional staffing available to Congress [Rogers 1941]. Many of Rogers's proposals later appeared among the Galloway committee's recommendations.) For the next four years, Galloway's committee, by his account, functioned "primarily as a catalytic agency, seeking to stimulate congressional interest in self-improvement and public interest in congressional reform" (Galloway 1950, 3–4). The committee conducted dozens of off-the-record meetings with senators and representatives to establish a range of perceived problems and suggested solutions. Under Galloway's leadership, it also sponsored, or otherwise encouraged, radio debates, magazine articles, newspaper editorials, and special studies. Drawing on his earlier ties to the renamed National Planning Association, Galloway arranged for Cleveland management analyst Robert Heller to prepare a provocative report entitled "Strengthening the Congress." The League of Women Voters also gave this topic special attention, sparking nationwide discussions of the reform opportunities (Byrd 1988, 539–47).

As a result of this agitation, Congress, in December 1944 created its own Joint Committee on the Organization of Congress and hired Galloway to direct a staff that included himself and one secretary.[3] In March 1945, the joint committee, cochaired by Wisconsin Senator Robert M. La Follette Jr. and Oklahoma Representative A. S. Mike Monroney, opened three months of hearings, with testimony from 102 witnesses forming the heart of a printed record that exceeded fifteen hundred pages. In its March 1946 final report, the joint committee offered thirty-seven specific recommendations grouped in broad categories such as committee structure and operation, party policy committees, research and staff facilities, congressional time management, lobby registration, and member pay increases (U.S. Congress 1946, 1–35).

The committee based its conclusions on the rise, since the First World War, of presidential government, which threatened the relegation of Congress to "a mere ceremonial appendix to bureaucracy . . . working with tools from the wig and snuff-box era" (U.S. Congress 1946, v). Concerned for the fate of parliaments in totalitarian nations, President Franklin Roosevelt's seemingly dictatorial actions in times of national emergency, the Supreme Court's apparent usurpation of legislative functions in declaring laws unconstitutional, and executive agencies that played an increasing role in drafting necessarily technical legislation (6), the reformers lamented that "During the nineteenth century, the great issues were legislative; today, administration is nine-tenths of the law" (12).

George Galloway was a master publicist. To add force to the joint committee's final report, he assembled a book entitled *Congress at the Crossroads* (1946). Issued late in 1946 by a major publisher and widely reviewed, the book bears the scissors-and-paste marks of its hurried construction. Written to appeal to those deeply dissatisfied with the national legislature, the book embedded the committee's specific recommendations in a generalized account of Congress's history and operations.

Much to Galloway's surprise, in August 1946 Congress accomplished a "legislative miracle" by passing the landmark Legislative Reorganization Act, just before adjourning for that year's midterm election campaigns. "In one quick leap," he concluded, "Congress jumped the hurdles of timidity, inertia, and vested interest and modernized much of its machinery and methods. All told, it added up to the most sweeping reorganization in congressional history." He noted that the legislation incorporated his recommendations for committee reorganization, professional staffing, and lobbyist registrations. It established a long-needed budget procedure with a ceiling on total appropriations, raised congressional salaries, and made members eligible to join the federal retirement system, "a step that will encourage super-annuated members to retire" (1946, 342–43).

While passage of the 1946 Legislative Reorganization Act achieved major institutional changes in staffing and committee structure, Galloway concluded "at best it was only a beginning, although a good one." He complained that the bill "was considerably diluted before it finally passed, and several important reforms never went beyond the discussion stage." Although its enactment just weeks before the appearance of *Congress at the Crossroads* reduced the book's immediacy, Galloway's volume set forth an ambitious agenda for more substantive reforms (1946, 343).

## Integration of Functions

In his activities with the joint committee and in his book, Galloway set his focus on the entire Congress—without singling out either chamber. This reflected his belief that the institution had become too fragmented; its fragmentation fostered its inefficiency. As an outsider coming to Capitol Hill, Galloway lacked the institutional biases of members and senior staff. He mistakenly minimized the chambers' vast differences with respect to their history, culture, rules, and customs. In his view, Congress could effectively tackle the problems of the postwar era only to the extent that it reduced its internal structural atomization and resulting duplication of effort.

Galloway directed his recommendations to eliminating the duplication inherent in Senate and House operations by creating in each body committees of identical structure and jurisdiction. He urged the fashioning for both houses and the various congressional support agencies of a single administrative system to handle disbursing, auditing, budgeting, and personnel management operations. Rather than emphasizing each institution's distinctiveness, he searched for their common elements. (Only later, in the late 1950s, did he focus on one body's uniqueness when the Committee on House Administration, aware of George Haynes's two-volume history of the Senate, asked Galloway to prepare a similarly organized work on the House of Representatives.)

Although Galloway did not write specifically on the Senate as an institution, his views of that body are evident in *Congress at the Crossroads*. Today, we accept many of his successful Senate-related proposals as well-established congressional operating features without realizing their relatively modern origin, or their parentage. These range from such essential features as the creation of professional staffs for senators and Senate committees, to establishment of regularized committee operating procedures and improved party agenda-setting through the vehicle of party policy committees.

Given Galloway's enduring stature as a preeminent congressional reformer, however, many of his 1946 proposals—just as earlier recipes by Rogers and Haynes—appear naïve and out-of-touch with the Congress of his time. Those based on his perception of the need for greater efficiency through administrative centralization seem particularly unrealistic. By its centralized and hierarchical structure, the executive branch was far better equipped to address the challenges that had increasingly confronted the nation since the beginning of the twentieth century. Congress had no choice, in Galloway's view, but to emulate the executive's organizational strengths, including a more clearly defined chain of command and expert staff resources. Presidential administrations such as Franklin Roosevelt's moved to address national emergencies with a speed and decisiveness unknown to Congress. Here is a brief inventory of Galloway's Senate-related proposals that time has shown to be out of touch with institutional reality.

## Appointment of Committee Chairmen

As an outsider to Senate operations who relied on George Haynes for a description of earlier reform efforts, Galloway missed the fundamental jurisdictional tension between floor leaders and committee chairmen; he neglected the institution's seeming pride in its lack of established hierarchy; and he ignored the profound sense of mutual distrust and latent antagonism so deeply embedded in Senate-House relations (Galloway 1946, 140, 144–45). Only someone new to the Senate's operations could believe, as he did, that committee chairmen would agree to be appointed by the majority leader (194), or that party leaders would agree to meet regularly and earnestly with their House counterparts, in a "legislative cabinet," (120, 195) to shape and pursue a congressional session's agenda. In proposing a centralized administrative structure for both houses, he disregarded the Senate's traditional preference for decentralization in such matters.

## Electronic Voting

Years later, the House of Representatives adopted Galloway's recommendation for electronic tabulation of roll call votes as a time-saving device (1946, 80). The Senate, less than a quarter of the size of the House, did not follow the House in adopting this innovation. It can be expected to carry its late eighteenth-century method of hand-tabulation well into the twenty-first century. As crowded schedules and ease of travel back to their home states leave senators less time for personal interaction than was available even in Galloway's day, they are not likely to give up the opportunity these roll calls offer for frequent unstructured interaction with colleagues of both parties.

## Consolidated Committee Operations

Galloway envisioned a single building dedicated to congressional committee and executive agency liaison operations (1946, 56, 81, 326). Although this plan never matured, the Senate in the late 1940s adopted its underlying purpose by designating that its second office building, then in the planning stages, would be devoted exclusively to committees. When that structure—today known as the Everett Dirksen Building—opened in 1958, it provided office suites and hearing rooms for the Senate's sixteen standing committees. As another example, however, of the difficulty of enforcing such seemingly logical plans in nonhierarchical institutions such as the Senate, some committees simply ignored the plan and remained in place. The new building soon began to resemble its predecessor in the mix of members' offices and committee suites.

## Party Policy Committees

The conservative coalition of southern Democrats and western Republicans struck Galloway as a serious impediment to government effectiveness because it reduced the responsibility and accountability of the individual parties. Bloc voting and shifting bipartisan coalitions served only to frustrate "the major popular will." Near the top of his list of reforms was the creation of party policy committees to establish clear party positions on major issues. After House Speaker Sam Rayburn scuttled these plans for his chamber, the Senate established its own policy committees. In the years ahead, each Senate party shaped its policy committee according to its particular needs and traditions (Ritchie 1997, 3–17).

## Debate Limitation

Galloway sensed that the Senate of his day had no taste for liberalizing its cloture rule to allow less than a two-thirds majority to end debate on specific legislation. (In fact, within three years, the Senate made cloture even more difficult to invoke by requiring a vote of two-thirds of the total number of senators, rather than just those present and voting.) In full disagreement with Lindsay Rogers, he noted impatiently that "Much precious time is wasted in long-winded Senate speeches consisting largely of long quotations from putative authorities made to empty seats and galleries. Arguments which could be summed up in thirty minutes or less are stretched out tediously to three or four hours until all but a small handful of members have retreated in boredom to the privacy of their offices leaving the loquacious orator to bellow almost alone" (Galloway 1946, 200). If a liberalized cloture rule were not possible, then perhaps the floor schedule could be structured to set aside periods in which "Senators might talk to their hearts' delight on anything under the sun without interrupting the regular order of legislative business" (81). Additionally, he suggested a stricter standard of germaneness and the radio broadcasting of floor proceedings along the lines proposed in 1944 by Florida Senator Claude Pepper. He believed that this public exposure would force speakers to condense their remarks or "run the risk of being retired from Congress by an outraged public" (200, 317).

## Committee Reform

Identifying "committee work as the heart of congressional activity," Galloway recommended setting aside Monday through Wednesday for committee meetings and Thursday and Friday for regular legislative sessions (1946, 81). With a view toward increased efficiency and the elimination of blurred jurisdictional boundaries, he described twelve broad public policy areas and recommended that the Senate restructure its committee system to establish one committee for each policy area. Under this plan, the House would also create twelve committees, whose names and jurisdictions would be identical to their Senate counterparts. He envisioned adoption of a practice then followed in the Massachusetts legislature of holding joint hearings and relying on joint staffs (76). "Rather than looking down at a forlorn performance before empty chairs, the public might well choose between attendance at one or more parts of a twelve-ring committee circus where questions and argument would be lively and real" (290). His desire for public access to committee hearings, however, did not extend to committee business meetings and markup sessions. These gatherings, he believed, should be closed to the public, for "Partisanship disappears behind closed doors, and secrecy improves the chances of compromise" (180).

### Other Constitutional Functions

Consistent with his belief—and that of Lindsay Rogers—that members of Congress "should not spend one working minute on anything that somebody else can do just as well," Galloway urged a sharp reduction in the number of federal officials subject to Senate confirmation (1946, 83). For top officials, he believed that the president should invite professional organizations to prepare panels of qualified candidates for offices within their competence. He also advocated removing Congress's constitutional power to decide on the fitness of its own members by proposing that panels of federal judges resolve contested congressional elections, with appeal to the Supreme Court (23). Similarly, with impeachment trials for federal court judges, he contended that the Senate was too busy to be diverted by such relatively insignificant matters. He proposed trial of federal judges, other than Supreme Court justices, by a three-member court with right of appeal to the Supreme Court. He acknowledged, however, that the Senate had shown no interest in abandoning this constitutional function (16–17).

With the hindsight of more than half a century, many of these reforms appear hopelessly unrealistic. At the time, however, they represented bold new approaches to fixing an institution that appeared increasingly anachronistic and incapable of meeting the burgeoning host of postwar challenges.

While Lindsay Rogers moved on to other topics after completing *American Senate*, and George Haynes turned to retirement activities, George Galloway remained on Capitol Hill to observe the afterlife of the Legislative Reorganization Act's reforms (Galloway 1951, 1952, and 1956). He did this from the perspective of the Library of Congress's Legislative Reference Service, where he served as a senior specialist until his retirement in December 1966.

Rogers, Haynes, and Galloway each advanced his era's critical understanding of Senate operations and vulnerabilities. Trained in the Columbia and Johns Hopkins tradition that valued historical documentation as a resource for the study of Congress, these political scientists explored the Senate's founding principles and their subsequent confrontation with the demands of an expanding nation. Today, only Haynes's more historically based work retains much reference value, but all three books influenced a generation or more of political scientists and their students (Riddick 1949).

In 1953 the American Political Science Association, with the encouragement of Lindsay Rogers and George Galloway, established a congressional fellowship program. For nine months, early-to-mid-career fellows "serve on congressional staffs and acquire 'hands on' experience while gaining insight into the legislative process . . . to improve the quality of scholarship on and teaching of Congress and American national politics, thereby enhancing public understanding of Congress and policymaking" (American Political Science Association 2000). The opportunity for outside scholars to learn from and to teach seasoned insiders is perhaps the best legacy of John Burgess and Herbert Baxter Adams, and their scholarly successors—Rogers, Haynes, and Galloway.

## NOTES

1. For an account of relations between Adams and Wilson, see W. Stull Holt's *Historical Scholarship in the United States, 1876–1901: As Revisited in the Correspondence of Herbert B. Adams* (1938, 88–94).

2. This practice dates back at least to 1797, when Vice President Thomas Jefferson wrote a former senator, "You and I have formerly seen warm debates and high political passions [in the Senate]. But gentlemen of different politics would then speak to each other and separate the business of the Senate from that of society. It is not so now." Thomas Jefferson to Edward Rutledge, June 30, 1797 (Washington 1854, 4:191).

3. Albert Somit and Joseph Tanenhaus make the following observation: "The fortuitous conjunction between the 1945 report of the Association's Committee on Congress (under George Galloway) and the provisions of the 1946 Legislative Reorganization Act tempted other [Association] committees to come up with reports of equal 'consequence' " (1982, 150, n. 8).

# Reflections on Forty Years of the Senate

## DONALD R. MATTHEWS

The study of the U.S. Senate flourishes—that's the first conclusion I draw from this book. Not only are the various chapters well done, they even tend to agree. Extreme individualism and bitter partisanship—a curious combination of conflicting attitudes and behaviors—characterize the contemporary upper house, making leadership and policymaking excruciatingly difficult. The Senate of the 1950s, which I tried to describe in *U.S. Senators and Their World* (1960), has changed.

So has the study of the Senate. In the 1950s, the handful of scholars studying the Congress worked alone with little knowledge of each others' work. The previous literature on the Senate seemed old, naïve, and inadequately scientific to those of us excited by the "behavioral revolution." Today, the circle of active congressional researchers is very large and an imposing infrastructure facilitates their work. There is a journal, *Legislative Studies Quarterly,* and a *Handbook of Legislative Studies.* The American Political Science Association's (APSA) Congressional Fellowship Program has introduced several young political scientists (plus others) to Congress every year for decades. A large and lively section of the APSA Annual Meeting is devoted to legislative studies (mostly research on Congress). The same is true of regional professional meetings. The *CQ Almanac* has developed into a full-fledged research service of great value to Congress watchers. C-SPAN televises the daily sessions of the House and Senate. The Congressional Budget Office, the Congressional Research Service, and the Senate Historical Office provide in-house expertise of a sort unknown a few decades ago. All roll call votes since the beginning of the institution are now available in machine readable form and most political scientists have the computing and statistical skills needed to analyze this mountain of quantitative data. The Senate and the House provide a fertile research arena for political scientists of all sorts.

In recent years, I have been studying another national legislature, the Norwegian Storting (Matthews and Valen 1999). Very different from either the U.S. Congress or the British Parliament, it has forced me to think about legislatures and legislative representation in new ways. For example, Norwegians believe that their national legislature should represent their nation symbolically as well as reflect their policy views. The Storting, in this sense, is one of the world's most representative legislatures, the U.S. Congress one of the least. Most Norwegians are appalled that women, blacks, Asians, and Hispanics have had such a hard time winning seats in Congress, especially the Senate.

Again, when viewed from the Norwegian perspective, the Senate appears to be one of the most unrepresentative legislatures in another sense. Visiting Americans explain that the equal representation of the states in the Senate was the price of union at the Constitutional Convention. But the large gap between our egalitarian rhetoric and the realities of Senate representation remain.

The costs and consequences of equal representation in the Senate has received surprisingly little attention from political scientists. But a legislature in which the largest states with 50 percent of the population have only 18 percent of the seats is a serious anomaly in a nation committed to the idea that equality of voting power for individual voters is mandated by the constitution!

There are signs that political scientists are beginning to work on this problem. Back in 1990 Donald J. McCrone came up with an ingenious way to grasp the magnitude of Senate misrepresentation (McCrone 1990). He hypothetically reconstitutes the Senate into a one-hundred-seat body with the states represented proportional to their population. States that receive less than one seat under this arrangement were given a seat. Then he compares the outcomes of roll call votes for this hypothetical Senate with the real thing. The results are striking. In 1981, seven of the fifteen votes classified as key votes by the *CQ Almanac* would have passed in the hypothetical Senate but were defeated in the real Senate. The next year there were six reversals out of fifteen key votes. Equality of state representation in the Senate may have different consequences at different times, but at this time it seems to provide a large obstacle that urban, minority, liberal, and Democratic groups must overcome to achieve their goals. Congress's failure to pass popular reforms in recent decades may have a simple explanation.

Finally, in 1999 Frances E. Lee and Bruce I. Oppenheimer published *Sizing up the Senate: The Unequal Consequences of Equal Representation,* the first book-length study of the topic. In this important work, they show how the size of states affects the relationships between senators and their constituents, the emergence of Senate candidates, fund-raising and elections, the senators' committee preferences, and other behaviors in Washington. They also demonstrate the small-state advantage in the distribution of federal tax dollars. The consequences of the Senate's unique apportionment scheme deserves still more attention.

While the study of the Senate is thriving, the institution itself seems to be in some trouble. Does a highly partisan, highly individualistic, easily deadlocked, and poorly representative legislature have a future? Certainly the Senate has suffered a loss of popular support in recent decades. But so have other political institutions in the United States and abroad. And it would be a mistake to assume that all the Senate's maladies are permanent. The Senate has changed in important ways in the last half century, and it will continue to do so in the future. So far it has survived massive changes in its political and economic environment while retaining much power and independence. Only future generations will learn how and how well the Senate performs in the twenty-first century.

# Bibliography

## AUTHOR INTERVIEWS

Robert B. Dove, U.S. Senate parliamentarian, Washington, D.C., June 25, 1998.
Senator Thad Cochran, Washington, D.C., July 27, 1996.
Will Feltus, former staff director, Senate Republican Conference, Washington, D.C., August 6, 1996.
Tony Fratto, communications director for Senator Rick Santorum, Washington, D.C., July 19, 1996.
Senator Rod Grams, Washington, D.C., July 29, 1996.
Senator James Inhofe, Washington, D.C., July 10, 1996.
Senator Jon Kyl, Washington, D.C., June 14, 1996.
Alex Pratt, press secretary to Senator Fred Thompson, Washington, D.C., May 3, 1996.
Laurel Pressler, chief of staff to Senator Mike DeWine, Washington, D.C., August 7, 1996.
Donald A. Ritchie, associate historian, Historical Office, U.S. Senate, Washington, D.C., June 24, 1998.
Senator Craig Thomas, Washington, D.C., May 13, 1996.
Jade C. West, staff director, U.S. Senate Republican Policy Committee, Washington, D.C., June 10, 1998.

## SENATE HISTORICAL OFFICE ORAL HISTORIES

"Gregory S. Casey: Chief of Staff of Senator Larry Craig, 1991–1996; Deputy Chief of Staff, Office of the Majority Leader, 1996; Senate Sergeant at Arms, 1996–1998."
"Roy L. Elson: Administrative Assistant to Senator Carl Hayden and Candidate for the United States Senate, 1955–1969."
"F. Nordy Hoffman: Senate Sergeant at Arms, 1975–1981."
"Pat M. Holt: Chief of Staff, Foreign Relations Committee."
"Kelly D. Johnston: Staff Director, Senate Republican Policy Committee, and Secretary of the Senate, 1992–1996."

"Carl M. Marcy: Chief of Staff, Foreign Relations Committee, 1955–1973."
"Stewart E. McClure: Chief Clerk, Senate Committee on Labor, Education, and Public Welfare."
"Roy L. McGhee: Superintendent of the Senate Periodical Press Gallery, 1973–1991."
"Floyd M. Riddick: Senate Parliamentarian."
"William A. Ridgely: Senate Financial Clerk and Assistant Secretary of the Senate."
"Darrell St. Claire: Assistant Secretary of the Senate."
"Francis R. Valeo: Secretary of the Senate."
"Rein J. Vander Zee: Assistant to the Senate Democratic Whip and Assistant Secretary of the Majority, 1961–1964."
"Jerry T. Verkler, Staff Director of the Senate Interior and Insular Affairs Committee, 1963–1974."
"Ruth Young Watt: Chief Clerk, Permanent Subcommittee on Investigations."
"Francis O. Wilcox: Chief of Staff, Foreign Relations Committee, 1947–1955."

## BOOKS, PERIODICALS, JOURNALS, AND WEB SITES

Adams, Herbert Baxter. 1887. *The Study of History in American Colleges and Universities.* Washington, D.C.: U.S. Government Printing Office.
Aldrich, John, and David Rohde. 1995. "Theories of the Party in the Legislature and the Transition to Republican Rule in the House." Political Institutions and Public Choice Working Paper 95-05. Institute for Public Policy and Social Research, Michigan State University, East Lansing, Michigan.
———. 1996. "A Tale of Two Speakers: A Comparison of Policy Making in the 100th and 104th Congresses." Political Institutions and Public Choice Working Paper 96-04. Institute for Public Policy and Social Research, Michigan State University, East Lansing, Michigan.
American Political Science Association. <http://www.apsanet.org/about/cfp/index.cfm>. Accessed: February 24, 2000.
Auerbach, Stuart. 1987. "Colleagues Tell of Chiles' 'Martyrdom' on Bill." *Washington Post*, 18 July, D2.
Bader, John, B. 1998. "Partisanship in the U.S. Senate, 1969–1996." University of California, Los Angeles. Typescript.
Bailey, Christopher J. 1988. *The Republican Party in the U.S. Senate, 1974–1984: Party Change and Institutional Development.* Manchester, U.K.: Manchester University Press.
Baker, Richard A. 1988. *The Senate of the United States: A Bicentennial History.* Malabar, Fla.: Krieger.
Baker, Richard A., and Roger H. Davidson, eds. 1991. *First among Equals: Outstanding Senate Leaders of the Twentieth Century.* Washington, D.C.: Congressional Quarterly.
Baker, Ross K. 1980. *Friend and Foe in the U.S. Senate.* New York: Free Press.
———. 1999. *Friend and Foe in the U.S. Senate.* 2nd ed. Acton, Mass.: Copley Editions.
Baumer, Donald C. 1992. "Senate Democratic Leadership in the 101st Congress." In *The Atomistic Congress: An Interpretation of Congressional Change,* ed. Allen D. Hertzke and Ronald M. Peters Jr. Armonk, N.Y.: Sharpe.

Berdahl, Clarence A. 1939. "Review of *The Senate of the United States.*" *Political Science Quarterly* 54 (June): 298.

Beth, Richard. 1995. "What We Don't Know about Filibusters." Paper presented at the annual meeting of the Western Political Science Association, Portland, Oregon, March 20–23.

Binder, Sarah A. 1996. "The Disappearing Political Center." *The Brookings Review* 15 (Fall): 36–39.

———. 1997. *Minority Rights, Majority Rule: Partisanship and the Development of Congress.* New York: Cambridge University Press.

———. 1999a. "The Dynamics of Legislative Gridlock, 1947–96." *American Political Science Review* 93:519–33.

———. 1999b. *Dynamics of Legislative Gridlock.* Manuscript, Brookings Institution and George Washington University.

Binder, Sarah A., and Steven S. Smith. 1997. *Politics or Principle? Filibustering in the United States Senate.* Washington, D.C.: Brookings.

Blechman, Barry M. 1990. *The Politics of National Security: Congress and U.S. Defense Policy.* New York: Oxford University Press.

Brady, David W., and Craig Volden. 1998. *Revolving Gridlock: Policy and Politics from Carter to Clinton.* Boulder, Colo.: Westview.

Brady, David W., Richard Brody, and David Epstein. 1989. "Heterogeneous Parties and Political Organization: The U.S. Senate, 1880–1920." *Legislative Studies Quarterly* 14 (2): 205–23.

Bresnahan, John. 1998. "Senate Leader Defends His Performance." *Roll Call,* June 11, 34.

———. 1999a. "Daschle, Lott Argue about Notification on Amendments." *Roll Call,* June 21, 28.

———. 1999b. "Lott, Nickles Deny Friction over Health Care." *Roll Call,* July 5, 1.

Brownson, Anna L., and Charles B. Brownson, eds. 1979 and 1983. *Congressional Staff Directory.* Mt. Vernon, Va.: Staff Directories.

Bullock, Charles E. III, and David W. Brady. 1983. "Party, Constituency, and Roll-call Voting in the U.S. Senate." *Legislative Studies Quarterly* 8 (1): 29–43.

Burgess, John W. 1883. "Methods of Historical Study in Columbia College." In *Methods of Teaching History,* ed. G. Stanley Hall. Boston: Ginn, Heath.

Burns, James MacGregor. 1963. *The Deadlock of Democracy: Four Party Politics in America.* Englewood Cliffs, N.J.: Prentice Hall.

Byrd, Robert C. 1988. *The Senate, 1789–1989: Addresses on the History of the United States Senate.* Vol. 1. Washington, D.C.: U.S. Government Printing Office.

———. 1991. *The Senate, 1789–1989: Addresses on the History of the United States Senate.* Vol. 2. Washington, D.C.: Government Printing Office.

Cannon, Lou. 1977. "Hayakawa's Style." *Washington Post,* 27 February, A1.

Carroll, Holbert N. 1966. *The House of Representatives and Foreign Affairs.* Boston: Little, Brown.

Cassata, Donna. 1997a. "Lott's Task: Balance the Demands of His Chamber and His Party." *Congressional Quarterly Weekly Report,* 8 March, 567–71.

———. 1997b. "Sen. Jesse Helms, R-N.C.," *Congressional Quarterly Weekly Report,* 6 December, 2968.

Chirac, Jacques, Tony Blair, and Gerhard Schroeder. 1999. "A Treaty We All Need." *New York Times*, 8 October, A21.

Cohen, Richard E. 1996. "The Senate Broker." *National Journal*, 21 December, 2733.

*Congressional Record*. 1967. 90th Cong., 1st sess., vol. 113, pt. 19.

——. 1999. 106th Cong., 1st sess., vol. 145, no. 8.

——. 1999. 106th Cong., 1st sess., vol. 145, no. 70.

——. 1999. 106th Cong., 1st sess., vol. 145, no. 94.

——. 1999. 106th Cong., 1st sess., vol. 145, no. 106.

——. 1999. 106th Cong., 1st sess., vol. 145, no. 136.

——. 1999. 106th Cong., 1st sess., vol. 145, no. 137.

——. 1999. 106th Cong., 1st sess., vol. 145, no. 138.

——. 1999. 106th Cong., 1st sess., vol. 145, no. 139.

——. 1999. 106th Cong., 1st sess., vol. 145, no. 140.

——. 1999. 106th Cong., 1st sess., vol. 145, no. 141.

——. 1999. 106th Cong., 1st sess., vol. 145, no. 142.

——. 1999. 106th Cong., 1st sess., vol. 145, no. 143.

——. 1999. 106th Cong., 1st sess., vol. 145, no. 144.

——. 1999. 106th Cong., 1st sess., vol. 145, no. 152.

*Congressional Quarterly Weekly Report*. 1999. "Party Unity Background." 11 December, 2993.

Cook, Timothy E. 1997. *Governing with the News*. Chicago: University of Chicago Press.

——. 1999. "Senators and Reporters Revisited." Paper presented at the Robert J. Dole Institute for Public Service and Public Policy Conference on Civility and Deliberation in the United States Senate, Washington, D.C., July 16.

Cox, Gary W., and Mathew D. McCubbins. 1993. *Legislative Leviathan: Party Government in the House*. Berkeley: University of California Press.

Crook, Sara Brandes, and John R. Hibbing. 1997. "A Not-so-distant Mirror: The 17th Amendment and Congressional Change." *American Political Science Review* 91 (December): 845–53.

Crowley, Scott G. "The Effects of the Sixteenth and Seventeenth Amendments in Changing the Role of the States in the Federal System." *Brigham Young University Law Review* (1989): 161–73.

Dangerfield, Royden. 1940. "Review of *The Senate of the United States*." *The American Journal of International Law* 34:374–75.

Davidson, Roger H. 1985. "Senate Leaders: Janitors for an Untidy Chamber?" In *Congress Reconsidered*. 3rd ed. Ed. Lawrence C. Dodd and Bruce I. Oppenheimer. Washington, D.C.: CQ Press.

——. 1989. "The Senate: If Everyone Leads, Who Follows?" In *Congress Reconsidered*. 4th ed. Ed. Lawrence C. Dodd and Bruce I. Oppenheimer. Washington, D.C.: CQ Press.

Davidson, Roger H., ed. 1992. *The Postreform Congress*. New York: St. Martin's.

Davidson, Roger H., and Colton C. Campbell. 2000. "The Irony of the 105th Congress and its Legacy." In *The United States National Election and Transition of 1996–1997: Nominating, Electing, and Organizing Congress and the Presidency*, ed. Harvey L. Schantz. New York: Garland.

Davidson, Roger H., and Walter J. Oleszek. 1998. *Congress and Its Members*. 6th ed. Washington, D.C.: CQ Press.

Daynes, Byron W. 1971. "The Impact of the Direct Election of Senators on the Political System." Ph.D. diss., University of Chicago.

Deering, Christopher J. 1999. "Learning to Legislate: Committees in the Republican Congress." In *New Majority or Old Minority? The Impact of Republicans on Congress*, ed. Nicol C. Rae and Colton C. Campbell. Lanham, Md.: Rowman & Littlefield.

Deering, Christopher J., and Steven S. Smith. 1997. *Committees in Congress*. 3rd ed. Washington, D.C.: CQ Press.

Dewar, Helen. 1989. "Senate Foreign Relations Panel Founders." *Washington Post*, 10 October, A1.

———. 1995. "Senate GOP Urged to Shift Power, Solidify Policy Positions in Advance." *Washington Post*, 17 May, A21.

Dewar, Helen, and Michael Grunwald. 1999. "HMO Bills Suffer Setbacks on Hill; Parties Squabble for Lead Position." *Washington Post*, 24 June, A8.

Dirksen, Everett M. 1961. Radio/TV script, April 16.

Doherty, Carroll J. 1997. "Helms Calls Weld Unacceptable as Ambassador to Mexico." *Congressional Quarterly Weekly Report*, 7 June, 1328.

———. 1999. "How Will Congress Navigate the New Media Maelstrom?" *Congressional Quarterly Weekly Report*, 20 March, 682–86.

Doherty, Carroll, J., and Jeffrey L. Katz. 1998. "Bucking up: Many Democrats Thrive after Shock of '94." *Congressional Quarterly Weekly Report*, 4 July, 1818–24.

Evans, C. Lawrence. 1999. "How Senators Decide: An Exploration." Paper presented at the Norman Thomas Conference on Senate Exceptionalism, Vanderbilt University, Nashville, Tennessee, October 21–23.

Evans, C. Lawrence, and Walter J. Oleszek. 1997. *Congress under Fire: Reform Politics and the Republican Majority*. Boston: Houghton Mifflin.

———. 1999. "The Strategic Context of Senate Deliberation." Paper presented at the Robert J. Dole Institute for Public Service and Public Policy Conference on Civility and Deliberation in the United States Senate, Washington, D.C., July 16.

Fenno, Richard F., Jr. 1976. "Observation, Context, and Sequence in the Study of Politics." *American Political Science Review* 80 (March): 3–15.

———. 1982. *The United States Senate: A Bicameral Perspective*. Washington, D.C.: American Enterprise Institute.

———. 1995. "Senate." In *The Encyclopedia of the United States Congress*. Vol. 4. Ed. Donald C. Bacon, Roger H. Davidson, and Morton Keller. New York: Simon & Schuster.

Fessler, Pamela. 1992. "Helms Sweeps through Panel, Fires Nine GOP Staff Aides." *Congressional Quarterly Weekly Report*, 11 January.

Fite, Gilbert C. 1991. *Richard B. Russell, Jr., Senator from Georgia*. Chapel Hill: University of North Carolina Press.

Foerstel, Karen. 1999a. "GOP, Industry Try to Shift Attention from 'Patient Rights' to Aid for Uninsured." *Congressional Quarterly Weekly Report*, 8 May, 1079–80.

———. 1999b. "Debate on Managed Care Legislation Diverges along Familiar Lines." *Congressional Quarterly Weekly Report*, 20 March, 701.

Foley, Michael. 1980. *The New Senate: Liberal Influence on a Conservative Institution, 1959–1972.* New Haven, Conn.: Yale University Press.

Franck, Thomas M., and Edward Weisband. 1979. *Foreign Policy by Congress.* New York: Oxford University Press.

Galloway, George B. 1946. *Congress at the Crossroads.* New York: Thomas Y. Crowell.

——. 1950. *Congress and Democracy: A Lecture Delivered at the Ohio State University, February 27, 1950.* Columbia, Ohio.

——. 1951. "Proposed Reforms in Congressional Investigations." *University of Chicago Law Review* 18 (Spring): 478–502.

——. 1952. *Next Steps in Congressional Reform.* Urbana: University of Illinois Institute of Government and Public Affairs.

——. 1956. *Congressional Reorganization Revisited.* College Park: University of Maryland Bureau of Government Research.

Gamm, Gerald, and Steven S. Smith. 1999. "Emergence of Senate Party Leadership." Paper presented at the Norman Thomas Conference on Senate Exceptionalism, Vanderbilt University, Nashville, Tennessee, October 21–23.

Gettinger, Stephen, ed. 1999. "Between the Lines." *Congressional Quarterly Weekly Report,* 20 February, 424–25.

Greenberg Quilan Research. 1999. *Democracy Corps Poll.*

Goshko, John M. 1985. "Virtuoso Performance Surprises Hill." *Washington Post,* 3 November, A12.

Hamilton, Alexander, James Madison, and John Jay. 1961. Reprint. *The Federalist Papers,* ed. Clinton Rossiter. New York: Mentor.

Hatfield, Mark O, et al. 1997. *Vice Presidents of the United States, 1789–1993.* Washington, D.C.: U.S. Government Printing Office.

Haynes, George H. 1894. *Representation and Suffrage in Massachusetts, 1620–1691.* Baltimore: Johns Hopkins University Press.

——. 1896. "A Know Nothing Legislature." *Annual Report of the American Historical Association for 1896.* Washington, D.C.: U.S. Government Printing Office.

——. 1900. "Representation in State Legislatures." *Annals of the American Academy of Political and Social Science* 15 (March): 204–35.

——. 1906. *The Election of Senators.* New York: Henry Holt.

——. 1914. "The Changing Senate." *North American Review* 200 (August): 231.

——. 1924. "The Senate: New Style." *Atlantic Monthly* 134 (August): 252.

——. 1938. *The Senate of the United States.* 2 vols. Boston: Houghton Mifflin.

Henkin, Louis. 1972. *Foreign Affairs and the Constitution.* New York: Norton.

Henry, Ed. 1999. "Daschle Rakes in $1.3 Million." *Roll Call,* June 10, 1.

Hibbing, John R., and Elizabeth Theiss-Morse. 1995. *Congress as Public Enemy.* New York: Cambridge University Press.

Holt, W., Stull, ed. 1938. *Historical Scholarship in the United States, 1876–1901: As Revisited in the Correspondence of Herbert B. Adams.* Baltimore: Johns Hopkins University Press.

Hook, Janet, and Donna Cassata. 1995. "Low-key Revolt May Spur Thurmond to Give Colleagues a Freer Hand." *Congressional Quarterly Weekly Report,* 11 February, 466.

Hosansky, David. 1995. "GOP Conference Will Consider Limits on Seniority System." *Congressional Quarterly Weekly Report*, 20 May, 1392.

Hoxie, Gordon R., et al. 1955. *A History of the Faculty of Political Science Columbia University*. New York: Columbia University Press.

Huitt, Ralph K. 1954. "The Congressional Committee: A Case Study." *American Political Science Review* 48 (June): 340–65.

———. 1965. "The Internal Distribution of Influence: The Senate." In *The Congress and America's Future*, ed. David Truman. Englewood Cliffs, N.J.: Prentice Hall.

Hurley, Patricia A., and Rick K. Wilson. 1989. "Partisan Voting Patterns in the U.S. Senate, 1877–1986." *Legislative Studies Quarterly* 14 (2): 225–50.

Jones, Charles O. 1994. *The Presidency in a Separated System*. Washington, D.C.: Brookings.

Katzenbach, Nicholas deB. 1989. "The Constitution and Foreign Policy." In *A Workable Government? The Constitution after 200 Years*, ed. Burke Marshall. New York: Norton.

Kiewiet, D. Roderick, and Mathew D. McCubbins. 1991. *The Logic of Delegation: Congressional Parties and the Appropriations Process*. Chicago: University of Chicago Press.

Kirchhoff, Sue. 1999. "Insurers' Latest Advertising Blitz May Outdo 'Harry and Louise.'" *Congressional Quarterly Weekly Report*, 17 July, 1718–19.

Koszczuk, Jackie. 1996. "Democrats' Resurgence Fueled by Pragmatism." *Congressional Quarterly Weekly Report*, 4 May, 1205–10.

Krehbiel, Keith. 1998. *Pivotal Politics: A Theory of U.S. Lawmaking*. Chicago: University of Chicago Press.

Krikorian, Greg. 1999. "California and the West; Lawmakers Flock to Silicon Valley for Fund-raisers." *Los Angeles Times*, 28 November, A28.

Krutz, Glen. Forthcoming. "Tactical Maneuvering on Omnibus Bills in Congress." *American Journal of Political Science*.

———. Forthcoming. "Getting around Gridlock: The Effect of Omnibus Utilization on Legislative Productivity." *Legislative Studies Quarterly*.

Laski, Harold J. 1939. "Review of *The Senate of the United States*." *The Nation* (April): 384.

Lee, Frances E., and Bruce I. Oppenheimer. 1999. *Sizing up the Senate: The Unequal Consequences of Equal Representation*. Chicago: University of Chicago Press.

Lindsay, James M. 1999. "End of an Era: Congress and Foreign Policy after the Cold War." In *Domestic Sources of American Foreign Policy: Insights and Evidence*, ed. Eugene R. Wittkopf and James M. McCormick. Lanham, Md.: Rowman & Littlefield.

Link, Arthur, ed. 1983. *The Papers of Woodrow Wilson*. Princeton: Princeton University Press.

Loomis, Burdett A. 1988. *The New American Politician*. New York: Basic.

———. 1998. *The Contemporary Congress*. 2nd ed. New York: St. Martin's.

Luce, Robert. 1927. "Review of *The American Senate*." *American Political Science Review* 21 (February): 178–79.

Madison, James. 1999. *Writings*. The Library of America. New York: Penguin Putnam.

Malcolm, Ellen R. 1999. "Reaffirming Our Commitment to Choice." *Notes from EMILY* (December), 7.

Manley, John F. 1973. "The Conservative Coalition in Congress." *American Behavioral Scientist*, 17 December, 223–47.

Mann, Robert. 1996. *The Walls of Jericho: Lyndon Johnson, Hubert Humphrey, Richard Russell, and the Struggle for Civil Rights.* New York: Harcourt Brace.

Matthews, Donald R. 1960. *U.S. Senators and Their World.* Chapel Hill: University of North Carolina Press.

Matthews, Donald R., and Henry Valen. 1999. *Parliamentary Representation: The Case of the Norwegian Storting.* Columbus: Ohio State University Press.

Mayhew, David R. 1974. *Congress: The Electoral Connection.* New Haven, Conn.: Yale University Press.

McCrone, Donald J. 1990. "The Representational Consequences of State Equality in the U.S. Senate." Paper presented at the annual meeting of the Western Political Science Association, Newport Beach, April 15–17.

Mitchell, Alison. 1997. "Return of Partisanship to Capitol Hill." *New York Times*, 14 November, A1.

Nelson, Garrison. 1993. *Committees in the U.S. Congress, 1947–1992.* Washington, D.C.: Congressional Quarterly.

Newlin Carney, Eliza. 1997. "Running Interference." *National Journal*, 22 November, 2360–63.

*New York Times.* 1970. 28 November, 30.

Oleszek, Walter J. 1995. "Senate Leadership." In *The Encyclopedia of the United States Congress.* Vol. 3. Ed. Donald C. Bacon, Roger H. Davidson, and Morton Keller. New York: Simon & Schuster.

———. 1996. *Congressional Procedure and the Policy Process.* 4th ed. Washington, D.C.: CQ Press.

O'Neill, Tip. 1987. *Man of the House.* New York: Random House.

Oppenheimer, Bruce. 1985. "Changing Time Constraints on Congress: Historical Perspectives on the Use of Cloture." In *Congress Reconsidered.* 3rd ed. Ed. Lawrence C. Dodd and Bruce I. Oppenheimer. Washington, D.C.: CQ Press.

Ornstein, Norman J., Thomas E. Mann, and Michael J. Malbin. 1996. *Vital Statistics on Congress, 1995–1996.* Washington, D.C.: American Enterprise Institute Press.

———. 1998. *Vital Statistics on Congress, 1997–1998.* Washington, D.C.: Congressional Quarterly.

———. 2000. *Vital Statistics on Congress, 1999–2000.* Washington, D.C.: American Enterprise Institute Press.

Ornstein, Norman J., Thomas E. Mann, and Robert Peabody. 1993. "The U.S. Senate in an Era of Change." In *Congress Reconsidered.* 5th ed. Ed. Lawrence C. Dodd and Bruce I. Oppenheimer. Washington, D.C.: CQ Press.

Ornstein, Norman J., Robert L. Peabody, and David W. Rohde. 1985. "The Senate through the 1980s: Cycles of Change." In *Congress Reconsidered.* 3rd ed. Ed. Lawrence C. Dodd and Bruce I. Oppenheimer. Washington, D.C.: CQ Press.

———. 1993. "The U.S. Senate in an Era of Change." In *Congress Reconsidered.* 5th ed. Ed. Lawrence C. Dodd and Bruce I. Oppenheimer. Washington, D.C.: CQ Press.

———. 1997. "The U.S. Senate: Toward the 21st Century." In *Congress Reconsidered.* 6th ed. Ed. Lawrence C. Dodd and Bruce I. Oppenheimer. Washington, D.C.: CQ Press.

Patterson, Samuel C. 1995. "The Congressional Parties in the United States." Paper presented at the annual meeting of the American Political Science Association Conference, Chicago, April 15–17.

Patterson, Samuel C., and Gregory A. Caldeira. 1987. "Party Voting in the United States Congress." *British Journal of Political Science* 18:111–31.

Patterson, Samuel C., and Anthony Mughan, eds. 1999. *Senates: Bicameralism in the Contemporary World*. Columbus: Ohio State University Press.

Peabody, Robert L. 1981. "Senate Party Leadership from the 1950s to the 1980s." In *Understanding Congressional Leadership*, ed. Frank H. Mackaman. Washington, D.C.: CQ Press.

Pepper, Claude. 1939. "Review of *The Senate of the United States*." *Harvard Law Review* 52 (April): 1026–27.

Petrocik, John R. 1996. "Issue Ownership in Presidential Elections, with a 1980 Case Study." *American Journal of Political Science* 40:825–50.

Pomper, Miles. 1998. "The New Faces of Foreign Policy." *Congressional Quarterly Weekly Report*, 28 November, 3203–8.

Poole, Keith T., and Howard Rosenthal. 1997. *Congress: A Political-economic History of Roll Call Voting*. New York: Oxford University Press.

Preston, Mark. 1999. "With Fourth of July Recess over, Fireworks Begin." *Roll Call*, July 12, 38.

Rae, Nicol C. 1994. *Southern Democrats*. New York: Oxford University Press.

———. 1998. *Conservative Reformers: The Freshmen Republicans and the Lessons of the 104th Congress*. Armonk, N.Y.: M. E. Sharpe.

Riddick, Floyd. 1949. *The United States Congress Organization and Procedure*. Manassas, Va.: National Capital.

Ripley, Randall B. 1969. *Power in the Senate*. New York: St. Martin's.

———. 1985. "Power in the Post–World War II Senate." In *Studies of Congress*, ed. Glenn R. Parker. Washington, D.C.: CQ Press.

Ritchie, Donald A. 1982. "Beyond the *Congressional Record*: Congress and Oral History." *The Maryland Historian* 13 (Fall/Winter): 7–16.

———. 1991. "Alben W. Beckley: The President's Man." In *First among Equals: Outstanding Senate Leaders of the Twentieth Century*, ed. Richard A. Baker and Roger H. Davidson. Washington, D.C.: Congressional Quarterly.

———. 1997. *A History of the United States Senate Republican Policy Committee, 1947–1997*. Washington, D.C.: U.S. Government Printing Office.

———. 1998. "The Senate of Mike Mansfield." *Montana: The Magazine of Western History* 48 (Winter): 50–62.

Rohde, David W. 1991. *Parties and Leaders in the Postreform House*. Chicago: University of Chicago Press.

———. 1992. "Electoral Forces, Political Agenda, and Partisanship in the House and Senate." In *The Postreform Congress*, ed. Roger H. Davidson. New York: St. Martin's.

Rohde, David W., Norman O. Ornstein, and Robert L. Peabody. 1985. "Political Change and Legislative Norms in the U.S. Senate, 1957–1974." In *Studies of Congress*, ed. Glenn R. Parker. Washington, D.C.: CQ Press.

Rogers, Lindsay. 1916. *The Postal Power of Congress: A Study in Constitutional Expression.* Baltimore: Johns Hopkins University Press.

———. 1917. *America's Case against Germany.* New York: Dutton.

———. 1934. *Crisis Government.* New York: Norton.

———. 1939. "Review of *The Senate of the United States.*" *Saturday Review of Literature,* 4 February, 19.

———. 1941. "The Staffing of Congress." *Political Science Quarterly* 56 (March): 1–22.

———. 1949. *The Pollsters: Public Opinion, Politics, and Democratic Leadership.* New York: Knopf.

———. 1959. "The Filibuster Debate: Barrier Against Steamrollers." *The Reporter,* 8 January, 22.

———. 1968 [1926]. *The American Senate.* New York: Johnson Reprints.

Sellers, Patrick J. 1999a. "Leaders and Followers in the U.S. Senate." Paper presented at the Norman Thomas Conference on Senate Exceptionalism, Vanderbilt University, Nashville, Tennessee, October 21–23.

———. 1999b. "Winning Media Coverage in the U.S. Congress." Paper presented at the Norman Thomas Conference on Senate Exceptionalism, Vanderbilt University, Nashville, Tennessee, October 21–23.

———. 2000. "Promoting the Party Message in the U.S. Senate." Paper presented at the annual meeting of the Midwest Political Science Association, Chicago, April 15–17.

"Seventy Years of the Worcester Polytechnic Institute." <http://www.wpi.edu/Academics/ Library/Archives/SeventyYears/page143.html>. Accessed: December 28, 1999.

Shepsle, Kenneth. 1989. "The Changing Textbook Congress." In *Can the Government Govern?,* ed. John Chubb and Paul E. Peterson. Washington, D.C. Brookings.

Shepsle, Kenneth, and Barry Weingast. 1994. "Positive Theories of Congressional Institutions." *Legislative Studies Quarterly* 19:149–80.

Shelley, Mack C. 1983. *The Permanent Majority: The Conservative Coalition in the United States Congress.* Tuscaloosa: University of Alabama Press.

Silverberg, David. 1999. "Nasty, Brutish and Short: The CTBT Debate." *The Hill,* 8 December, 16.

Sinclair, Barbara. 1982. *Congressional Realignment: 1925–1978.* Austin: University of Texas Press.

———. 1989. *The Transformation of the U.S. Senate.* Baltimore: Johns Hopkins University Press.

———. 1995. *Legislators, Leaders and Lawmaking.* Baltimore: Johns Hopkins University Press.

———. 1997. *Unorthodox Lawmaking.* Washington, D.C.: CQ Press.

———. 1998. "The Plot Thickens: Congress and the President." In *Great Theatre: The American Congress in Action,* ed. Herbert Weisberg and Samuel Patterson. New York: Cambridge University Press.

———. 1999a. "Partisan Imperatives and Institutional Constraints: Republican Party Leadership in the House and Senate." In *New Majority or Old Minority? The Impact of Republicans on Congress,* ed. Nicol C. Rae and Colton C. Campbell. Lanham, Md.: Rowman & Littlefield.

———. 1999b. "Co-equal Partner: The U.S. Senate." In *Senates: Bicameralism in the Contemporary World*, ed. Samuel C. Patterson and Anthony Mughan. Columbus: Ohio State University Press.

———. 1999c. "The Sixty-vote Senate: Strategies, Process and Outcomes." Paper presented at the Norman Thomas Conference on Senate Exceptionalism, Vanderbilt University, Nashville, Tennessee, October 21–23.

———. 1999d. "Individualism, Partisanship and Cooperation in the Senate." Paper presented at the Robert J. Dole Institute for Public Service and Public Policy Conference on Civility and Deliberation in the United States Senate, Washington, D.C., July 16.

———. 2000. "Hostile Partners: The President, Congress and Lawmaking in the Partisan 1990s." In *Polarized Politics: Congress and the President in a Partisan Era*, ed. Jon Bond and Richard Fleisher. Washington, D.C.: CQ Press.

Smith, Steven S. 1989. *Call to Order: Floor Politics in the House and Senate*. Washington, D.C.: Brookings.

———. 1993. "Forces of Change in Senate Party Leadership and Organization." In *Congress Reconsidered*. 5th ed. Ed. Lawrence C. Dodd and Bruce I Oppenheimer. Washington, D.C.: CQ Press.

Smith, Steven S., and Marcus Flathman. 1989. "Managing the Senate Floor: Complex Unanimous Consent Agreements Since the 1950s." *Legislative Studies Quarterly* 15 (3): 349–74.

Somit, Albert, and Joseph Tanenhaus. 1982. *The Development of American Political Science: From Burgess to Behavioralism*. New York: Irvington.

Stewart, Charles III, and Jonathan Woon. 1998. *Congressional Committee Assignments, 103rd to 105th Congresses, 1993–1998*. U.S. Senate, 20 July.

Sundquist, James. 1968. *Politics and Policy*. Washington, D.C. Brookings.

Swift, Elaine K. 1996. *The Making of an American Senate: Reconstitutive Change in Congress, 1787–1841*. Ann Arbor: University of Michigan Press.

Thorson, Greg, and Tasina Nitzschke. 1999. "When the Majority Won't Listen: The Use of the Senate Filibuster by the Minority Party." Paper presented at the annual meeting of the Midwest Political Science Association, Chicago, April 15–17.

Thurber, James A. 1997. "Centralization, Devolution, and Turf Protection in the Congressional Budget Process." In *Congress Reconsidered*. 6th ed. Ed. Lawrence C. Dodd and Bruce I Oppenheimer. Washington, D.C.: CQ Press.

*Time Magazine*. 1962. "The Leader." 14 September, 27.

Torcom, Jean. 1973. "Minority Leadership in the United States Senate: The Role and Style of Everett Dirksen." Ph.D. diss., Johns Hopkins University.

Towell, Pat. 1998. "Will Warner Challenge the White House from the Helm of Armed Services?" *Congressional Quarterly Weekly Report*, 21 November, 3181–83.

Turner, Robert F. 1989. "Restoring the 'Rule of Law': Reflections on the War Powers Resolution at Fifteen." In *The War Power after 200 Years: Congress and the President in a Constitutional Impasse*, 100th Congress, 2d. sess. Washington, D.C.: U.S. Government Printing Office.

U.S. Congress. 1946. Joint Committee on the Organization of Congress. *Organization of Congress*. Senate Report 1011. 79th Cong., 2nd sess., March 4.

Uslaner, Eric M. 1993. *The Decline of Comity in Congress*. Ann Arbor: University of Michigan Press.

Warren, Charles. 1928. *The Supreme Court in United States History*. Boston: Little, Brown.

Washington, H. A., ed. 1854. *The Writings of Thomas Jefferson*. Vol. 4. Washington, D.C.: n.p.

*Washington Post*. 1996. 18–21 January.

———. 1999. 24 June, A8.

White, William S. 1957. *Citadel: The Story of the U.S. Senate*. New York: Harper & Brothers.

# Index

*Italic* numbers refer to illustrations and tables.

abortion rights: PBA and, 35–36, 37–38
Abraham, Spencer, 9, 110
Accountability Act, 145
Adams, Herbert Baxter: political science
  and, 147–48
administrative assistants: staff issues and,
  138
Africa trade bill, 118, 122
agricultural appropriations, 81
airplane travel: and deliberations, affects
  on, 134
Aldrich, John, 110
ambassador nominations: FRC and, 43
amendment tree: CFR and, 122; charts
  and, 126n10; Democratic Party and,
  126n5; Ed-Flex Act and, 122; gun-
  control legislation and, 122; juvenile
  justice reform and, 114; lockbox bill
  and, 86, 122; majority leaders and, 87,
  121–22; majority party and, 122;
  media coverage and, 122; minority
  leaders and, 86, 121–22; minority
  party and, 122; 103rd Congress and,
  86; party politics and, 121–23, *123,*
  125, 126; Y2K Act and, 122
American Federation of Labor and
  Congress of Industrial Organizations
  (AFL-CIO), 83
American Historical Association, 148
American Political Science Association
  (APSA), 148, 160, 166, 167

*The American Senate* (Rogers), 150, 151,
  153
Armed Services Committee (ASC):
  authorizations and, 48; history of, 51;
  ideology and, *53,* 54–55, *55;*
  individualism issues and, 58;
  membership turnover and, 52–55;
  polarization and, *56*
arms-reduction agreements: and
  observers, senators as, 27

Bader, John B.: on voting trends, 7
Baker, Howard H., Jr., 54, 95
bargaining tactics: CTBT and, 26–28
Baucus, Max, 70
Bayh, Evan: PBA and, 38
Bennett, Robert: CFR and, 32
Biden, Joseph R., Jr.: courtesy and, 29;
  CTBT and, 24, 25, 27, 39; FRC and,
  124; PBA and, 38; policy agendas
  and, 59
Binder, Sarah A., 5, 45, 50, *56,* 96
Blair, Tony: CTBT and, 25
Bond, Christopher S. "Kit," 111
Boxer, Barbara: CFR and, 31; PBA and,
  36, 37, 38, 39
Breaux, John: PBA and, 38
Brownback, Sam: CFR and, 33
budget issues: minority leaders and, 96–98
Burgess, John W.: political science and,
  147–48, 166

Burke, Sheila, 71

Byrd, Robert C.: amendment tree and, 86; constituencies and, 93; *CQWR* and, 99, 101; CTBT and, 24, 28; leadership issues and, 67, 70; media coverage and, 99, 101; minority leaders and, 94, 95; "morning business" and, 126n1; PACs and, 102; PBA and, 38

campaign finance issues: education campaign pamphlet and, 158

campaign finance reform (CFR): advocates for, 30–31; amendments and, 32; amendment tree and, 122; cloture provision and, 120; defensive strategies and, 31–32; deliberations and, 21–22, 30–34; majority party strategies and, 86; 105th Congress, 86; party politics and, 33–34, *40, 42*

Case, Clifford, 54

Casey, Gregory S.: on patronage positions, 145

Chafee, John H.: CFR and, 33; CTBT and, 29; patients' bill of rights and, 80; PBA and, 38

Chiles, Lawton, 66

Chirac, Jacques: CTBT and, 25

*Citadel: The Story of the U.S. Senate* (White), 139

civil rights movement: regionalism and, 4

civil service: staff issues and, 137

Clinton, Bill: ambassador nominations and, 43; CTBT and, 22, 23, 26, 44, 124; minority leaders and, 105; PBA and, 35, 36

cloture provision: CFR and, 120; Democratic Party and, 88, 118–19, *119;* education bills and, 120; GOP and, *119;* history of, 45, 50; lockbox bill and, 120, 126n9; majority leaders and, 116; majority party strategies and, 86; managed health care issues and, 119–20; party politics and, 116, 118–21, *119,* 125; political scientists and, 150–51; Rule XXII and, 150, 151; "sunshine" reform and, 131; votes and, 164

Coats, Dan, 78

Cochran, Thad: on Republican Conference reforms, 10–11

coffee agreement: party politics and, 137

Collins, Susan, 33, 38, 78, 84

Columbine High School shootings, 84, 85, 114

committee system: decentralization and, 141; executive agencies and, 153, 163; House and, 165; majority leadership issues and, 141–42; offices and, 163–64; party politics and, 165; political scientists and, 142; reforms and, 131, 136–37, 142, 152, 162, 164–65; Sixty-fifth Congress and, 152; staff issues and, 139–40; "sunshine" reform and, 140. *See also* staff issues

Comprehensive Test Ban Treaty (CTBT): bargaining tactics and, 26–28; deliberations and, 21–29; Democratic Party and, 22, 124, 125; GOP and, 22–23; and impeachment hearings effects on, 28, 29; 107th Congress and, 23; UCA and, 124

computers: impeachment hearings and, 144; staff issues and, 144; staff salaries and, 139

Congress: administrative centralization and, 162–63; foreign policy and, 57; ideology and, 52–53, 60n11; liberalism and, 52, 54, 55; membership turnover and, 52; political scientists and, 167–68; and presidents, expediency of, 163; reforms and, 162; staff issues and, 135–36. *See also under* number of session

*Congress at the Crossroads* (Galloway), 161

Congressional Accountability Act of 1995: and salaries, congressional, 131–32; staff issues and, 144–45

*Congressional Quarterly Almanac,* 167
*Congressional Quarterly Weekly Reports
 (CQWR),* 99, 101
Connally, Tom: foreign policy and, 136
Conrad, Kent: PBA and, 38
conservatism: leadership issues and, 66
constituencies: leadership issues and,
 94–96; minority leaders and, *93,*
 93–94; senators and, 159; television
 coverage and, 144; voting trends and, 7
Cook, Timothy E., 98–99
courtesy, senatorial: deliberations and, 16,
 28–29, 41–42; impeachment hearings
 and, 41
Coverdell, Pat, 26, 29, 108, 110
Craig, Larry: on leadership issues, 75, 88
C-SPAN, 167
C-SPAN2, 81
Cuba: ships and, 66

*Daily Report,* 74
Danforth, John C., 54
Daschle, Tom: amendment tree and, 114,
 121–22; CFR and, 32, 34; *CQWR*
 and, 101; CTBT and, 27; juvenile
 justice reform and, 114; leadership
 issues and, 75; media coverage and,
 99, 101, 105; minority leaders and,
 14–15, 94, 95, 103, 104–5; minority
 leadership issues and, 71; PACs and,
 102; party politics and, 11; patients
 bill of rights and, 78, 81–82; PBA
 and, 38
Dawes, Charles: cloture provision and,
 150–51
debates. *See* deliberations
Deconcini, Dennis: individualism and, 50
Deering, Christopher J., 10
deliberations: airplane travel and, 135;
 CFR and, 21–22, 30–34; cloture
 provision and, 45; courtesy, senatorial
 and, 28–29; CTBT and, 21–29;
 leadership issues and, 65–67; 106th
 Congress and, 21, 22; PAB and,
 21–22, 34–38; party politics and,

39–42, *40*; radio broadcasts and, 164;
 scheduling and, 39; television coverage
 and, 131, 143–44; time constraints
 and, 40; UCA and, 68–69
Democratic Party: amendment tree and,
 126n5; cloture provision, 88; cloture
 provision and, 118–19, *119*; CTBT
 and, 22, 29, 124, 125; education
 policies and, 110; ideology and, *53;*
 individualism issues and, 11;
 leadership issues and, 14; liberalism
 and, 11; lockbox bill and, 120; 104th
 Congress and, 11, 110; 105th
 Congress and, 11; 106th Congress,
 15, 68; party collective action and, 74,
 75; party politics and, 11, *12,* 110–13,
 *113;* and party unity, plan for, 15–16,
 *15–16;* patients' bill of rights and,
 77–85; regionalism and, *3;* Rule XIV
 and, 116; UCA and, 125
Democratic Policy Committee (DPC),
 74, 142–43
DeWine, Mike, 36, 110
direct elections, 132, 152–53, 155, 157
Dirkson, Everett: constituencies and, 94;
 on individualism issues, 16; leadership
 issues and, 91, 92–93; media coverage
 and, 99, 103–4; minority leaders and,
 94, 95, 103–4
Dodd, Christopher J., 49, 104
Dole, Robert: *CQWR* and, 99;
 individualism and, 67; institutionism
 and, 13; media coverage and, 96, 98,
 99, 101; minority leaders and, 94, 95,
 96; PACs and, 102
Dorgan, Byron: party politics and, 124;
 PBA and, 38; and Senate, character of,
 88
Durbin, Richard: CFR and, 30; PBA and,
 35, 37

Ed-Flex Act: amendment tree and, 86,
 122; cloture and, 121; Democratic
 Party and, 112; GOP and, 111; party
 politics and, *113;* UCA and, 88, 121

education policies: cloture provision and, 120; Democratic Party and, 110, 111; 106th Congress and, 111

*The Election of Senators* (Haynes), 155

election system: direct elections and, 132, 152–53, 155, 157; and judges, federal, 165; party politics and, 18; reforms and, 155–56; state size and, 156–57

electoral politics: membership turnover and, 45; minority leaders and, 101–2

electronic voting, 163

Elson, Roy L.: lobbyists and, 141

e-mail system: impeachment hearings and, 144

EMILY's List, 38

Everett Dirksen Building: committee system and, 163

executive agencies: committee system and, 153, 163

executive branch: and faith in, 142; FRC and, 140–41; investigations and, 151; staff issues and, 135

Fair Labor Standard Act: staff issues and, 144

Family and Medical Leave Act: staff issues and, 144

federal appropriations: Olympic Games and, 32

federal grants: WTO and, 32

Feingold, Russell: CFR and, 30, 39

Felton, Rebecca, 134

filibusters: foreign policy and, 50; leadership issues and, 66; minority leaders and, 92, 96, *97*; national security policy and, 50; party politics and, 7–8

floor rules *See* deliberations

foreign policy: Congress and, 57; consolidated deterrence and, 46, 47, 60n5; influences on making, 43; membership turnover and, 50–55, 59; and observers, senators as, 27–28; policy agendas and, 57, *58*, 59; presidential powers and, 47, 60n3;

and Senate, role of, 44; Seventy-third Congress and, 48; staff issues and, 135–36

Foreign Relations Committee (FRC): ambassador nominations and, 43; authorizations and, 48; executive branch and, 140–41; history of, 51; ideology and, 52–53, *53*, 53–54, *54*; individualism issues and, 58; liberalism and, 52, 54, *54*; membership turnover and, 52–55; negative legislative power and, 51, 59; party politics and, *56*; policy agendas and, 59; staff issues and, 137–38; "sunshine" reform and, 140; television coverage and, 143

freshmen "fly-arounds," 9

Freshmen Focus groups, 109

freshmen senators, 8, 9, 27. *See also* senators

Frist, Bill, 78, 84, 110

Fulbright, J. William: FRC and, 51

gallery visitors, 153

Galloway, George: administrative centralization and, 162–63; biography of, 160–62; on cloture provision, 164; committee system and, 162, 164–65; on delegation of work, 165; electronic voting, 163; executive agencies and, 162; executive branch and, 162; and judges, federal, 165; on LRA of 1946, 161; media coverage and, 160; on media exposure, 164; party policy committees and, 164; party politics and, 165; political scientists and, 148–49, 166; on reforms, Congressional, 162; on senator qualifications, 165

Gephardt, Richard A. "Dick," 104, 109

Gillette, Guy: administrative assistants and, 138

Gingrich, Newt: media coverage and, 98, 99, 108; on Senate, role of, 146

Goldwater, Barry G., 51, 103

Gorbachev, Mikhail: INF and, 27
Gore, Al, 114
Gramm, Phil, 78
Greenberg-Quinlan polls, 110–11
Griffin, Robert P., 54
gun-control legislation, 84, 85, 114, 118, 122

Hagel, Chuck: on CTBT, 25; policy agendas and, 59
Hamilton, Alexander, 43–44, 47, 60n4
Harding, Warren, 150
Harkin, Tom: lockbox bill and, 87; PBA and, 36, 38
Hatch, Orrin, 114
Hatfield, Mark, 9, 76
Hayakawa, S. I., 54, 60n12
Hayden, Carl: patronage positions and, 138
Haynes, George H.: biography of, 154–56; campaign finance reform and, 158; on elections, direct, 157; election system and, 155–56, 156–57; political scientists and, 148–49, 154–59, 166; on prestige of senators, 158–59; and Senate, opinion of, 159; on Senate, size of, 156
Health, Education, Labor and Pensions (HELP) Committee, 78–79
Health Benefits Coalition, 83
Heller, Robert, 160
Helms, Jesse: CTBT and, 22, 24, 25, 27, 29, 39; foreign policy and, 43; FRC and, 51, 54, 58, 60n12; negative legislative power and, 59
Hoffman, F. Nordy: computers and, 144; on television coverage, 143–44
Hollings, Ernest F.: PBA and, 38
Holt, Pat N.: coffee agreement and, 137; deliberations and, 135; FRC and, 140; on television coverage, 143
House of Representatives: character of, 1, 17, 45, 145–46; committee systems and, 165; ideology and, 2, 5, 7; impeachment hearings and, 13, 41; leadership issues and, 68; majority

party and, 107; media coverage and, 108; membership turnover and, 7, 45; 106th Congress and, 41; party policy committees and, 164; party politics and, 1, 10, 16, 41, 42, 52; policy agendas and, 107; reforms and, 162; Rules Committee and, 87; television coverage and, 131; women and, 134; WTO and, 45, 59
Humphrey, Hubert, 52
Hunt, Lester C., 52
Hurley, Patricia A.: on voting trends, 7
Hutchison, Kay Bailey: CTBT and, 25

ideology: ASC and, 52–53, 54–55, *55;* Congress and, 52–53, 60n11; FRC and, 52–53, 53–54; House and, 2, 5, 7; majority leadership issues and, 88; membership turnover and, 6–7; party politics and, 2, 5, 18; political parties and, 52, *53. See also* party politics
impeachment hearings: computers and, 144; and courtesy, senatorial, 41; CTBT and, 28, 29; House and, 13, 41; media coverage and, 73; minority leaders and, 104; party politics and, 13; television hearings and, 143
impeachment trials: of judges, federal, 165
individualism: 106th Congress and, 58; party politics and, 167
individualism issues: ASC and, 58; deliberations and, 49–50; Democratic Party and, 11; FRC and, 58; leadership issues and, 66–67, 69–71, 76, 89; majority leadership issues and, 68; media coverage and, 72–73; party collective action and, 73–76; party politics and, 1, 4, 16; PCT and, 50, 60n7; UCA and, 68–69. *See also* leadership issues
Individuals with Disabilities Education Act (IDEA), 112, 113, *113*
Inhofe, James M.: and courtesy, senatorial, 41; courtesy and, 29; CTBT and, 23, 25

institutionism, 13
interest groups, policy-oriented, 4, 18, 66, 67
Intermediate Nuclear Force (INF) Treaty, 27

Jackson, Henry M., 52
Javits, Jacob K., 55
Jay, John, 46, 47, 60n5
Jefferson, Thomas: on prestige of senators, 166n2; on Senate, role of, 45
Jeffords, James M.: CFR and, 33; CTBT and, 29; managed health care issues and, 79; PBA and, 38
jet airplanes. *See* airplane travel
*John Hopkins Studies in Historical and Political Science,* 148
Johnson, Lyndon B.: as constituency, 94, 105; individualism and, 3; leadership issues and, 91; majority leadership issues and, 141
Johnson, Timothy P., 38
Johnston, Kelly D.: RPC and, 143
Joint Committee on the Organization of Congress, 160
judges, federal: and elections, contested, 165; and impeachment trials of, 165
juvenile justice reform, 114–15

Kennedy, Edward M., 79, 84, 121
Kennedy, Robert F.: on television coverage, 143
Kissinger, Henry: CTBT and, 26
Knowland, William, 91
Kohl, Herb: individualism issues and, 70
Kyl, Jon: committee system and, 110; CTBT and, 23, 25, 27; freshmen senators and, 8, 9; GOP discipline and, 9

labor issues: staff issues and, 144–45
La Follette, Robert M., Jr., 161
lame-duck sessions: reforms and, 134
Landrieu, Mary: PBA and, 37, 38
Laski, Harold, 159

Lautenberg, Frank: PBA and, 37
leadership issues: conservatism and, 66; constituencies and, 94–96; deliberations and, 65–67; Democratic Party and, 14; filibusters and, 66; GOP and, 14; House and, 68; individualism issues and, 66–67, 69–71, 76, 89; and interest groups, policy-oriented, 66, 67; liberalism and, 66; media coverage and, 66, 67, 99, 106n3; membership turnover and, 66; 106th Congress and, 69–71; party collective actions and, 75–76; party politics and, 13–16, 65, 67–68, 72, 111. *See also* individualism
League of Women Voters, 160
Leahy, Patrick: PBA and, 38
Lee, Frances E., 168–69
legislation: majority leadership issues and, 68–69
Legislative Directors (LDs): party politics and, 11–13
*Legislative Notice,* 74
Legislative Reorganization Act of 1946: administrative assistants and, 138; committee system and, 131, 136–37, 142; reforms and, 161, 166n3; staff issues and, 135
Legislative Reorganization Act of 1970: staff issues and, 139–40
liberalism: Congress and, 52, 54, 55; Democratic Party and, 11; FRC and, 52, 54, *54*; leadership issues and, 66; membership turnover and, 44, 52, 60n9; PBA and, 38; procedural revolution and, 4
Lincoln, Blanche: PBA and, 38
lobbyists: "sunshine" reform and, 141
lockbox bill: amendment tree and, 86, 122; cloture provision and, 120, 126n9; Democratic Party and, 120; GOP and, 120; party politics and, 108
Long, Russell B.: on regionalism, 3

Lott, Trent: amendment tree and, 114, 121–22; CFR and, 34; cloture provision and, 118, 126n9; CTBT and, 22, 23, 24, 26, 28; gun-control legislation and, 118; individualism issues and, 70, 71; juvenile justice reform and, 114; majority party strategies and, 86, 104; managed health care issues and, 85–86; party politics and, 13, 108; patients bill of rights and, 78, 80–82; roll call votes and, 108; Rule XIV and, 125; time constraints and, 40; UCA and, 125
Luce, Robert, 153
Lugar, Richard G.: CTBT and, 29; FRC and, 54, 60n12

Mack, Connie, 9–10, 108
Madison, James, 17, 43–44, 145
majority leaders: role of, 4
majority leadership issues: amendment tree and, 121–22; cloture provision and, 116; committee system and, 141–42; history of, 91; ideology and, 88; individualism issues and, 68; legislation and, 68–69; minority leaders and, 93; party politics and, 68, 71–72, 88–89, 89; policy agendas and, 98; reforms and, 145
majority party: amendment tree and, 122; House and, 107; policy agendas and, 107; Rule XIV and, 115; strategies, 85–88
managed health care issues: cloture provision and, 119–20; party politicsand, 77–85. *See also* patients' bill of rights
Mansfield, Mike, 4, 139, 141
Marcy, Carl M., 136–37, 138, 143
Matthews, Chris, 99
Matthews, Donald R.: "club" tradition and, 139; on individualism, 167; on leadership issues, 14; on party politics, 1; party politics and, 91; on regionalism, 2–3

McCain, John: CFR and, 33, 39; and courtesy, senatorial, 41; CTBT deliberations and, 30
McCain-Feingold Bipartisan Campaign Finance Reform Act (CFR): advocates for, 30–31; amendments and, 32; amendment tree and, 122; cloture provision and, 120; defensive strategies and, 31–32; deliberations and, 21–22, 30–34; majority party strategies and, 86; 105th Congress, 86; party politics and, 33–34, *40, 42*
McClure, Stewart E.: administrative assistants and, 138; on reforms, 139; on staff growth, 140; on television coverage, 133
McConnell, Mitch: CFR and, 31, 32, 33, 39
McCrone, Donald J.: and representation, egalitarian, 168
McGhee, Roy L.: on television coverage, 133, 143
McGovern, George, 52
media coverage: amendment tree and, 122; Congress and, 167; constituencies and, 144; C-SPAN, 167; C-SPAN2, 81; deliberations and, 108, 131, 143–44; FRC and, 143; House and, 108, 131; impeachment hearings and, 73; individualism issues and, 72–73; leadership issues and, 66, 67, 99, 106n3; minority leaders and, 92, 98–101, *100,* 103–4, 105; party collective action and, 74–75; patients' bill of rights and, 81, 83, 85; procedural revolution and, 4; radio broadcasts and, 164; radio broadcasts and, 164; reforms and, 143, 160; senator qualifications and, 133–34; "sunshine" reform and, 131, 140, 141; television coverage, 131, 133–34, 143–44, 167
Meehan, Martin T.: CFR and, 32
membership turnover: ASC and, 52–55; Congress and, 52; electoral process

and, 45; foreign policy and, 50–55; FRC and, 52–55; House and, 7, 45; ideology and, 6–7; leadership issues and, 66; liberalism and, 44, 52, 60n9; national security policy and, 50–55; 105th Congress and, 6; party politics and, 122, 125; policy agendas and, 57

message politics. *See* party politics

Mikulski, Barbara, 35

minimum wage bill, 121, 122

minority leadership issues: amendment tree and, 121–22; budget issues and, 96–98; constituencies and, *93*, 93–94; electoral politics and, 101–2; filibusters and, 92, 96, *97*; history of, 91; influences of, 103–5; majority leaders and, 93; media coverage and, 92, 98–101; 103rd Congress and, 8; party politics and, 68, 71–72, 94–95, *95*; policy agendas and, 98; presidents and, 92, 94, 95–96, 97, 105; role of, 4, 14–15

minority party issues: amendment tree and, 122; 103rd Congress and, 77; party politics and, 112, 124; Rule XIV and, 115, 125; strategies and, 76–77

minority representation: Norwegian Storting and, 168; political scientists and, 168; reforms and, 168; and states, size of, 168–69

missile defense system, 108

Mitchell, George: media coverage and, 98, 99

Monroney, A. S. Mike, 160, 161

"morning business": party politics and, 108–9, *109*; speeches and, 126n1

Moynihan, Daniel Patrick: on CTBT, 25; PAB and, 38

Muskie, Edmund, 52

National Federation of Independent Business, 83

National Rifle Association, 84

national security policy: authorizations and, 49; Congress and, 46;

consolidated deterrence and, 46, 47; influences on making, 43; membership turnover and, 50–55, 59; policy agendas and, 57, 59; presidential powers and, 46–47; and Senate, role of, 44

*New York Times,* 99, 105; CTBT and, 24–25; policy agendas and, 56

Nickles, Don, 78, 80, 84, 110

Nineteenth Amendment: senate reforms and, 134

Ninety-first Congress: party politics and, 67

Nixon, Richard M.: impeachment trial and, 143

North, Oliver, 58

Northeast Dairy Compact, 70–71

Norwegian Storting: and representation, egalitarian, 168

Nunn, Sam A., 51

Occupational Health and Safety Act: staff issues and, 144

Olympic Games: federal appropriations and, 32

103rd Congress: amendment tree and, 86; minority leadership issues and, 8; minority party issues and, 77

104th Congress: Democratic Party and, 11, 110; freshmen senators and, 9; GOP and, 8; party politics and, 17; reforms and, 2

105th Congress: CFR and, 86; Democratic Party and, 11; membership turnover and, 6

106th Congress: deliberations and, 21, 22; Democratic Party and, 15, 78; education policies and, 111; House and, 41; individualism and, 58; leadership issues and, 69–71; party politics and, 109; policy agendas and, 75; senator qualifications and, 109

107th Congress: CTBT and, 23

O'Neill, Thomas P. "Tip," 99, 105, 108

Oppenheimer, Bruce I., 168–69

Pacificus-Helvidius debate, 43–44

Panama Canal Treaty (PCT), 27, 50, 60n7

Partial-birth Abortion Ban (PAB): abortion rights and, 35–36; amendments and, 37–38; anecdotal references and, 36; deliberations and, 21–22; liberalism and, 38; party politics and, *40, 42;* personal references and, 37

partisanship. See party politics

party policy committees, 162, 164

party politics: amendment tree and, 121–23, *123,* 125, 126; cloture provision and, 118–21, *119,* 125; coffee agreement and, 137; committee system and, 165; CTBT and, 44; deliberations and, 17; Democratic Party and, 110–13, *113;* education bills and, 110; election issues and, 18; GOP and, 109–10, 110–13, *113,* 126n8; House and, 1, 10, 16, 41, 42, 52; impeachment hearings and, 13; individualism and, 167; leadership issues and, 2, 65, 67–68, 72, 111; lockbox bill and, 108; majority leadership issues and, 68, 71–72, 88–89, 89; managed health care issues and, 77–85; membership turnover and, 122, 125; minority leaders and, 94–95, *95;* minority leadership issues and, 68, 71–72, *95;* minority party and, 112, 124; "morning business" and, 108–9, *109;* negative legislative power and, 4–5; Ninety-first Congress and, 67; 104th Congress and, 17; 106th Congress and, 109; party policy committees and, 162, 164; patients' bill of rights and, 77–85; polarization and, 52–55, *53, 54, 55, 56;* polling and, 111, 112; roll call votes and, 120, 125; Rule XIV and, 115–16, *116,* 125, 126n7; Senate procedures and, 107–26; staff issues and, 136, 140; UCA and, 123–25, 126; Vietnam War and, 137. *See also* ideology

patients' bill of rights: media coverage and, 81, 83, 85; party politics and, 77–85. *See also* managed health care issues

patronage positions: staff issues and, 138–39, 145

Paul, Ron: WTO and, 44–45

Pearson, James B., 54

Pell, Claiborne D.: FRC and, 51

Penrose, Boise: direct elections and, 132

Pentagon, 48

Pepper, Claude, 159, 164

Percy, Charles H., 55, 104

Petrocik, John R., 110

Phillips, David Graham, 155

Pinchot, Gifford: direct elections and, 132

policy agendas: foreign policy and, *58;* FRC and, 59; House and, 107; majority leaders and, 98; majority party and, 107; minority leaders and, 98; 106th Congress and, 75; policy changes and, 56–57, 61n13

policy committees: political scientists and, 142–43

political action committees (PAC), 94, 101–2

political science: national politics and, 147–48, 166

*Political Science Quarterly,* 147, 149, 160

political scientists: cloture provision and, 150–51; committee system and, 142; Congress and, 167–68; historic documentation and, 166; policy committees and, 142–43; reforms and, 148–49, 148–54, 154–59; and representation, egalitarian, 168

polling: party politics and, 111, 112

Poole, Keith T.: voting analysis and, 52

pork-barrel legislation, 32

power, political: negative legislative, 44–45, 51, 59; party politics and, 4–5. *See also* presidential powers

presidential powers, 46–47, 60n3, 60n4, 60n5. *See also* power, political presidents: and Congress, expediency of, 163; minority leaders and, 92, 94, 95–96, 97, 105

procedural revolution, 4

radio broadcasts: deliberations and, 164. *See also* media coverage

Rayburn, Sam, 142, 164

Reagan, Ronald: INF and, 27; policy agendas and, 94

reforms: committee system and, 152, 162; Congress and, 162; DPC and, 142–43; effects of, 145; and elections, direct, 132, 157; House and, 162; majority leadership issues and, 145; media coverage and, 160; 104th Congress and, 2; political science and, 147–48; political scientists and, 148–49, 148–54; and representation, egalitarian, 168; RPC and, 142–43; staff issues and, 162; television coverage and, 143; traditions and, 142

regionalism: civil rights movement and, 4; Democratic Party and, *3*; party politics and, 2–3

Reid, Harry: CFR and, 33, 34; lockbox bill and, 87; party collective action and, 75; patient's bill of rights and, 82; PBA and, 38

Republican Conference reforms: effects of, 10–11; party discipline and, 9–10

Republican Party (GOP): cloture provision and, 118–19, *119*; CTBT and, 22–23, 29, 124; freshmen senators and, 9; ideology and, *53*; leadership issues and, 14; lockbox bill and, 120; 104th Congress and, 8; party collective action and, 74, 75, 76; party politics and, 9–10, 109–10, 110–13, *113*, 126n8; patients' bill of rights and, 79–85; Rule XIV and, 116; Super Ed-Flex Act and, 111; UCA and, 124

Republican Policy Committee (RPC), 13–14, 74, 142–43

Riddick, Floyd M.: direct elections and, 132–33

Robb, Charles S., 85

*Roe v. Wade*, 35, 38

Rogers, Lindsay: biography of, 149–50; committee investigations and, 151; committee system and, 152; on delegation of work, 152; on direct elections, 152–53; on elections, direct, 152–53; executive branch and, 153; on Haynes, 159; political scientists and, 148–54, 166; on Senate, role of, 151; on Senate, size of, 156; staff issues and, 160; on treaties, review of, 153

Rohde, David W., 110

roll call votes, 108, 120, 125, 167

Roosevelt, Franklin, 161, 163

Rosenthal, Howard, 52

Rule XIV: Democratic Party and, 116; GOP and, 116; majority leaders and, 125; majority party and, 115; minority party and, 115, 125; party politics and, 115–16, *116*, 125, 126n7

Rule XXII: cloture provision and, 150, 151

Russell, Richard B.: ASC and, 51; authorizations and, 49; individualism issues and, 3

Russell Amendment, 49

Russert, Tim, 99

Rutledge, Edward: on prestige of senators, 166n2

Salt Lake City 2000 Winter Olympics, 32

Saltonstall, Leverett, 51

Santorum, Rick: anecdotal references and, 36; on CFR deliberations, 34; committee system and, 110; and courtesy, senatorial, 41; patients' bill of rights, 78; PBA and, 34–35, 37, 38, 39; personal references and, 37

Sarbanes, Paul S., 87

scandals: investigations and, 150

Schlesinger, James: CTBT and, 26

Schroeder, Gerhard: CTBT and, 25

Scott, Hugh: minority leaders and, 4, 95
Sellers, Patrick J., 105, 111; party politics
    and, 110
Senate: institutional change and, 47–56,
    169; role of, 17, 44, 45, 146, 151; size
    of, 156
*Senate of the United States* (Haynes), 154,
    156
Senate Resolution 60: staff issues and, 140
senators: constituencies and, 159;
    courtesy and, 16, 28–29, 41–42;
    duties of, 159; as observers, 27–28;
    prestige and, 158–59, 166n2;
    qualifications and, 109, 133–34, 165;
    women, 134. *See also* freshmen
    senators
Seventeenth Amendment: and elections,
    direct, 132, 152–53, 155; prestige
    and, 158
Seventy-third Congress: foreign policy
    and, 48
sexual harassment issues: staff issues and,
    145
Shays, Christoper: CFR and, 32
Sinclair, Barbara: cloture provision and,
    116; on filibusters, 8; majority party
    issues and, 96; on Senate, changes in,
    49
Sixty-fifth Congress: committee system
    and, 152
*Sizing up the Senate: The Unequal
    Consequences of Equal Representation*
    (Lee and Oppenheimer), 168
Smith, Bob: PBA and, 37
Smith, Gordon H.: CTBT and, 29
Smith, Steven S., 45, 50, 96
Snowe, Olympia: CFR and, 33; patients
    bill of rights and, 85; PBA and, 38;
    Republican Conference and, 110
social security lockbox bill: amendment
    tree and, 86, 122; cloture provision
    and, 120, 126n9; Democratic Party
    and, 120; GOP and, 120; party
    politics and, 108
Somit, Albert, 166n3

Speaker of the House, 68, 72
Specter, Arlen: CFR and, 33; CTBT and,
    29; PBA and, 38
St. Claire, Darrell: patronage positions
    and, 139; staff issues and, 138; on
    television coverage, 133–34, 143
staff issues: administrative assistants and,
    138; civil service and, 137; committee
    system and, 139–40; computers and,
    139, 144; executive branch and, 135;
    foreign policy and, 135–36; FRC and,
    137–38; growth and, 139–40; labor
    issues and, 144–45; party politics and,
    136, 140; patronage positions and,
    138–39, 145; reforms and, 160, 162;
    salaries and, 139; sexual harassment
    issues and, 145; unions and, 144–45.
    *See also* committee system
states: and representation, egalitarian,
    168–69
Stennis, John C.: ASC and, 51
Stevens, Ted: PBA and, 38
stimulus program, 77, 86
"Strengthening the Congress" (Heller), 160
Summers, Larry, 83
"sunshine" reform: cloture provision and,
    131; committee system and, 140; FRC
    and, 140; lobbyists and, 141
Super Ed-Flex Act: GOP and, 111
Supreme Court: legislation and, 161
*The Supreme Court in United States
    History* (Warren), 154

Taft, Robert, 91
Tanenhaus, Joseph, 166n3
television coverage, 167; constituencies
    and, 144; deliberations and, 131,
    143–44; FRC and, 143; House and,
    131; reforms and, 143; senator
    qualifications and, 133–34. *See also*
    media coverage
Thomas, Craig: party politics and, 109,
    110
Thompson, Fred, 31, 33
Thurmond, J. Strom, 51, 58

*Time* (magazine), 103–4
tobacco subsidies, 32
Tower, John G.: ASC and, 51; secretary of defense and, 58
traditions: "club" tradition and, 139; patronage positions and, 138–39; reforms and, 142; senatorial courtesy and, 16, 28–29, 41–42
transcontinental jet travel: deliberations and, 134
"Treason of the Senate" (Phillips), 155
treaties, review of, 153
Treaty of Versailles, 27, 153
Truman, Harry, 133
Twentieth Amendment: lame-duck sessions and, 134

unanimous consent agreement (UCA): CTBT and, 23, 24, 124; Ed-Flex Act and, 88, 121; GOP and, 124; individualism issues and, 68–69; juvenile justice reform and, 114; party politics and, 123–25, 126; patients' bill of rights and, 83, 85
unions: staff issues and, 144–45
U.S. Chamber of Commerce, 83
*U.S. Senators and Their World* (Matthews), 139, 167

Valeo, Francis R., 139, 140, 143
Vandenberg, Arthur G., 51, 136
Verkler, Jerry T.: on majority leadership issues, 141–42
Versailles Treaty, 27, 153

Vietnam War, 137, 142
visitors, gallery, 153
voting analysis: constituencies and, 7; ideology and, 52, 60n9; party politics and, 5–7, *6*

Warner, John W.: CTBT and, 25, 39; FRC and, 58; policy agendas and, 59
Warren, Charles, 154
*Washington Post:* on leadership issues, 66
Watergate scandal, 142
Watkins, Charles: direct elections and, 132–33
Watt, Ruth Young, 134, 140, 143
Weicker, Lowell, 66–67
Weld, William, 43
Wellstone, Paul: CFR and, 31, 32
White, William S., 2–3, 139
Wilcox, Francis O., 135, 136
Wiley, Alexander, 138
Wilson, Rick K.: on voting trends, 7
Wilson, Woodrow: cloture provision and, 150; political science and, 147–48; on senators, prestige of, 159; Versaille Treaty and, 27
women: Congress and, 134
World Trade Organization (WTO) 1999, 32, 44–45, 59
Wyden, Ron, 88

Y2K Act, 86, 114, 118, 122

Zee, Rein J. Vander: on television coverage, 133

# About the Contributors

RICHARD A. BAKER, the historian of the U.S. Senate Historical Office, is the author of *Conservation Politics: The Senate Career of Clinton P. Anderson* (1985) and *The Senate of the United States: A Bicentennial History* (1987).

COLTON C. CAMPBELL is an assistant professor of political science at Florida International University, and is currently a visiting assistant professor of political science at American University. He is the coeditor of *New Majority or Old Minority? The Impact of Republicans on Congress* (1999). He served as an American Political Science Association (APSA) congressional fellow in 1998–1999 in the office of Senator Bob Graham (D-Fla.).

ROGER H. DAVIDSON, an emeritus professor of government and politics at the University of Maryland, College Park, is now a visiting professor of political science at the University of California, Santa Barbara. On Capitol Hill, he has served on House and Senate committee staffs and as senior specialist at the Congressional Research Service. He is the coauthor of *Congress and Its Members* (2000), the standard textbook on the subject. His articles on the Senate have addressed such subjects as committees, leadership, multiple referrals of bills, and the chamber's relations with the executive branch.

CHRISTOPHER J. DEERING is a professor of political science at George Washington University. He is the coauthor of *Committees in Congress* (1997) and editor of *Congressional Politics* (1989). He served as an APSA congressional fellow in 1984–1985 in the office of Senate Majority Leader George Mitchell (D-Maine).

C. Lawrence Evans is an associate professor of political science at the College of William and Mary. He is the author of *Leadership in Committee: A Comparative Analysis of Leadership Behavior in the U.S Senate* (1989) and the coauthor of *Congress under Fire: Reform Politics and the Republican Majority* (1996). He served as an APSA congressional fellow in 1991–1992.

Burdett Loomis is a professor of political science at the University of Kansas. He has written extensively on Congress, interest groups, and policymaking. He served as an APSA congressional fellow in 1975–1976, and helped to establish the Robert J. Dole Institute at the University of Kansas. His recent books include *The Sound of Money* (with Darrell West) (1998) and the edited collection, *Esteemed Colleagues: Civility and Deliberation in the United States Senate* (2000).

Donald R. Matthews is an emeritus professor of political science at the University of Washington. He is the author of numerous books, including *U.S. Senators and Their World* (1960), *Yeas and Nays: A Theory of Decision-making in the U.S. House of Representatives* (1975), and *The Party's Choice* (1976).

Walter J. Oleszek is a senior specialist in American national government at the Congressional Research Service. He is the author of *Congressional Procedures and the Policy Process* (1996) and the coauthor of *Congress and Its Members* (2000). He has served as policy director of the Joint Committee on the Organization of Congress.

Nicol C. Rae is a professor of political science at Florida International University. He is the author of *The Decline and Fall of the Liberal Republicans from 1952 to the Present* (1989), *Southern Democrats* (1994), and *Conservative Reformers: The Republican Freshmen and the Lessons of the 104th Congress* (1998). He served as an APSA congressional fellow in 1995–1996 in the office of Senator Thad Cochran (R-Miss.).

Donald A. Ritchie, associate historian of the U.S. Senate Historical Office, is the author of *James M. Landis: Dean of the Regulators* (1986) and *Press Gallery: Congress and the Washington Correspondents* (1991). He is the winner of the Forrest C. Pogue Award for significant contributions to the field of oral history.

Barbara Sinclair is the Marvin Hoffenberg Professor of American Politics at the University of California, Los Angeles. She is the author of numerous books, including *Transformation of the U. S. Senate* (1989), *Legislators, Leaders, and Lawmaking* (1995), and *Unorthodox Lawmaking: New Legislative Processes in the U.S. Congress* (1997). She served as an APSA congressional fellow in 1978–1979 in the office of Speaker of the House Thomas P. O'Neill (D-Mass.).